Approaches to Actor Training

Approaches to Actor Training

International Perspectives

Edited by John Freeman

methuen | drama
LONDON • NEW YORK • OXFORD • NEW DELHI • SYDNEY

METHUEN DRAMA
Bloomsbury Publishing Plc
50 Bedford Square, London, WC1B 3DP, UK
1385 Broadway, New York, NY 10018, USA
29 Earlsfort Terrace, Dublin 2, Ireland

BLOOMSBURY, METHUEN DRAMA and the Diana logo are trademarks of
Bloomsbury Publishing Plc

First published in Great Britain 2019 by Red Globe Press
Reprinted by Methuen Drama 2022

Copyright © John Freeman and The Authors, under exclusive licence to Springer Nature Limited, 2019

John Freeman has asserted his right under the Copyright, Designs and Patents Act, 1988, to be identified as Author of this work.

All rights reserved. No part of this publication may be reproduced or transmitted in any form or by any means, electronic or mechanical, including photocopying, recording, or any information storage or retrieval system, without prior permission in writing from the publishers.

Bloomsbury Publishing Plc does not have any control over, or responsibility for, any third-party websites referred to or in this book. All internet addresses given in this book were correct at the time of going to press. The author and publisher regret any inconvenience caused if addresses have changed or sites have ceased to exist, but can accept no responsibility for any such changes.

A catalogue record for this book is available from the British Library.

A catalog record for this book is available from the Library of Congress.

ISBN: HB: 978-1-137-60772-0
       PB: 978-1-137-60771-3

To find out more about our authors and books visit www.bloomsbury.com and sign up for our newsletters.

In memory of Tony Jones

Contents

Acknowledgements ix
Contributors xi

1 Perspectives and Provocations, Prescriptions and Principles 1
  John Freeman

Part 1 Preparing the Ground 25

2 Whole Actor, Whole Person Training: Designing a Holistic Actor Training Programme for Individual Career Longevity and Well-Being 26
  Andrea L. Moor

3 Being Human 44
  Adrian James

4 All Those Words: Why Bother with All Those Old Plays? 64
  Annie Tyson

5 What Are You Saying? An Approach to Teaching Text in an Era of Language Loss 84
  Laura Wayth

6 Mind the Gap: Gōng Fēng Shuǐ and the Missing Teeth (Ma) 100
  Robert (Draf) Draffin

Contents

Part II Training and Production — 117

7 The British Tradition in Acting Shakespeare: Challenges to Teaching the Acting of Shakespeare in a UK Conservatoire in the Twenty-First Century — 118
Stephen Simms

8 An Actor's World: People, Space, Time and Text — 136
Jeff Janisheski

9 Approaches to Acting and Interacting in Immersive and Interactive Performance — 158
Klaus Kruse

10 Yoga in a Circle: Actor Training Across Borders — 177
Diane M. Sadak

Part III The Body and the Word — 195

11 The Architecture of Action: Late Stanislavski in Contemporary Practice — 196
Hugh O'Gorman

12 Standing on the Outside Looking In — 216
Michael McCall

13 An Eye on the Exit: Actor Training in a Liberal Arts Environment — 233
Ellen Margolis

Bibliography — 248
Index — 257

Acknowledgements

Influences come from many places: articles, books, conversations, performances, workshops and, above all, from people. The idea for this book came from my former head of school, Larry Lynch. Without that prompt, this book would never have been; for that and a great deal more, I am indebted to him.

Nicola Cattini and subsequently Sonya Barker and Emily Lovelock at Red Globe Press (formerly Palgrave) took the proposal and developed it into workable shape. Their expertise was invaluable and much appreciated. I am indebted too to the outstanding students and colleagues I have been fortunate enough to work with at universities and conservatoires, primarily in the United Kingdom and Australia.

The recent death of Tony Jones, whose memory this book is dedicated to, brings to mind the other people who have taught and supervised me; for their patience, perseverance and knowledge, I thank them here. The long list includes Derek Akers, Susan Broadhurst, Pete Brooks, Ian Brown, Margaret Eddershaw, Barry Edwards, Bernard Gilhooly, Gerry Harris, Baz Kershaw, John Singleton, Keith Sturgess and Geoff Sutton.

The panel on the education and training of actors at the 7th Annual International Conference on Visual and Performing Arts organized in Athens by ATINER was significant in the way it opened up dialogue between actor trainers from around the world. While most of the following chapters do not come from its participants, the conference was a catalyst for a series of conversations of which this book is a clear part.

The editor and publisher would also like to thank the following for the use of copyright text material in the book:

Ian Maxwell for the main recommendations directed to drama schools from Maxwell et al (2015), 'The Australian Actor's Wellbeing Study: A Preliminary Report' in Chapter 2, Whole Actor, Whole Person Training: Designing a Holistic Actor Training Programme for Individual Career Longevity and Well-Being.

Lyn Darnley for quotations from unpublished PhD and MPhil theses, 'Artist Development and Training in the Royal Shakespeare Company'

(2013) and 'A History of Voice Teaching in Britain' (1994) in Chapter 7, The British Tradition in Acting Shakespeare: Challenges to Teaching the Acting of Shakespeare in a UK Conservatoire in the Twenty-First Century.

Larry Wilde for quotations from an interview conducted with Ellen Margolis (2016) in Chapter 13, An Eye on the Exit: Actor Training in a Liberal Arts Environment.

Contributors

Andrea L. Moor is senior lecturer and course coordinator in acting at the School of Creative Practice at Queensland University of Technology (QUT), where she is engaged in teaching, directing and curriculum design across all three years of training. Moor holds a doctorate of creative industries (QUT), specializing in contemporary actor training in Australia. As an actor, her credits are extensive, working across theatre for most of Australia's leading companies, as well as in film, television and radio. Her work has taken her to London's West End, the Edinburgh Festival and Los Angeles. With Queensland Theatre Company, she was resident director (2014–2015) and artistic associate (2015). Moor is a National Institute of Dramatic Art (NIDA) graduate (1985, acting) and studied at East 15 (1979) and with Atlantic Theater Company (1994). Moor introduced the acting technique called Practical Aesthetics to Australia, teaching at NIDA, the Western Australian Academy of Performing Arts (WAAPA) and QUT and as an on-screen performance coach. Moor identifies as a practitioner teacher because she continues to work as an actor across all mediums, bringing the industry to the classroom and the classroom to the industry.

Adrian James trained at the Drama Centre London and worked as an actor in the United Kingdom and Europe. He taught at East 15 under its founder Margaret Bury Walker and directed productions in London. He taught at Arts Educational Schools, London, leading the United Kingdom's first vocational MA in acting. He gained his fellowship of the higher education academy from The Royal Central School of Speech and Drama and his PhD from City University of London. James teaches at East 15 Acting School, University of Essex, where he leads the certificate of higher education in theatre arts. He is a fellow of the Royal Society of Arts. James's chapter outlines the underlying principles and practical exercises for a first term of actor training in behavioural realism. Suggesting that the schooling systems from which most students emerge can sometimes discourage the reflective, critical self-awareness essential for creative development, the chapter describes an attempt to stimulate students' non-judgemental awareness by focusing on the felt sensations of their own past, examining the nature of narrative and social relationships through the techniques of professional discipline, preparation and object relation exercises. The discovery and sensitizing of the students' own experienced sense of 'truth' and trust in their own being is emphasized by using aspects of each's own biography and experiences and their shared biographies and experiences.

Annie Tyson read drama and theatre arts at Birmingham University before training at Drama Centre London, then spent the first years of her professional life as an actor in theatre and television; Tyson continues to work as an actor. She taught at Rose Bruford and the Drama Centre, where she was course director before joining the Royal Academy of Dramatic Art (RADA) as an acting tutor and director. Tyson was part of the core team for the Royal Shakespeare Company's project Open Stages. She has a long-standing relationship with the Carnegie Mellon School of Drama, where she directs and gives masterclasses in Restoration comedy. Tyson runs classical and contemporary audition workshops for The Mono Box, for whom she is a patron and is a mentor for the diversity in actor training initiative Open Door. Tyson's chapter explores the need for actors in training to develop confident ownership of complex language. The chapter addresses techniques for working with rich, metaphorical, poetic and articulate dramatic language applied here to plays of the Restoration, demystifying the wit and rhetorical structures that are characteristic of the genre. The chapter includes an actor's analysis of a piece of Etheredge's *The Man of Mode*, identifying the language structures, devices and imagery that provide clues to character and action. This is followed by examples of exercises that prepare actors for this work.

Laura Wayth has an MFA from the American Repertory Theatre Institute for Advanced Theatre Training at Harvard University and the Moscow Art Theatre School Institute in Russia. Wayth is the author of *The Shakespeare Audition* and *A Field Guide to Actor Training*. She was a 2002–2003 Fulbright fellow to Moscow and a 2012 senior Fulbright scholar to Romania. She has worked internationally as a teacher and coach in Italy, Morocco, China and London and is currently associate professor and coordinator of the Actor Training Programme at San Francisco State University. Wayth's chapter begins with the premise that in an era of increasing reliance on visual information, the recognition of the power of language is suffering. As actors in training drift further away from the poignancy of language, Wayth suggests ways in which acting instructors might help students to discover and better understand the challenges and possibilities of working with heightened text. The chapter explores some of the ways in which Wayth reinvented her own teaching and the methods she uses to work with emerging actors on a decidedly modern problem.

A professional footballer before moving into theatre, **Robert (Draf) Draffin** has subsequently created a body of internationally acclaimed work. He has trained actors at the Victorian College of Arts (VCA); Shanghai Theatre Academy; Monash University; Latrobe University; Deakin University; the Theatre Training Research Programme, Singapore; and the Shanghai Theatre Academy. A recipient of the prestigious Kenneth Myer Medallion (outstanding services for the performing arts), a three-year fellowship from The Australia Council of the Arts and an Asialink residency, for the last decade Draffin has been researching actor training through the philosophical and practical lens of tai'ji. This has run alongside research into the harvest ritual with Aboriginal Amis tribe in Taiwan and the design and facilitation of workshops with major businesses, business schools and associations, hospitals and organizations, including the Defence Material Organisation, Air Services and the Red Cross. Draffin's work with actors in training is defined by the corporeal and kinaesthetic state of liminality: the embodied creative energy held in thresholds and moments of flux. Accordingly, his chapter discusses the importance of foundation actor training based on traditional Asian somatic practices. The chapter describes the principles and practical exercises underpinning this training and highlights the use of repetition in knowledge making, the need to embrace experience and the contemporary and neurological applications of those practices in the imaginative and creative process of the actor.

Stephen Simms is vice principal of the Royal Birmingham Conservatoire (RBC), head of acting and professor of actor education, the only person to hold this title in the United Kingdom. An honours degree graduate of RADA, Simms received the George Bernard Shaw scholarship, the Beerbohm-Tree Prize and the RADA silver medal. He was an actor with the Royal Shakespeare Company for several years, a member of Declan Donnellan's multi-award-winning company Cheek by Jowl, director and tutor with the Shakespeare Birthplace Trust and a member of the acclaimed theatre group Actors from the London Stage. He has appeared in the West End, in television series and major international feature films. Simms's chapter negotiates ways in which the RBC trains actors to deal with postmodern, postfeminist, postcolonial and post-dramatic worlds where previous cultural certainties are no longer taken for granted; and it deals with conforming to industry aesthetics, which students must meet if they wish to work. The chapter addresses the conservatoire's training as students move through a production of the 1603 quarto *Hamlet*. Central to this production was whether actors trained in the British tradition could embrace a postmodern approach to production and create a theatrical whole. The challenge of the production was therefore one which tested the flexibility of training.

Over the past 20 years, **Jeff Janisheski** has taught and directed in Australia, England, Japan, Korea, Russia, Vietnam and the United States. He is a chair and professor of theatre arts at California State University Long Beach, and artistic director of their California Repertory Company. Janisheski's previous roles have included head of acting at NIDA; artistic director of the National Theater Institute at the Eugene O'Neill Theater Center; associate artistic director at New York's Classic Stage Company and cofounder of the New York International Butoh Festival. Janisheski is a recipient of the Theatre Communications Group New Generations/Future Leaders fellowship. Janisheski's chapter outlines an approach to actor training that he developed at NIDA, an approach which fuses Stanislavski, Viewpoints, *butoh* and *noh*. Through études, improvisations and group compositions, students explore the four main building blocks of theatre – people, space, time and text – to create three-dimensional worlds with detailed physical and psychological life, a playful and creative connection with space and time and a curiosity and hunger for language and the written word. Through concrete examples of his work with NIDA students on *Antigone* – which involved intensive choral, character and composition work – Janisheski demonstrates the application of these steps and the interrelationship of different methods needed to train actors so that they become truthful, transformational and theatrical.

Klaus Kruse is a director, designer, performer and senior lecturer in the theatre department at Falmouth University's Academy of Music and Theatre Arts, where he co-developed the BA acting programme. Kruse has taught at the London School of Economics, Academy of the Arts Reykjavic, the University of Plymouth and the Berlin University of the Arts; he is an artistic director, scenographer and writer for the international performance collective Living Structures, which he cofounded in 2007. With specialisms in designing and directing immersive theatre productions, Kruse has a particular interest in the significance of the audience's physical position in the performance space. These interests are front and centre in Kruse's chapter, which describes the acting programme at Falmouth University. Kruse addresses this through an example of professionally informed teaching practice, which emphasizes the distinctive and contemporary ethos of the university's approach to training. The chapter focuses on workshop preparation for a site-specific production of Dan Farrelly's translation of Goethe's *Urfaust*. The studio exercises are at the same time an integral part of the programme. This is where the workshop explores audience–performer relationships and the actor's use of eye-contact in intimate, immersive and one-to-one performance situations; it also speaks to an innately twenty-first-century philosophy of actor training. The idea of actors as creators as well as interpreters exists in the space between each of Kruse's lines.

Diane M. Sadak is associate professor of acting and directing at Towson University's department of theatre arts. Before this, Sadak was visiting professor of acting and voice at the Korean National University of Arts. She has acted and directed throughout the United States and taught at several international institutions, including Dartington College, UK; the University of Rajasthan and Jaipur College, Rajasthan, India; NIDA, Australia; Theatre of Changes, Greece; and the Accademia dell'Arte, Italy. Sadak has studied extensive vocal techniques at the Banff Centre for the Arts, Canada and the Roy Hart International Centre for Voice, France, where she has conducted new research on Buddhist workbooks as a foundation for advanced actor training. These activities form part of Sadak's work with the International Federation of Theatre Research (IFTR) and her leadership of the working group Theory and Practice of Performing in St. Petersburg, Russia. A certified teacher of Vinyasa Power Flow yoga, Sadak's 25 years of research into the cross-cultural integration of movement and vocal training informs her approach to acting without borders. Connecting yoga to actor training combines chakra work, the yoga sutras of Patanjali and Vinyasa Power Flow, and training in Bikram yoga. Embedding these into actor training, Sadak's chapter explores a seemingly simple and extremely beneficial integration between a piece of yoga flow as a regular practice for actors in their training and the rehearsal process.

Hugh O'Gorman is an actor, director and teacher active in professional theatre, film and television. He has appeared on Broadway, off Broadway and at dozens of regional theatres and Shakespeare festivals across the United States; his many television credits include AMC's critically acclaimed, award-winning show *Remember WENN* (SAG award nomination) and HBO's *John Adams*. O'Gorman is co-executive director of the National Alliance of Acting Teachers; head of acting at California State University Long Beach (CSULB); a faculty member of the Michael Chekhov Association (MICHA); owner of The Praxis Acting Studio in Los Angeles; and author of *The Keys to Acting*. O'Gorman's chapter explores the multi-pronged, holistic acting process called active analysis, which Stanislavski developed over the final stretch of his career. Because Stanislavski did not publish formally on the subject, relatively little is known about this work outside of Russia. The chapter provides a rough sketch of some of the essential elements from that technique, with particular focus on *action* and how theatre faculty at CSULB integrate active analysis and its accompanying architecture of action into their actor training programmes.

A graduate of NIDA's acting course and with a doctorate in performing arts from WAAPA, **Michael McCall** is course coordinator of communications and media at the University of Notre Dame Australia (Fremantle), where he is head of film and screen production and theatre studies. He has taught and directed at WAAPA and across the theatre, screen and writing faculties of Curtin University. McCall works professionally as an actor, director, script editor and producer for stage and screen and invests considerable time into arts advocacy through active roles in various arts bodies across Australia. McCall's chapter describes the process of working with WAAPA students on a production; it draws on insights gained across several years of training actors, the writer's commitment to plays that advocate strong dramatic content and the challenges to acting students' learning through production. At the heart of the chapter is concern that student actors are able to harness the powerful substance of the plays they perform in. This is worked through via the application of a shorthand (albeit not simplistic) process that addresses the pressures between text, movement and voice and encourages actors to translate text into purposive action.

Ellen Margolis serves as chair of theatre and dance and director of theatre at Pacific University in Oregon and is a member of the Dramatists Guild. She works as an actor, director, playwright and voice and dialect coach. Her scholarship focuses on acting history and culture, and along with Lissa Tyler

Renaud, she is co-editor of *The Politics of American Actor Training*. Margolis's plays – including *Pericles Wet, Hide, American Soil, What We Thought, Prime* and *A Little Chatter* – have been produced at theatres and festivals throughout the United States. Margolis has received commissions from *Proscenium Theatre Journal*, the Portland Shakespeare Project, Teen West, Mile Square Theatre, Shaking-the-Tree Studio and the Susan G. Komen Foundation. In her chapter 'An Eye on the Exit: Actor Training in a Liberal Arts Environment', Margolis addresses the particular challenges of teaching acting in an American four-year college. Starting from the question, what do I do for a living? Margolis first examines her own training as an undergraduate and graduate student. She then considers the vision and values of the liberal arts mission before going on to investigate the conflicting demands and multiple priorities at play in any given moment in the acting studio.

1

Perspectives and Provocations, Prescriptions and Principles

John Freeman

Blurred Lines

This book begins with what might seem like a sentence against itself. Actors need no formal qualifications. The qualities that matter most are generally considered to be a good, empathetic imagination; a retentive memory; a sharp brain; a clear, resonant voice; and control over breath, body and gestures. Actors must also develop their sense of truth, a faculty that means different things in different schools, styles, countries and systems. As Jeff Janisheski suggests in his chapter in this book on actor training at National Institute of Dramatic Art (NIDA), 'Truth is elastic, expansive and elusive – not limited to a specific style, method or form of acting. It is what *fills* that form – through the actor's energy, imagination and action.'

Qualifications are unnecessary, and yet no matter how cogent the arguments about innate ability and learned technique might appear and no matter how urgently publicists stir the twin pots of accident and instinct, actors invariably need to be trained.[1] Only very rarely do actors of discernible quality arrive unschooled, thrown into the professional world as Martin Heidegger would have it, and even these rare few invariably seek training out as they progress.[2] This book reveals approaches to training that are described by the very people who map out, manage and deliver it. Their contributions are unique and uniquely valuable.

Accounts from people who train actors are precious in the largely ephemeral histories of performing arts, and this book allows a dozen of these to be heard. The historical influence of training is not sidestepped in the following chapters so much as given space to speak for itself and to speak differently through different approaches. Doing so invites the reader to meet and interact with a range of ideas, providing as visceral an understanding of actor training at diverse institutions in the United Kingdom, United States and Australia as words on the page can provide.[3]

The book focuses on training for actors as something that takes place over a prescribed period of time, usually but not always amounting to three or four uninterrupted years, and it places practical knowledge at its core.[4] The chapters come directly from actor trainers, with each providing a genuine sense of being in the studio. Writing can never capture everything it describes, and yet words can do things that moments in time might struggle to hold. Words can help convey a sense of different locations, intentions, strategies, philosophical underpinnings and practical concerns.

In straddling the world of teacher needs and student needs, the book provides value to overlapping groups: to students and their advisors, who look for ideas on how schools develop training philosophies; to teachers, who look to weigh their ideology against other programmes and increase their own knowledge and craft; and to working actors, who can draw usefully on many of the ideas herein. The chapters are substantial in length, allowing for explanation rather than (just) description. This is important because this book does not attempt to teach readers how to act. There are many books that claim to do this, as there are books that try to teach people swimming and ballroom dancing; and as with a teach-yourself-tango book, some are good and some are bad.[5] While reading is a practice, and a creative one at that, when it comes to acting, it can only function as suggestion or support; it can never be a substitute for *doing*, not even its shadow. 'We learn to walk by walking', Robert Wilson reminds us, and 'you can read all the books about it you want, but you learn by doing. I've learned theater by making theater.'[6] The maxim of 10,000 hours of practice as a necessary precursor to expertise is a good one. Although reading this book will provide readers with information and inspiration, it makes no attempt to masquerade as training. The chapters address practice *through* practice, engaging implicitly with aspects of practice as research, itself a byproduct of learning by doing, kinesthetic and experiential learning. All of these approaches are concerned in differently nuanced ways with discovery resulting from one's own actions rather than with learning from watching others' performances or reading their instructions or descriptions. This amounts to the idea of proof upon practice, which is central to actor training.

A number of national and international movements have been set up which share ideas around training.[7] It is within this context of opening up hitherto private approaches that this book works, allowing readers access to core beliefs in training. This amounts to not quite a collective idea of the responsibility that institutions hold but rather a snapshot, a record of a key moment in time. This moment in time is one when more students are undertaking vocational actor training at universities than at drama schools. Certainly in the United Kingdom, this is a recent and potentially game-changing phenomenon.[8] With some notable exceptions, university programmes in acting are new, and compared to institutions such as East 15 and RADA, they are not widely, or let us say *internationally*, known.[9] Whereas some chapters will describe work undertaken at recognizably 'elite' schools, others will focus on work elsewhere. This is central to the book and in its own way is an attempt at diversity. It challenges the idea that only those who teach at famous places (and who train the famous faces) have insights worth sharing. By the same token, the contributors are at different stages of their careers, linked by a willingness to share their approaches and to encourage a community of artists, academics and practitioners to debate current issues in the expanding disciplines of actor training. This is a choice, a decision to accommodate voices that do not belong to only the established old guard. It would be naive to argue that a sense of elitism does not exist in actor training institutions; nevertheless, perpetuating that forms no part of this book's agenda.

Books that have their origins in universities are almost always defined by a thesis that prescribes the way they are approached, read and given value: by a big idea. If one of this book's concerns is to avoid the uniformity of big voices, another is to resist corralling language into something that speaks only to a select echo chamber of like-minded readers. Readers are invited to encounter the following chapters without prescription and without feeling that they need to buy into the particular values of either this editor or those contributors. That the chapters to come differ in content, context and kind is a result of contributions from people who were not selected based on uniformity in ideas, training techniques or beliefs; their differences as much as their similarities do much to reflect the variety of experiences that students encounter during their training.

Although it would be simple to refer to drama schools as providing training and universities as dealing with education, it would be also reductive and false.[10] It would be false too to suggest that drama school training is automatically better by dint of reputation, facilities and contact hours. These things matter, but they are not always clear barometers of quality. The convergence of universities and drama schools has in some ways muddied the once-clear waters between academic and vocational study. A consequence of this is that actors in training now have considerably more choice than they had at any time in the past. Not too long ago, a UK university programme called a bachelor of arts in theatre (BA theatre) could fairly safely suggest a concentration on the *why* of theatre, just as a BA in acting at a drama school might be said to look at the *how* of acting. Those clear differences or assumptions no longer exist in quite the same way.[11]

Inevitably, the perspectives offered here exclude more than they cover, and the book functions as part of an expanding chorus of work to be read alongside rather than in lieu of other texts. It can also be classed as a form of co-generative dialogue inasmuch as the chapters provide more than space for a group of people to speak their mind; they provide the book with a noetic sense of the immediate, the bodily and the authentic. The chapters address practical approaches, and the detailed exercises can be taken off the page and worked through in the studio. The caveat here is that none of the approaches in this book exist in isolation, with each forming part of ongoing programmes of training. Indeed, one of the consistent features of actor training is repetition, where patterns of behaviour are absorbed and refined over long periods of time. It may seem contradictory to state that while any of the contributors' exercises can be followed and adapted by readers, they are not included here to turn the following pages into a recipe book. Rather, the exercises add to the chapters they are part of by giving a suggestion of how things might work on the studio floor. The exercises can be used independently, which is a useful byproduct rather than an intention.

Contributors, Chapters and Changing Times

At a time when 25% of university students are using or waiting to use counselling services and when the United Kingdom's Office for Students regards mental health as a 'top priority', it is inevitable that the contemporary training of actors encompasses self-esteem, awareness of the potential for emotional and mental trauma, self-care, the support and generation of mental and emotional resilience and wellness in all participants.[12] As Mark Cariston Seton sees it, actor training requires 'appropriate and sustainable ethical training practices' in order to avoid the 'potential for and actual accounts of misuse of power by teachers over students in a highly intimate and vulnerable context of learning, exploration and risk-taking.'[13]

Best intentions notwithstanding, actor training has been relatively slow to move towards this, rooted as it is in traditions that can appear so established as to be fixed. Nevertheless, training does not take place in a vacuum, and concerns of widening participation, diversity, devised work, new dramaturgical and interdisciplinary paradigms, inclusion, welfare, teacher–student ethics and safe practice impact all aspects of actor training.[14] Some of the contributors focus closely on these issues: Diane M. Sadak explores wellness in training; Andrea L. Moor considers ways of reshaping the actor training curriculum to ensure longevity of career and ongoing mental, emotional and spiritual well-being; Klaus Kruse wrestles with the ethics of control and consent; and Ellen Margolis addresses gendering as it plays out in students' experiences of actor training and in the ways 'we may be inadvertently reinforcing gender in exercises, scene assignments, even warm-ups.'

In many ways, the exercises described in this book speak to a practice that is in the process of being radically reworked; to a time when traditional patriarchal methods of knowledge transfer as handed down in the teacher-as-expert mode are being questioned and reshaped into differently considered formats; to a reimagining of what Persephone Sextou describes as a context within which the tutor is the 'authority' and the student is the 'ignorant'.[15] Shifra Schonmann tells us that although 'There are no simple rules to ensure that teachers are doing the *right things* all the time … one should aim at doing the *things right*.'[16] Where theory allows a certain distance, vocational training is immersive, which is to say that students learn through a type of tutor-led doing. How, then, should students be led into new learning without also leading them into distress? How should they be led into the *right* kind of difficulty in the *right* kind of ways? The chapters by Moor and Margolis that bracket this book do much to articulate a new dawn in the ways that actors are being trained, led and listened to.

If there is a shift in the way many of us train actors in order to address (if not quite fully ensure) their well-being as well as their burgeoning skills, we need to acknowledge that this shift is taking place within the context of broad similarities in what remains at many places a conservative approach to training. A consequence of this is that there are elements of overlap between chapters. Where some contributors revisit similar territories about character work, this reflects a consistency of approach based on Stanislavskian principles. Anne Bogart's impact is notable too through the widespread adoption of the Saratoga International Theater Institute (SITI) Company's training through Viewpoints and Suzuki, and she emerges as a key influence, particularly with US-trained teachers.[17] Readers are invited to regard these overlaps as reiteration rather than repetition, as indicators of deeply-rooted tendencies.

Theatre thrives on conventions, and it is a short hop from this to the conventional. The contributors to this book were selected in no small part because their approaches to training link tradition with innovation and because they are engaged in the training of actors in different ways at different institutions. They can each lay claim to expertise, and while actor trainers at this level are innately engaged in theatre scholarship, the expertise offered in this book relates to activity and *doing* rather than a type of writerly discussion that is largely divorced from action. Certainly it is the case that none of the contributors position themselves here as theorists writing from behind the safety of a desk about how actors *should* be trained. Chapters inevitably come from an 'in-the-know' perspective, and yet in totality, this book allows little more than a fraction of the practice that makes up studio training.

The processes in this book are not intended to be prescriptive, and they remain the work of the writers rather than the institutions they represent. Books outlast teaching careers and remain largely fixed, whereas practice and practitioners move on. Indeed, some of the contributors describe processes that took place at institutions they no longer work at. Jeff Janisheski, for example, writes about training at NIDA in Sydney, where he was head of acting, whereas he is currently a chair and professor in the theatre arts department at California State University Long Beach;[18] Michael McCall is currently course coordinator of communications and media at the University of Notre Dame in Fremantle, whereas his chapter describes teaching undertaken at the Western Australian Academy of Performing Arts (WAAPA). My own work on this book began when I was head of theatre at Falmouth University; at the time of publication, I am employed at the University of Huddersfield, with an adjunct position at the University of Notre Dame. Though we carry who we are to where we go, we also shed our skins and change.

Just as the contributors speak for themselves, so too does this introductory chapter, which should not be read as a recruitment drive for the institutions represented here. The book is not about which type of training best equips students for industry employment. Were such to be the case, the chapters with a UK focus might well be on unrelated programmes at Oxford and Cambridge, as graduates of these universities disproportionately dominate the acting profession, particularly in positions of influence and power.

In the majority of contexts, actors use their voices to deliver text; and matching vocal skill with body movement is a given of the approaches detailed in the chapters to come. Some chapters have a particular focus on one aspect or another (speaking text in Restoration theatre for example) but even in these instances, voice cannot be thought of as an isolated skill, so much as something that requires coordination of the entire body.

Student actors develop techniques and strategies for training the voice and body in a variety of performance contexts, the majority of which involve working with text. Understanding the interdependence of breath, voice, physicality and text is required for actors in order to translate the concepts of writers and directors into action. Most teachers will have specialisms at the same time as they share a commitment to the integration of all aspects of acting. This book's contributors have an implicit belief in a collaborative training process; this amounts to a type of speech, text and body training that all teachers and students will be familiar with. The book is broken down into a tripartite structure in order to acknowledge these three elements at the same time as creating an overall sense of the type of collective perspective common to most types of training.

Chapters are grouped in loosely connected ways with the understanding that voice cannot be separated from movement any more than movement can be separated from text or text separated from production. Actors generally require the voice and body to communicate a character's inner life through an externally written dramatic text. Because of this, actors in training are encouraged to develop a deep kinesthetic mind/body awareness that sees physical and verbal qualities as interdependent. Students are expected to grow as actors who are confident in body and voice as a combined instrument.

None of the borders between chapters and approaches are watertight, nor should they be.

Chapters contain ideas that reinforce and others that contradict: some imply a quasi-militaristic autocracy, and others locate actor training as a space in which students develop their own ways of working under the care of guides rather than gurus. Where some of the contributors prefer the imperative 'must' over the discretionary 'might', this speaks as much perhaps to the differences between the way we teach and the way we subsequently write about it as it does to any sense of autocracy.[19] Nevertheless, in all cases, the intention behind the book has been to allow people to speak to their own concerns rather than to some homogenized version of what actor training is.

It is axiomatic that the ideas in some chapters are more or less familiar than those in others. Robert Draffin's chapter, for example, opens up notions of somatic training in Indonesian and Singaporean contexts, which stand in stark relief to the core training methods undertaken in pursuit of the behavioural realism described by Adrian James in his chapter on work at East 15. The curricular choices we make play a significant role in shaping students' values; accordingly, the choices we make over *what* and *how* to teach are generally reflective of the attitudes and beliefs of particular cultures and institutions. In this sense, optimal training environments tend to not only reflect the diverse cultures, perspectives and experiences of students but also balance the expectations of traditional Western curricular perspectives and pedagogical strategies with more internationally varied learning expectations and values.[20] Draffin's chapter speaks to the importance of ancient traditions, and it says a lot about Western ethnocentricity that so much of it will strike many readers as new.[21]

New Forms for New Times

Actor training has an obligation to produce technically knowing, investigative, flexible, responsive, resilient, inquiring and innovative performers – graduates who have the potential to not only sustain careers in their discipline of choice but also redefine what acting might be and what might be done with it, not least in applied and increasingly technological forms.[22] Actors are always working in the now, according to and alongside the need to tackle historical and modern texts and working with the techniques of realism (e.g. chapters by McCall, Wayth and O'Gorman) students are likely to encounter traditions where the language is in a register other than that of mainstream theatrical performance (e.g. chapters by Kruse, Simms and Janisheski). Many drama schools and universities include practices developed out of the concerns of fine art; digital theatre's fluid coexistence of the live and the mediatized; Indigenous activism and performance; work that challenges the orthodoxies of theatrical content, form and event; and the postmodern and the post-dramatic.

While Stanislavski remains the point of departure for much current thinking about actor training, in some ways the very traditions of artifice and knowing theatricality that his work unsettled have re-emerged in a contemporary theatre that at times has little or no interest in a fictional fourth wall between actor and audience. They have been unsettled too by contemporary technologies which promote ideologies of the present in ever-shifting futuristic forms, by a swathe of twenty-first-century technologies with the capacity to present multiple and overlapping versions of the now from different time frames, scales and countries.

This comes, as Alice Tuppen-Corps might see it, when practice embraces embodied as well as aesthetic notions of intimacy and identity, where actors and spectators engage in the interactive navigation of sites that are often as digitally mediated and dreamlike as they are actual. Immersive theatre is thus able to assume a dialogical space that positions the spectator and actor as both participant and observer.[23] Immersive theatre also carries with it the promise of a type of authenticity that differs in kind from the sustained pretence that comes with behavioural realism taking place behind its notional fourth wall.[24] In Erika Fischer-Lichte's terms, immersive theatre carries a different kind of presence too:

> Spectators sense a certain power for the actor that forces them to focus their full consideration on him without feeling overwhelmed, perceiving it as a source of energy .... Spectators sense that the actor is present in an unusually intense way, granting them, in turn, the intense sensation of themselves as present.[25]

Patrice Pavis locates presence similarly:

> To have 'presence' ... is to know how to capture the attention of the public and make an impression; it is also to be endowed with a *je ne sais quoi* which triggers an immediate feeling of identification in the spectator.[26]

Erving Goffman introduced an idea of identity construction in the study of human interaction through the use of metaphors that borrowed heavily from dramaturgy. In his best-known work, *The Presentation of Self in Everyday Life*, Goffman explored interpersonal interaction and how individuals 'perform' in order to project desirable images of who they are, and he stayed with theatre metaphors in his illustration of individuals' contrasting *front stage* and *back stage* behaviour. In front stage mode, a person, an *actor*, is acutely conscious of being observed by people, by *spectators*, and will consciously perform to those who are watching by observing certain rules and conventions. This actorly behaviour will be necessarily different in a private backstage environment. Goffman's front stage, then, is the observable space, the location in which deliberately contrived performances are displayed, where individuals act out their parts and where explicit and implied cues and patterns to the exchange are part and parcel of the actor–spectator relationship. As with immersive theatre, online performances are differently mediated and codified, blurring the lines between front and back stage. Consequently, the most intimate and private domestic locations can become wilful backdrops to the gaze of a large and often unknown audience, and the strictures of front stage and back stage are relaxed to disappearing point.

Online environments not only provide their users with the means to perform and present different identities but also merge the real and the fabricated to a hitherto unimaginable extent. The distance between actor and spectator provided by an absence of physical contact makes it easy to conceal aspects of the offline self and embellish an online persona, while the virtual spaces for these portrayals of alternate identities seem endless. That individuals perform their identities is not a radical concept. As Zizi Papacharissi notes,

> In environments that are both *privately public* and *publicly private*, the sequential arrangement of backstage and front stage is upset. The backstage no longer signals privacy and the front stage does not guarantee publicity…. allowing privately intended information to be broadcast to multiple public audiences, and delivering publicly produced information to private and intimately known audiences. Moreover, the individual must assess not one situation, but potentially an infinite number, in which the same self–performance must maintain authenticity, coherence, and relevance.[27]

When it comes to actor training, practice has always been prioritized over theory. No argument is being made here that online identity construction should form an embedded part of all actor training, but it does speak to digital performance modes, which are reimagining relationships between actors and spectators and between intimacy and distance. Tracey Moore sees theatre as something considered, communal and physical and as a form that is an antidote to what ails us in the digital world, which in forcing us to disconnect from technology and connect with one another can remind us what it is to be human.[28] But if any discipline is to be relevant in the current world, it needs to understand and engage with both the contemporary and the contextual.

Helenna Ren suggests that contemporary life is a state where 'all human activity could be considered as "performance", or at least all activity carried out with a consciousness of itself'.[29] In this sense, being and acting 'lie not in the frame of theatre versus real life but in an attitude'.[30] Of course, new technologies have massively influenced the ways in which identities and roles are created, received and understood, and these ways are not limited to overtly mediated situations. According to Steve Dixon, the human self has always been multiple; however, new virtual environments have allowed for a deeper engagement with these numerous identities.[31] Knowingly constructed online performances inevitably allow for smaller and in some ways more delicate encounters than we find in conventional theatres; yet the seeming intimacy of digitally structured one-to-one exchange, while fundamentally different to physical meetings, can create a sense of being present that is at odds with geographical distance. The experience positions actor and spectator in a shared and relational space that is at once private and public as well as engaged and detached.[32]

It remains a peculiarity of mainstream drama that events happen for reasons: A = B = C. In life, as we know, the accidental is writ large, and sometimes *things just happen*. In life, not every action has a reason and not every action has a consequence: good people do bad things for no discernible reason; the moralistic tell lies; loving parents kill their children; decorated soldiers rape civilians; random acts of violence are wrought by passive people; people act *out of character*. Because we know that the real is real, we accept the inevitability of not always knowing why events occurred in the ways that they did. To this extent, courtrooms act like theatres in their desire not primarily to punish but to know.

Unlike 'real life', drama, like other forms of fiction, is expected to make sense, and actors are the instruments through which this sense is communicated. If drama is characterized by narrative and dialectics, post-dramatic theatre occurs when internal logic no longer forms the centre, when composition is no longer experienced as an organizing quality but as an artificially imposed manufacture. The post-dramatic theatre theorized by Hans-Thies Lehmann and initially proposed by Richard Schechner eliminates the ideas of sustained representation and fictionality, privileging instead the spectator's individual experience in the moment of presentation. Squeezed between the aesthetics of mainstream theatre and a postmodern love of theory speak, Stanislavski's commitment to, even obsession with, finding the truth of fictional words might no longer feel particularly *necessary*. A dramatist's words may not always have as their intention the suspension of our collective disbelief; they may indeed seek to do just the opposite.[33]

Postmodernism's treatment of theatre can appear disconcertingly tame alongside Lehmann's description of the post-dramatic as that which is no longer *dramatic* and where unified character, plot, setting and the representation of a fictive cosmos is ruptured and even relinquished altogether. The result of this is not a play with characters and a recognizably stable setting so much as a composition of potentially meaningful moments which echo and evoke numerous situations, feelings and states. This book's chapters from Klaus Kruse and Stephen Simms on students learning through participation in overtly immersive productions remind us that however individual institutions might describe themselves, actor training is training for the now and for the future; or at least it should be. Simms describes, in his chapter in this book, the role of training as the creation of transformative actors, people who can 'respond to changing requirements and are not tied in time or ideology to any particular method or approach', stressing that 'there is no single industry for which students are being trained.' In a similar vein, the ever-astute Richard Gough sees training as a process concerned with nurturing 'practitioners not for the profession as it currently exists but rather for how it might be – in the future, as yet, unforeseen and unimagined.'[34]

The United Kingdom's Federation of Drama Schools recently determined to undertake training sessions in order to understand the right of consent and the complexities of permission, ethical caring, appropriate physical contact and personal integrity in and out of classes and the rehearsal room, particularly in circumstances where there is a power imbalance.[35] Their guidelines state that 'Consent can neither be presumed or expected or given under pressure, by peers or teachers/directors … where there might seem to be or there is an unequal power balance.'[36] For those institutions only recently beginning to engage with formal actor training, the ground is shifting before a firm foothold has been established. Committed as many universities are to providing students with contemporary, forward-looking training for contemporary and forward-looking careers, these shifting grounds make for exciting and positive times.[37] Writing about practice always locks the past into a kind of endless present. In many ways, this book chronicles the present as a near-past which is turning day by day into something that will never return.

Recent Histories, Current Contexts

The first drama department in the United States was established at the Carnegie Institute of Technology. In 1945, Oxford University sent a group of its scholars to the United States in order to explore the possibility of including drama in their own curriculum; the commission's report, published in 1948, stated that any attempts to include drama in ways that followed the US pattern 'would not be easily assimilated with the aims and traditions of their university' and that many of the programmes were inconsistent with 'the element of rigorous intellectual discipline'.[38] The Oxford dons felt that the US system was too vocational and that when acting in plays, students would become engrossed in the demands of the role at the expense of focusing on 'the significance of the play as a whole'.[39] The report suggested that it would be interesting to see productions at Oxford performed by a school of players 'under the aegis of the university but without any reference to any university degree.'[40] This interest has come to fruition with Oxford mounting approximately 30 student-cast shows each term supported by a full-time university drama officer, who helps students to plan, programme and publicize their productions. In addition to this, each year a major theatrical figure is appointed as the Cameron Mackintosh visiting professor of contemporary theatre to give a series of lectures and workshops for students. Previous holders of this position include Richard Attenborough, Nicholas Hytner, Diana Rigg, Kevin Spacey and Patrick Stewart.

Tyrone Guthrie was a member of a committee that presented a document called *The Universities and the Theatre* (1952), which was arranged to discuss the matter of Bristol University's following the United States' lead. Guthrie suggested that in its elementary state, the subject of drama might better belong not to a university but to a technical school or dramatic academy, and he bemoaned 'the dangerous tendency of universities to become not seats of learning, but training centres for jobs'.[41] The academic study of performance in the United Kingdom began then not at an Oxford college but with a handful of drama students at Bristol University in 1948. When it emerged as a UK subject, BA theatre was linked to both the educational vision and the etymology of learning through doing; while BA theatre studies tended to look towards the more abstract notions of *Theaterwissenschaft*, or the science of theatre. Many theatre programmes in the United Kingdom, the United States and Australia were subsequently rebranded as performance studies, for no better reason in some cases than that it was seen as an early-twenty-first-century sensationalization of nomenclature.

In the United Kingdom alone, the Higher Education Funding Council supports over 2,000 degree courses with 'acting', 'theatre' or 'drama' in their title.[42] Even though these university courses may appear to have a direct connection with the acting and theatre industry, some of them do not,[43] and it is impossible to accurately count how many aspiring graduate actors there are in the world. In the United States, many thousands of graduates of academic and professional acting schools are added to the total each year.[44] A recent UK report found that 86% of performers working in the profession had received formally accredited professional training.[45] Many of the remaining 14% come to acting from a form of celebrity recognition elsewhere: reality television, sports, music, fashion etc., often bolstered by personal coaching. This leaves precious little room for graduates from fully or quasi-academic programmes at universities.[46] To compensate for this, many graduates add postgraduate study at a drama school to their BA theatre qualifications.

Equity figures show that in the United Kingdom, as in the United States, the unemployment rate for actors is consistently around 90%, and if 86% of actors have been professionally trained – that is, at an accredited school – then the space for graduates from university programmes is tighter still.[47] In light of this and despite the high visibility wrought by occasional successes, taking a university degree that implies a route to the professional stage can at some institutions become an exercise in near futility.[48] Alan Eisenberg, the executive director of Actor's Equity, is forthright in his belief that universities are turning out graduates 'for whom there is no work' and that universities are preparing students for 'a career that has no interest in them'.[49] It is better and more honest perhaps to recognize, as Mike Pearson suggests, that universities are working with 'an increasing number of students who may never work in the theatre industry, and (they) have to offer them something else.'⁵⁰ That 'something else' is often the type of support that encourages graduates to set up their own theatre companies and to carve out careers as independent theatre-makers and facilitators. To this end, university theatre programmes tend to encourage students to explore and develop their own practice and to pursue non-mainstream employment opportunities in line with what Deirdre Heddon and Jane Milling describe as a 'university contemporary theatre language'.⁵¹ In a theatre climate that is rapidly evolving, these distinctions are eroding, but traditionally this has led to work in applied drama contexts and the kind of practice variously described as alternative, experimental, visual or contemporary. The boundaries blur from both sides: just as universities are making serious inroads into vocational training, so too have established drama schools such as NIDA diversified their approach to training to include electives in physical, applied and musical theatre.

Drama schools tend to offer many more hours of training than universities do, and this time to learn gives their students an inevitable advantage.⁵² Once again, it can be difficult for prospective students to pick a path through the ways in which universities advertise their acting programmes. Not all issues are made transparent to prospective students. Every programme will have recruitment targets for enrolment numbers. Other targets exist, often in relation to widening participation: information on applicants' age, postcode, gender, race and nationality will be monitored by human resources, and institutions from the grand to the barely known will need to demonstrate that their application and selection processes are fair, equitable and in line with strategic plans. With actor training, this is a serious matter. When diversity within the performing arts has been subject to so much serious and strenuous public debate in recent years, it is right and proper that institutions do what they can to make access to training available to rich and poor alike, with the knowledge that limited progress has so far been made in terms of class, wealth and social as well as cultural diversity. Institutions are aware of the need to attend to the unconscious and structural biases that still impact approaches to training. Although selection process still have room for improvement, having actors emerging from programmes with cohorts that reflect contemporary life in all its colours, shapes, sounds, beliefs, values and sizes is doing much to challenge still-narrow perceptions of what an actor *looks like* and how an actor *is*.

Widening participation works because it encourages institutions and the members of staff who populate them to challenge an often unconscious bias; what matters too is that the gates of access are not opened without concern for what lies within. It is never enough to assume that training and education work as a one-size-fits-all approach. Being accepted into a programme and being included in it are in no way the same thing; we know too that the institutional language of inclusivity can mask real prejudice, whether conscious or not.[53]

The United Kingdom's Conference of Drama Schools comprises the country's most established training establishments. Its purpose is to strengthen the voice of the member schools and to maintain the standards of training within the vocational drama sector. It also serves to distinguish some of the differences between drama schools and universities and to make it easier for prospective students to understand the application process. The fact that many previously independent UK drama schools are now part of universities complicates this situation: East 15 is part of the University of Essex; Guildhall is part of City University of London; Guildford is part of the University of Surrey; the Royal Birmingham Conservatoire is part of Birmingham City University; Drama Centre London is associated with Central Saint Martins, which is a constituent college of the University of the Arts London.[54] Under circumstances such as these, it is easy to confuse drama school approaches with university approaches.

Regardless of whether a drama school is part of a university, all UK drama schools have their higher education validated by universities; without this, they are unable to offer degree qualifications. RADA, for example, while maintaining its independent status, has its degrees validated by Kings College London. All BA students in the United Kingdom have a grade band attached to their degree, a first class degree or an upper second, a lower second or a third. For graduates of drama school, this type of distinction tends to be less important than for graduates of university courses. It is much more common, for example, to hear a graduate say that they trained at Guildhall, RADA, East 15 et al. and to say whom they were taught by than that they graduated with a 1st or a 2:2. In this regard, the purpose of the majority of drama schools is clear and has not altered significantly as students have started to graduate with degree qualifications: they exist to train actors and turn them into better performers. Theory and contextual studies classes will usually form part of this training, but the focus is on learning and being trained to *do*.

Training and Value

Not everyone is convinced that actors need training at all. Speaking at a Westminster Forum Projects meeting, the National Youth Theatre's artistic director Paul Roseby claimed that 'Most actors do not require years of drama school to learn their craft'; people, he suggests, 'can either act or they can't'.[55] The theatre producer Richard Jordan sees things differently, arguing that if actors are to have sustainable careers, then being trained is necessary, given that training is 'not just in acting technique but also in the techniques of getting a job, building a career and surviving in the longer term.'[56] The reality may be somewhat more nuanced. Dee Cannon suggests in speaking to her work at RADA that 'the untrained actor often fares badly on stage' before echoing something of Roseby's views: drama schools can teach people timing and how to stand without being able to teach students to be in touch with their own spirit, and learned technique is useful, but it needs to be applied to some innate qualities.[57] Writing about which students are admitted to the Actors Studio, David Mamet argues that 'The Studio ... *chose* them; it did not *make* them. The best actors, passing through a rigorous and extensive audition process, were admitted .... The accomplished actors, young, vital, talented and hearty, succeeded and succeed *in spite of* their training.'[58] Certainly, it could be (and often is) said that the more rigorously selective drama schools are taking good actors rather than making them. But the same could be said of a university that sets high academic standards at the point of entry and then produces intellectually impressive graduates, recruiting the most academically potent at age 18 and almost inevitably graduating the most academically able at 21.

Mamet is adamant in his belief that 'most teachers of acting are frauds, and their schools offer nothing other than the right to consider oneself part of the theatre.'[59] Mamet has an ally in Elia Kazan, who takes aim at the Actors Studio, drawing attention to what he regards as the degeneration of Stanislavski's ideology through distortion:

> Most method teaching is corrupt ... it is not connected with a theatre. Stanislavski himself was connected with a theatre – always. It's a racket. Since they have to make money. they work the racket. They become show horses of authority in order to establish the reputation necessary to draw students.[60]

Through the method or otherwise, Stanislavski's influence dominates debates about acting in the West.[61] Stanislavski created a detailed process for the appearance of inspiration by means of the will, producing a purposive environment for artistic stimulation during the creation and performance of a role: stimulation in pursuit of simulation, as it were. For actors to behave onstage as truthfully as in their offstage lives, a roadmap of sorts is necessary, and Stanislavski's urgings continue to provide actors with the tools to work in new ways and new worlds and with new forms.[62]

Whether we like it or not, the new world we are in is the post-truth era: a time of fabrication, fabulation and mimeticism in which political debate is framed by emotional appeals that are largely disconnected from policy details. Low-level mendacity has become endemic in all realms of public, professional and social life. Facts play second fiddle to euphemisms, and deception and spin have started to reign. A 2017 lecture in the Distinguished Lecture Series at the University of Southampton entitled 'The truth, the post truth, and nothing but no truth, so help me God' (written and delivered by Jon Sopel) sounds as apposite as it does ironic.

One truth we do know is that regardless of differences in background and experience, acting students enter into programmes of training with some fairly consistent expectations. Students are likely, quite reasonably, to expect to work on their voices and bodies; to work on dramatic scripts from the past and present; to go deeply into supported scene study; and to be cast in a range of plays; to gain experience in acting for the camera and for radio. They can expect that their work will be seen by casting agents, directors and producers; that they will be taught by people with sharp-end professional experience; that they will have long and intensive contact hours; and that they will learn primarily through doing. Students will assume, again with some justification, that their process of application was in some way a measure of the programme they have joined and that if they were asked to audition in a certain way, then that 'way' would be reflective of the programme's aims. Being asked to prepare a three-minute soliloquy for presentation on an empty stage would suggest a particular programme focus (and I am aware that that the example is extreme), whereas spending half a day on group exercises would suggest something altogether different.

People choosing acting as a career are entering a world with countless ways in; deciding whether to go to university or drama school is a key decision, but no more key than being able to determine whether a programme feels appropriate, rigorous and *right*. No route can provide all of the answers, and no institution can guarantee its graduates' success. The chapters that follow offer no golden answers to the questions of where or how one should study and train, because such answers can be determined only by students, on an individual basis; they are, however, written by teachers/trainers articulating what they do and why. The value of the chapters lies in the way they offer insight into what goes on in their programmes, workshops, classes and studios. No words can replicate the experience itself; nevertheless, the following chapters open doors to training processes. Readers are invited to walk through these doors and discover for themselves what different forms of actor training mean, what they intend and how the road to professional accomplishment is mapped and travelled.

Notes

1   Stories of actors, particularly those in film, stumbling into careers are regularly spun. The stories make good copy, but the reality is almost always different.
2   This is more obviously the case in theatre than in television and film.
3   Every decision is also a loss, and this book's focus on training at institutions in the United Kingdom, United States and Australia is not intended to be read as exclusive. The 12 institutions addressed in this book are in these three countries; other books with equal claim to offering international perspectives might just as usefully focus on work elsewhere. The decision to include four chapters from each of the countries highlights differences as well as similarities. These might have been overlooked had the chapters focused on work in 12 different countries; that is, the book might have seemed to suggest that *this* is how actors are trained in *that* country.
4   This choice excludes institutions such as the Actors Studio. Founded in 1947, the Actors Studio is a non-profit organization for professional actors, directors and playwrights; thus, it differs in kind from the broadly pre-professional training programmes addressed in this book. The Actors Studio has entered into partnership with Pace University New York to offer a three-year master in fine arts (MFA) degree based heavily on Stanislavski's system. The best-known Actors Studio is in New York, with a West Coast branch in Los Angeles.
5   Others still are exceptional at the same time as they are slightly undone by their own publicity. John Gillett's excellent 2014 book *Acting Stanislavski: A practical guide to Stanislavski's approach and legacy* (London & New York: Bloomsbury Methuen) has on its opening page a testimonial from Marina Calderone that Gillett's book 'will give you all the tools you need in your "Acting" kit' and that it will provide 'a process whereby you can create truthfully'. As good as the book is, it cannot do that.
6   Safir, M. A. (2011) *Robert Wilson from Within*. Paris: The American University of Paris. p. 320.

7   These include but are in no way limited to the Actors Center Alliance of Teachers; the International Platform for Performer Training; the American Society for Theatre Research; the Australasian Drama Studies Conference; the Performing Arts Scoping Study; Theatre and Performance Research Association; The Standing Conference of Drama Departments; Practice as Research in Performance; and Performing Arts Learning and Teaching Innovation Network.
8   The term 'drama school' refers here to institutions that are dedicated to a clear focus on the training of actors, as compared with institutions (often universities) that include the training and education of actors alongside a range of other programmes and subject areas.
9   Bretton Hall College is an obvious example. Founded in 1949, the college specialized in innovative courses in design, music and the visual and performance arts. Bretton Hall merged with the University of Leeds in 2001 and was subsequently sold off in 2006. Founded in 1961, Dartington College of Arts is another example. Dartington had a focus on a performative and multidisciplinary approach to the arts. Its teaching staff were all active arts practitioners, including Rudolph Laban, John Cage, John Hall, Gavin Bryars and Michael Checkov.
10 A degree in acting says vocation and implies intent. To train students to be actors means to be measured in large part, if not exclusively, by how many graduates go on to long-term and credible careers as actors. While some BA acting programmes at UK universities have recognized that a vocational degree requires vocational hours (as well as sufficiently and sometimes *differently* qualified members of staff), others continue to offer 10 or 12 hours of timetabled staff contact time. Many students in these programmes are talented, intelligent and driven, but it is understandably difficult to convince directors and casting agents that the training they have received is as valid and useful as a minimum of 30 hours a week of staff contact time at a drama school.
11 There are some financial benefits to students from this. Historically, students at UK drama schools did not qualify for support through government grants. When drama schools began to wrap their training around programmes that led to earned degrees, their students became eligible. Before this, drama school students were funded either privately or, more rarely, through competitive scholarships from local education authorities and/or from charitable trusts. Grants have been replaced by a student loans system, but the principle of eligibility remains the same.
12 Vaughan, R. (2018) 'Mental health crisis among students must be top priority'. Published originally in the *i*. 12 August, p. 6. Retrieved from The Office for Students (OfS) https://inews.co.uk/news/education/student-mental-health-top-priority-watchdog
13 Seton, M. (2010) 'The ethics of embodiment: Actor training and habitual vulnerability'. *Performing Ethos* 1(1), pp. 5–20. https://www.researchgate.net/publication/233497041_The_ethics_of_embodiment_actor_training_and_habitual_vulnerability
14 Susan Robson suggests that companies need to be more than ready for disruption; they need to have the courage to self-disrupt: https://utilityweek.co.uk/event-review-the-customer-of-the-future-roundtable/. Actor training has been slow to change, but in recent years, this courage is becoming more evident.
15 Sextou, P. (2016) 'The Pedagogy of Drama Supervision in higher education'. *Brookes eJournal of Learning and Teaching* 3(1). http://bejlt.brookes.ac.uk/paper/the_pedagogy_of_drama_supervision_in_higher_education-2/

16 Schonmann, S. 'Ethical Tensions in Drama Teachers' Behaviour'. https://view.officeapps.live.com/op/view.aspx?src=http%3A%2F%2Fwww.theatroedu.gr%2Fportals%2F38%2Fmain%2Fimages%2Fstories%2Ffiles%2FArthra%2FSCHONMANN_Ethical%2520Tensions%2520in%2520Drama%2520Teachers.doc

17 Anne Bogart developed a version of an improvisational, ensemble-building technique called Viewpoints; she coupled this with the physical acting training developed by Tadashi Suzuki. The training methods of Bogart's company SITI are widespread tools of actor training, with classes taught in universities and colleges across the United States, as well as internationally.

18 Jeff Janisheski took up his California State University post after being commissioned to contribute a chapter to this book on his work at NIDA; the fact that he is now at Long Beach with another of the book's contributors, Hugh O'Gorman, occurred quite by chance.

19 Peter Sardi's LinkedIn article 'When acting techniques become dogma and acting teachers become gurus' includes incisive video clips of Edward Norton and Robert Benedetti discussing teachers of acting and their methods: https://www.linkedin.com/pulse/when-acting-techniques-become-dogma-teachers-gurus-peter-sardi.

20 'Western' generally refers to living in or originating from the West, in particular Europe, Canada, the United States, Australia and New Zealand. Australia is southeast of much of Asia, and yet the vast majority of its settled population are of European origin, and most of the country's gross domestic product (GDP), education, healthcare, tax rates, court system, form of government and regulatory systems are in line with other Western countries. In many ways, then, location is not significantly applicable. 'Western' speaks to an overall attitude, way of living and outlook. In this context, many people now regard Japan as Western.

21 For a provocative and telling take on this, see particularly page 7 of Richard Gough's 2018 paper 'Future Proof (With Courage & Curiosity): Training for a theatre that does not yet exist' *Polish Theatre Journal* 1(5), pp. 1–12 (www.polishtheatrejournal.com) https://pure.southwales.ac.uk/files/2162979/166_1108_1_PB.pdf.

22 This cuts both ways, inasmuch as the rise in technology has not necessarily resulted in committed digital artists but a generation of *why not me?* raised on a diet of immediacy. While the optimism of much modern life brings students its own undoubted rewards, it has also led, in the worst cases, to a peculiar combination of laziness and vanity, to an obsession with the self far removed from the disciplines of study or training. As Geoffrey Colman, head of acting at London's Central School describes it in 2008 in 'Reality TV Taking Over Acting Talents', the result is 'a lot of [applicants] who are, quite frankly, deluded ... and who are presenting themselves in an unprepared way': http://www.youtube.com/watch?v=scHZJmcFB8I.

23 Tuppen-Corps, A. (2017) https://www.alicetuppencorps.com/about.

24 The difference is in kind rather than quality. No argument is being made here that one form of presentation has a greater claim to authenticity than any other.

25 pp. 108–109.

26 Pavis, P. (1987) *Dictionary of the Theatre: Terms, Concepts, and Analysis*. Toronto, ON: University of Toronto Press, p. 9.

27 Papacharissi, Z. (2010) *A Private Sphere: Democracy in a Digital Age*. Malden, MA: Polity Press, p. 142.
28 Moore, T. (2016) 'Why Theater Majors are Vital in the Digital Age'. *The Chronicle of Higher Education*. http://www.chronicle.com/article/Why-Theater-Majors-Are-Vital/235925.
29 Ren, H. (2016) Unpublished MPhil thesis Brunel University: *Digital Performance: How representations of physical and virtual bodies inform identity construction/deconstructio*n.
30 Ibid.
31 Dixon, S. (2007) *Digital Performance*. Cambridge, MA: MIT Press, p. 269.
32 Virtual reality (VR) has been used in performance contexts for several years now, and practitioners continue to challenge notions of what is 'real', what is 'virtual' and what occupies the spaces in between. Through this, VR has created new performance paradigms, not least in terms of reimagining existing theatre work and boosting collaborations between actors, artists and engineers. New performance environments are being created within VR in order to change the ways in which audiences engage with performance. From an actor's perspective, VR involves more than the technical aspects of wearing camera rigs attached to their heads; the National Theatre used VR to help actors prepare for their roles in *The Plough and the Stars* by learning about the Easter Rising from the perspective of a young man who lived through it. See 'National Theatre uses virtual reality to get actors into character' in *The Telegraph*, 2 August 2016. http://www.telegraph.co.uk/news/2016/08/02/national-theatre-uses-virtual-reality-to-get-actors-into-character/.
33 It is worth noting that one of the key shifts in postmodern and post-dramatic theatre is the way that performers' relationships are often primarily with spectators rather than characters.
34 Gough, R. (2018).
35 Snow, G. (2018) *Drama schools commit to ethical guidelines to tackle sexual harassment*. 19 April 2018. https://www.thestage.co.uk/news/2018/drama-schools-commit-ethical-guidelines-tackle-sexual-harassment/.
36 Ibid.
37 The temptation here is to write 'all universities'. This might, however, be an exercise in optimism rather than reality.
38 Cumberlege, G. (1948) *Report of the Oxford University Drama Commission*. Oxford: Oxford University Press.
39 Ibid.
40 Ibid.
41 James, D. J. (1952) *The Universities and the Theatre*. Sydney: Allen & Unwin, p. 21.
42 In light of the fact that entries for drama at the General Certificate of Secondary Education (GCSE), generally undertaken at a UK high school, have dropped significantly over the five years to date, it is difficult not to see university numbers as a type of saturation point. See Kershaw, A. and I. Jones 'More pupils are shunning GCSEs in creative arts.' *The Independent*, 3 August 2018, p. 10.
43 See http://www.theactingwebsite.com/should-i-go-to-drama-school-to-become-an-actor-c229.html.

44　See http://theatredoconacting.blogspot.com.au/.
45　NCDT. (2010). http://www.ncdt.co.uk/files/Voc_Guide_June_10.pdf
46　Elkin, S. (2011). *University or Theatre School*. http://blogs.thestage.co.uk/education/2011/03/university-or-theatre-school/.
47　The situation is somewhat less bleak in Australia, although competition for professionally paid work is still high.
48　This statement needs to be qualified. In Australia, for example, Queensland University of Technology (QUT) offers a bachelor of fine arts (BFA) in acting and is consistently placed by industry leaders in the top four acting schools in Australia. As Andrea L. Moor's chapter shows, the QUT programme is strictly vocational with intense industry involvement and considerable graduate success. There are similar high-quality and successful university programmes in the United Kingdom and the United States.
49　McMahon, B. (2012) 'Unemployment is Lifestyle for Actors': http:www.huffington-post.com/Brendan-mcmahon.
50　Tysome, T. (2004) 'Focus Theatre' in *Times Higher Education*. 16 April (23–24), p. 24.
51　Heddon, D. & J. Milling (2015) *Devising Performance: a Critical History*. Basingstoke: Palgrave Macmillan, p. 249.
52　This is a tendency, not a given. BA acting programmes at some UK universities are beginning to increase the week-by-week hours of study; however, many others are not. Quantity does not always equate to quality, but it is often a useful measure of a university programme's commitment to the genuine demands of training.
53　This was addressed in a 2017 report, *Acting Up*, exploring the class barrier in UK drama schools and highlighting the cost of auditioning for drama school as one of many key barriers to entry. The report cites Guildhall's audition fee of £64 for prospective students to audition; the Royal Central School of Speech and Drama charges £55; RADA charges early applicants £46, rising to £86 for those applying later in the year; Bristol Old Vic Theatre School charges £45 per audition, rising to £65. The report's conclusion is that audition fees make the application process 'totally unaffordable for many students.' https://www.thestage.co.uk/news/2017/diversity-industry-challenge-not-just-one-drama-schools-claims-training-sector/. RADA is not alone in offering waivers based on financial hardship as well as holding regional auditions. Nevertheless, given that charging fees for auditions is a standard drama school rather than university practice and that potential students will routinely audition at several schools, this is an issue that runs counter to claims of valuing and promoting diversity. Requesting the waiving of fees based on one's financial position comes with its own costs in terms of emotions and confidence.
54　The Western Australian Academy of Performing Art is part of Edith Cowan University at Mount Lawley in Perth. WAAPA students are part of the university. From direct experience, I know that WAAPA students regard themselves as distinct from the wider university population. When they apply, they do so because of WAAPA's reputation and standing rather than Edith Cowan's. The Victorian College of the Arts (VCA) is part of Melbourne University, and VCA students likewise feel part of a distinct and separate

institution. This is not to discredit either Edith Cowan University or Melbourne University, which are both fine institutions. A similar situation exists in the United Kingdom: students are not significantly applying to East 15 because it now forms part of the University of Essex. What distinguishes programmes like these is that they are run according to drama school values. As an example, East 15 students will receive considerably more by way of timetabled staff contact hours than 'regular' Essex students. The University of Essex is interesting inasmuch as across its three campus locations, two (Loughton and Southend-on-Sea) house the East 15 programmes, while one (Colchester) is the site for BA theatre as well as MA and PhD routes. Notwithstanding the fact that the theatre programmes are taught by some experienced and active practitioners, being a theatre student at the University of Essex is a radically different experience in content and approach than that of being an acting student at East 15. In this way, the University of Essex provides a useful comparison between a university course, which combines theory and practice, and a drama school approach, where practice is always paramount. Interestingly and tellingly, there is little or no overlap between work that takes place at Southend/Loughton and work at Colchester.

55 Merrifield, N. (2013) 'Three-year drama training not needed by "majority of actors"'. *The Stage*, 24 October 2013. https://www.thestage.co.uk/news/2013/three-year-drama-training-needed-majority-actors/.
56 Gardner, L. (2008) 'Not puppets, but thinking actors'. *Guardian*, 15 July 2008. https://www.theguardian.com/education/2008/jul/15/highereducation.uk1).
57 Cannon, D. (2009) 'Character building and what makes a truly great actor'. *Guardian*, 9 May 2009. https://www.theguardian.com/stage/2009/may/09/character-building-great-actor.
58 Mamet, D. (1997) *True and False: Heresy and Common Sense for the Actor*. New York: Pantheon Books, pp. 14–15. Method acting receives something of a bad press in the United Kingdom, where many actors and trainers are sceptical, cynical even, about what is seen (and not always accurately) as the prioritizing of immersion over technique; there is some widespread caution too over a method being referred to as *the* method.
59 Ibid., p. 43.
60 Gray, P. (1965) *Stanislavski and America*. New York: Hill and Wang, p. 174.
61 These debates run also into spellings of his name, and these can be fiercely defended. For some it's always Stanislavski and for others Stanislavsky; for some it's Konstantin and for others Constantin. For the purpose of uniformity, it's Konstantin Stanislavski in this book's pages, other than where a bibliographic reference demands a different spelling.
62 It is worth remembering that Stanislavski was not widely regarded as a great actor, which is to say that being in possession of knowledge is not the same thing as being in control of one's art to the extent of transcending technique and form in pursuit of the mercurial. We bring who we are to what we do. If training teaches technique, it also serves to strip away many of the barriers between who we are and what we are prepared to show.

Part 1

Preparing the Ground

2

Whole Actor, Whole Person Training: Designing a Holistic Actor Training Programme for Individual Career Longevity and Well-Being

Andrea L. Moor

Introduction

This chapter analyses how the Queensland University of Technology (QUT) bachelor of fine arts (BFA) acting course is addressing actors' well-being as the philosophical underpinning of the curriculum design through WAWPT: Whole Actor, Whole Person Training. The measures taken are meant to support the student actor during the intensive three-year training and prepare them for the unpredictable nature of the industry they are entering. QUT acting is a vocational, conservatoire-style training programme that equips graduates for work in theatre, film and television. The programme has an extensive skills component, with each student engaging in seven full theatre productions, two studio television projects, two location shoots, extensive self-testing training, stand-up and voice-over training. QUT acting is regarded in the top four BFA acting programmes in Australia, with graduates achieving significant success in Australia and internationally, including in Hollywood.

Recommendations to Drama Schools

There is global awareness around the need to support and facilitate measures to ensure the well-being of actors within training and professional situations as evidenced by the establishment of well-being initiatives in Australia, the United Kingdom and the United States. Industry unions, private therapists and publications are getting on board to expose the disturbing statistics of poor mental and emotional wellness; to provide possible solutions to cooling off after a performance (2017, American Theatre) and the stress of the industry (Wellbeing for the Arts, UK); and to develop clear strategies for long-term wellness in the profession (Artsminds, UK). Australia has taken a leading position in the establishment of initiatives to address these problems. The Australian Actors Wellbeing Study (Maxwell et al., 2015) made several recommendations to actor training institutions regarding best practices in regard to actors' well-being. These recommendations included paying close attention to the actors' psychological health throughout all areas of training and performance as well as issues related to financial and career stability. The study proposed that many issues related to the ongoing mental and financial well-being of actors could be best addressed in the drama school setting:

> How actors are adequately prepared for their lifetime of work can be a vexed issue. However, what is emerging in the field is data that suggests more can be done to prepare those entering the acting profession and to support actors throughout their career development. … [T]eaching staff, support staff and industry partners might usefully enter into conscious dialogue with each other about ensuring a healthier interplay between students' developmental needs, course expectations and workplace culture.
>
> (Prior et al., 2015, p. 1)

Robb and Due clearly marked areas for specific attention:

> While there are various definitions of wellbeing, the current study utilises Ryff's empirically validated indicators of positive functioning, specifically autonomy (the ability to resist social pressure), environmental mastery, personal growth, positive relationships, purpose in life, and self-acceptance.
>
> (Robb, Due, 2017)

This chapter will outline how improvements both to the delivery of core actor training methodologies and the implementation of additional individual well-being programmes can improve indicators for students in these identified areas. Recommendations have been implemented in the BFA acting curriculum at QUT to shape a holistic, entire degree approach to actor training. This holistic approach marries two main areas of investigation: individual well-being programmes and core actor training. Initiatives involving mindfulness, relaxation, warm-up, warm-down and financial literacy will be discussed and their efficacy addressed.

Recent Development in the Awareness of Actor's Mental Health and Well-Being

Since the publication of *The Australian Actors Wellbeing Study* in 2015, there have been significant developments in the awareness of mental health of performers in Australia. The recent establishment of Entertainment Assist is the most notable development. The organization is the first lobby and education foundation to dedicate their energies specifically to 'research, education and training initiatives, identification of appropriate resources and promotion of appropriate mental health practices in performing arts and entertainment industry workplaces' (2018). The Australian Society for Performing Arts Healthcare (ASPAH) is broadening their focus to incorporate the mental health of performers, focusing at their 2018 conference on 'performance preparation and recovery'. Researchers are addressing the topic in great detail. Alison E. Robb and Clemence Due examined the well-being of acting students at two sites of training in Adelaide for their paper *Exploring psychological wellbeing in acting training: an Australian interview study* (2017); American researcher Brian C. Hite dedicated his doctoral thesis to the subject in *Positive Psychological Capital, Need Satisfaction, Performance, and Well-Being in Actors and Stunt People* (2015); Susan Leith Taylor dedicated her doctoral thesis to *Actor Training and Emotions – Finding a Balance* (2016); Mark Seton has established the Actors Wellbeing Academy; and the Media Entertainment and Arts Alliance (MEAA) has established a wellness committee, co-written a code of conduct with Screen Producers Australia (SPA) and with the Confederation of Australian State Theatre Companies (CAST).

The clear choreography of intimacy by an experienced intimacy choreographer is now being suggested as the most appropriate way to deal with intimacy onstage and on-screen, and theatre companies are considering expression of intimacy and subject topics as part of their risk assessment of a production. This comes at a time when performers, particularly women, are finding their voice and speaking out against systemic coverups concerning boundary crossing and abuse. It is the time of the #MeToo movement and the calling out of those in positions of power. Drama schools must take on board all of these developments by instituting both specific tools for actors' well-being and implementing philosophical underpinnings that make clear the roles and responsibilities of all teaching and directing staff in regard to student well-being and ethical conduct.

Recommendations into Practice

The main recommendations directed to drama schools from *The Australian Actors Wellbeing Study* were the following:

1. Actor training should systematically address aspects of actors' well-being, including the maintenance of psychological health and the imbedding of skills and techniques not only in warming up for performance – something that appears to be well-established in the field – but in cooling down and debriefing after performance.
2. Actors' financial literacy and capacity to engage in career planning should be addressed as a priority both by training institutions and by industry stakeholders.
3. The assertion of an industry-wide obligation to provide actors with structured opportunities to cool down and debrief after performance.
4. The urgency of raising actors' awareness about the industry-specific challenges of depression, anxiety, stress and both alcohol and drug use.
5. Training institutions and industry stakeholders should develop, implement and maintain strategies to develop actors' capacity both to recognize these challenges and to foster appropriate behaviours and practices in response.

I have conflated the above recommendations with the main points from the current literature to come up with the following categories that give us the best framework for addressing well-being and issues of mental health within the acting cohort:

- Identity – establishing a nurturing and supportive place for the student actor within the group and the school.
- Autonomy – the student actor takes control of their own learning from feedback and reflection to determine their own progress and steps for progression.

- Agency – developing the ability for each student actor to recognize issues and act on them for themselves and others.
- Knowledge – establishing clear knowledge of the student actor's craft in order to remedy anxiety and stress through clear acting processes.
- Skills – attaining the skills for personal and group well-being and the measures to take when mental health issues become apparent.

Identity: Establishing and Supporting Identity

Identity building is vital from day one of a student's arrival in any acting institution. Within the training at QUT acting, we adopt many strategies to make sure the student feels like a part of the family. Young actors entering a prestigious drama school will acknowledge that they are incredibly nervous on their first day, believing that everyone else is probably better than them and that the second- and third-year students are in a completely different stratosphere of ability. We attempt to level the playing field as quickly as possible through several informal gatherings both on and off campus in student-led initiatives, allowing the first years to form some social ties early on. We set them up with third-year mentors who are there to support them through the rigour of that first year. Once they graduate, these mentors will have had two years in the industry and will be a fountain of knowledge regarding how to survive that challenging first year.

In the first week, we establish the way students will be treated and the way they will treat each other for the next three years. As course coordinator, I meet with new students to share my perspective on actor training from a practitioner's point of view. Because one quarter of our students are on scholarships, it is made clear from day one that while these people did a great audition and did well to achieve the scholarship, there is no hierarchy in a drama school. One person may be brilliant in their first opportunity to work and then flail around as they process new information while others appear to overtake them.

It is important to clarify that arriving in the programme via a scholarship makes students neither better nor worse than anyone else. Students are also reassured that I will be their advocate for the full three years. This is vital. Students have often commented that this moment was significant to them. Students are told that I will always believe in them, especially when they might not be capable of believing in themselves. Students are assured at this point that they are all talented; otherwise, they would not have succeeded in gaining a place in such a competitive course and that each of them will have their own individual journey through their time at QUT.

This approach is drawn from the Montessori Education System, in which students' achievements are measured in terms of their understanding of the work. A student will always be in one of the three phases of understanding:

1. introduction to the work
2. repetition of the work, increasing understanding
3. mastery of the work.

Mastery of the work assumes many different levels and dimensions as the student actor takes on greater challenges. This scale assumes that each actor has the ability to be masterly and that each actor will achieve that mastery at their own pace, depending on many external and some internal factors. I assure them that by the day they present their showcase scenes to industry leaders they will all be masterly and that it does not matter what their journey is through the three years as long as they are striving for that. This introduction makes clear that acting is a process of learning and not some innate talent. They are assured they already have the talent and that their on-going journey will be one of learning how to extend, stretch and deepen that talent. By the end of day one, they should all feel that they are on an even playing field and that they are about to embark on a journey together. This entry into the environment is vital. The first day sets the tone for how a student's *identity* will be supported throughout the training.

Over the next three weeks, the cohort is taken on a deep process that sets them up for the entire three years. Facilitator Margi Brown Ash introduces them to relational impulse cultural collaborative (RICC) training. This is a process that Brown Ash has developed by synthesizing her experience as an actor, storyteller, theatre-maker, therapist and researcher. Much has been said in the literature about how ill-equipped acting teachers are to deal with the psychological complexities of young people's lives. Brown Ash holds a bachelor of arts (BA) with a diploma in education, a graduate diploma in adolescent health and welfare, a graduate diploma in experiential and creative arts therapy, a master of arts (research) and a masters in counselling. Brown Ash has also just completed her PhD thesis. Most importantly, she is a practising actor, director and theatre-maker, having trained in the United States and Australia. The work is underpinned by extensive research and many years of counselling experience. In this process, the students learn through both visual arts–based exercises and actor impulse training. They learn to acknowledge their individuality and at the same time accept the differences in the group. Gender and cultural perspectives are encouraged, and the group becomes aware of how power could potentially shift if each member of the group is not given a voice. Different styles of leadership are explored through play, and emphasis is placed on good manners and reflexive listening. The group determines their own guidelines of engagement to optimize excellence within the whole group. Brown Ash introduces them to the bridging in and bridging out process as a way of entering and exiting the work.

This process has now been adopted by many of the core teachers in the programme and offers everyone a way of checking in and leaving the day's work. After this initial three weeks, the student actors all feel empowered, and almost without knowing, they have been introduced to a healthy process of staying open and free in the work. Breath work, meditation and yoga are introduced and then implemented by the students as they go on to run their own warm-ups. Brown Ash sees herself much as a facilitator and mentor, allowing the students to gain mastery over the principles of the work.

Establishing Autonomy

The QUT acting curriculum has several foundational elements. As is the case at other Australian drama schools, we embrace wholeheartedly the notion of autonomy influenced by a uniquely Australian approach pioneered by Lindy Davies. Davies developed the original curriculum for the acting programme at Victorian College of Arts (VCA), The Autonomous Actor. In my doctoral research, I focused on QUT, National Institute of Dramatic Art (NIDA), VCA and Western Australian Academy of Performing Arts (WAAPA) from 2000 to 2012, and it was the VCA graduates who had studied under Davies who expressed the highest level of course satisfaction. They noted that they were well equipped to move into the industry with a clear idea of their own process, values and personal empowerment. The principles of unconditional positive regard and the focus on process clearly made a winning combination. As Davies describes it,

> I've set up a model of working which is based upon the Rogerian principle of unconditional positive regard. That means that the atmosphere of permission has to exist in the room in order for the work to take place, so that if any judgement or projection is going on, in terms of making the director/teacher the monster or the goddess or whatever, it gets exposed.
>
> (Ginters, 2008, p. 89)

In week four of the first semester, the QUT actors present scenes that they have chosen and staged without any influence from teaching staff, seeking feedback from their peers only. This forms a diagnostic tool that each staff member feeds into. The emphasis here is on gauging each actor's skills and the areas that need development. All of the teacher feedback is synthesized into an online platform that the student can continue to refer to throughout the three years of training. It is important that the student sees this as a diagnostic tool and not an evaluation. The work in these scenes usually reflects their high school drama class or any other teaching that they have had prior to entering the course and mostly does not incorporate the clear and uncluttered pursuit of action.

I then spend six weeks working with the students, retuning their awareness into the clear pursuit of action through the acting technique called practical aesthetics. The focus here is again not on how well they can act the scene but on how well they can explore each element of the technique. After six weeks, we want them to be able to use a simple process to analyse a scene, play a scene action with multiple tactics and bring a sense of personalization to the work that is informed by their own life but not based on past experience. The end result of this exercise is that they all see how simple adjustments in how they approach the work will make a significant difference to the outcome and see that it has nothing to do with 'talent'. They can then autonomously determine the outcome of their own work by making simple adjustments to the process. In this process, they coach each other and direct each other, owning the process as the means to an end. This again reflects the Montessori notion that once a student has mastered an activity, they can teach it to others. In this instance, the coaching reinforces their own understanding and gives them confidence in leading a process as a director or teacher would. They also come up against the bits they don't fully understand in the process. We set clear guidelines for coaching and point out the difference between coaching and directing, discouraging criticism and encouraging positive feedback. Through coaching, each actor starts to develop their own critical eye and the ability to articulate what they see. This of course feeds into all of their group work and is the foundation of the group-devised work that follows later in their first year.

Developing Agency

By the sixth week of their first year, the actors will have established their *identity* in the knowledge that the group supports their expression of themselves and will know how to support the identity of others in the group. They will have routinely experienced the check-in and check-out process from each day's work and often from individual classes. Through these various processes, the actors become aware of their own mental, physical and emotional responses to the work and can determine whether they need or one of their cohort needs support. They will have clear lines of reporting any issues, starting with their mentor, moving up to their individual teacher, onto me as course coordinator and then to the study area coordinator. If students have psychological issues, they can use the university's free counselling service. If we deem that their issue needs to be supported by Brown Ash, we can bring her back to work with an individual or to work with the whole group. This has proved to be invaluable when the group dynamics were for some reason unsettled.

Skills for Well-Being: Mindfulness Practices

In the first three weeks, the students learn several mindfulness and relaxation practices and are taught how to lead the group in these practices. Each student has the ability to lead a deep relaxation, a mindful meditation and a simple yoga sequence. Further relaxation and breathing techniques are incorporated in voice and movement training. They are also exposed to a specialist mindfulness trainer who extends their knowledge of these areas, incorporating sessions on mindset, empathy and resilience. The feedback from these sessions included students saying that with so much on their plate in the first semester they found the active meditations in yoga the most beneficial; it was in these sessions that students were best able to forget the competing demands on their time and just focus on the exercise.

Second- and third-year students were particularly hungry for these sessions and appreciated the time to escape from the demands of their rehearsals. There was great benefit in having the whole school participate together in yoga and mindfulness sessions as it aided in bonding the students and in reassuring the first years that they were not the only ones feeling the pressure of the rigorous programme.

Knowledge: Establishing a Clear Understanding of Acting Methodologies

The students continue their first-year progress, accumulating new skills through exposure to more acting methodologies, always using the foundational work of action pursuit as a guide. Throughout the year, the diagnostic report will be added to by both core staff and guest teachers and directors. The students are constantly referring to the diagnostic to track their progress and reflect on how each small outcome has assisted them in reaching their goals. Goal setting is an important part of the course structure throughout the three years. Each student sets a series of goals for their next project based on the feedback from staff, directors and their peers. At the end of each project, the student reflects on how well they reached those goals and looks to incorporate new challenges set by the most recent director. Goal setting and goal achieving has proven to be a productive way of encouraging autonomy in each student. They always achieve their goal to some degree, and this sense of achievement allays performance anxiety. In several cases, there have been students who were on medication to deal with anxiety, and through this knowledge- and skills-gathering process, with support from their medical professional, they have been able to go off their medication and instead use mindfulness principles to alleviate panic and unease. Angela Duckworth believes that through goal setting for our 'low-level and mid-level goals', we can clearly achieve our 'top-level' goal, claiming that 'the more unified, aligned, and coordinated our goal hierarchies, the better' (2017, p. 66).

There has been much debate about the possible harmful effects of some acting-training methodologies and how they are imparted. Prior et al. assert that

> It may be possible to witness questionable training practices in actor training today where students are taken into traumatic psychological states without adequate support. The power and control that many actor trainers either wittingly or unwittingly exercise seems evident.
>
> (2015, p. 65)

When I first read Seton's research in 2008, as I was writing my thesis, I felt the problem was overwhelmingly impossible. How could we eradicate systemic power abuse and firmly held beliefs from the training space? The answer now seems simple. Through a collective, conscious open discussion, we, the trainers, owe it to our student actors to provide the most supportive and enriching environments possible. Most trainers in this country have themselves graduated from a leading drama school, with many of us extending our studies overseas and regularly upskilling through master classes. Many teachers either have studied at the same drama school or teach the same methodologies. In my doctoral study, I noticed that the deciding factor for student success was not what was taught but how it was delivered. While one student may criticize a methodology taught by one teacher, when in the hands of another teacher it was highly rated.

Method-based teaching was considered a limiting approach by the industry leaders, and students from one school spoke of their intense discomfort with having to expose their emotional selves in the classroom setting. While some students acknowledged that sharing one's deepest secrets was often a bonding experience, they also said it laid them open to then having to deal with that information being made relatively public, sometimes issues that had never been talked about openly before. Students feel unable to express their discomfort due the hierarchy of relationships in the room:

> Such mysteries contributed to the asymmetrical relations of power that ensured teachers seemed always in possession of knowledges. Students implicitly understood that they must submit and become vulnerable in order to be recognized. They would thus gain the cultural capital necessary to establish themselves in the professional field.
>
> (Seton, 2010, p. 12)

Robb and Due make a salient point in the following:

> The second theme in the domain of acting training deals with students' experiences of destabilisation of self. This manifested as three clear types: challenging one's beliefs, accessing uncomfortable material, and blurring the boundary between self and character. Firstly, acting school was described as a place in which long-held beliefs were fundamentally challenged.
>
> (2017, p. 305)

The question is how we challenge these beliefs and what is within our rights in this process of destabilization. In their first year, the QUT actors are destabilized through the diagnostic exercise and then quickly shown a practical approach to achieving success in their scene, allowing them to remain autonomous throughout. They reach a basic level of mastery in just six weeks, thereby quickly alleviating the destabilizing sensation.

Drama schools have struggled with which techniques to teach, being criticized for adopting too eclectic an approach and equally judged harshly if they concentrate on just one approach. I am attempting to introduce a variety of approaches at QUT but with a clear underpinning so that one never cancels out another. Actors experience anxieties when they feel confused about how to approach the work, when one teacher gives them a strict prescription that conflicts with another teacher's approach. This confusion can make the student actor miserable and make them want to throw it all away. The methodologies used must be clear with apparent goals so the actor always knows why they are exploring each step. I introduce the core steps of analysis, listening, action pursuit, tactic playing and personalization early in the process. These are the black lines of the drawing. What follows gives the drawing colour and dimension and finally animates it into a full-bodied, full-flavoured, expressive performance.

The Teacher

My Own Experience: Practitioner/Teacher

As I suggested above, anxieties around an actor's work can be diminished when they have a clear approach and an array of approaches on hand that may suit a certain project. At QUT we are keen for actors to remain fluid in the work and to resist 'working it all out'. In my own earlier work, I had it all worked out. I knew what action I was playing on every line, and it did not matter what I was getting from my fellow actors. I would confidently play the same actions every night. I would be upset if another actor changed things because this was like going off script for me. My work appeared assured, confident and totally choreographed. There was no spontaneity and no window into who I was as a person. I got away with it onstage, but on-screen there was nothing real about it. When I learnt practical aesthetics, it terrified me because I was asked to 'be in the moment'. I would determine a scene action from the character's objective but not determine what tactics (transitive verbs) I should use in each moment until I was clear what I had just received from my fellow actors in that moment. Then I would need to determine what effect that had on me and then what tactic would be appropriate to achieve my scene action in the next moment. The technique forced me to listen and respond in the moment, informed by well-thought-out scene analysis.

Finally, I started to experience what 'being in the moment' was, and it was thrilling! The big adjustment for me was the personalization aspect. I had experienced all sorts of 'interventions' from directors and acting teachers trying to get me to be emotional in the scene. I had been yelled at and shamed; I had had my onion peeled; I had been asked to re-create moments from my life for half an hour before going onstage to ensure that I was in the right 'state' for this director's production. I never felt that I was empowered to find an emotional place myself, and I was always terrified that it might not come on the night. There was no surety in repeatability. Most processes left me feeling vulnerable and at the mercy of the director or teacher, looking for approval as to whether I got it or not and often experiencing intense shame if I did not. I perpetuated the expert/apprentice relationship, never acknowledging that I could find my own way if given the chance.

With practical aesthetics, I was asked to consider the scene action and ask myself if I needed to do that action what would it be 'as if'? If I needed to get someone to respect my space, what would that mean to me? I would find something that was real to me or that was imaginary but could possibly happen, to come up with a driver for that action. I found this work incredibly freeing as I suddenly had easy access to my emotional involvement in the scene. The 'as if' is not always comfortable and may indeed ask me to consider something quite personal, but no one in the room knows what that thing is. There is complete privacy around this personalization.

In teaching this process, I ask my students not to share their 'as ifs' if they are personal because it is none of our business and because a personal 'as if' may lose its fire if it is made public. I ask them to use the 'as if' as their personal fuel for the action. In this work, the personalization is directly linked to the 'doing' of the action. There is no re-creation of an 'emotional state' or delving into past memories to create a pure emotion. Emotion will arise from the need to pursue that action from the heat of the personalization. There is an imaginary element to this work, and the work is also part of the preparation or rehearsal process of a play. When I am in a run of a play, I may dip back into an 'as if' to make sure that need exists in me today, or it may be an automatic trigger from having repeated it so many times in rehearsal. The 'as if' is a trigger rather than a deep, experiential process. The actor is empowered to turn this trigger off and on. If the trigger is too intense, the actor may choose an 'as if' that will not overwhelm them and cause unnecessary anguish.

At QUT we hold the belief that the actor needs to be in charge of bringing any personalization to the work. They are introduced to the principles of emotional recall and instructed on how to use this work in certain situations. The student actor must always have agency within the teaching environment to decide what is appropriate for them. This creates a negotiation process between the teacher/director and actor where appropriate entry processes can be discussed and explored.

Teaching Practices: The New Model

It is my belief that we are now moving away from the teacher-as-expert model to the teacher-as-facilitator model. In the teacher-as-expert model, it is assumed that the teacher/director is all-knowing and that if the student actor is talented or clever enough, they will absorb the learnings from the teacher but never be as knowledgeable as the teacher. The teacher maintains the position of expert, and the student continues to need the teacher to achieve the appropriate outcomes. The student actor remains dependent on the teacher. In the teacher-as-facilitator model, the teacher shares their considerable expertise with the student actor but allows that student to process the knowledge through their own filters. The teacher remains open to the material not being appropriate to the student and is able to adjust the work accordingly. In this model, it is possible for the student actor to achieve mastery over the particular work and to own the processes as their own. This approach encourages autonomy and mutual respect: actor for teacher and teacher for actor. It is also my experience that the practitioner teacher is more likely to be able to adopt the teacher-as-facilitator model since in the process of being a working actor or director, one is always faced with the need to be adaptive and open.

Reeve and Jang highlight the positive effect of autonomy-supportive teachers in contrast to controlling teachers:

> When controlling, teachers have students put aside their inner motivational resources and instead adhere to a teacher-centred agenda, to encourage students to adhere to their agendas, teachers offer extrinsic incentives, impose external goals, utter pressuring communications, make external evaluations salient, and generally influence students' ways of thinking, feeling, and behaving in ways consistent with behaviour modification programs. The general idea is to establish an agenda of what students should and should not do and then shape students toward that agenda by using external contingencies and pressuring language. Hence, when controlled, students are motivated by external contingencies and pressuring language, not by their inner motivational resources …. Empirical research has shown that students with autonomy-supportive teachers, compared with students with controlling teachers, experience not only greater perceived autonomy but also more positive functioning in terms of their classroom engagement, emotionality, creativity, intrinsic motivation, psychological well-being, conceptual understanding, academic achievement, and persistence in school. (2006, p. 210)

The Academy Supporting the Conservatoire

There is a new development in the elite drama schools in Australia which is improving the rigour of the curriculum. In the past, there was a clear divide between the vocational training of the conservatoire model schools and the more academic processes taught at universities. Those who taught in the conservatories were teachers, and those at the universities were academics. It was quite an insult to be looked upon as an academic in the vocational space. One 'does' and the other 'theorizes' about the doing. As postgraduate research has evolved in recent years to acknowledge and even value practice-led research, a meeting of minds has taken place between the academy and the conservatoire. I am aware of several teachers in the

Australian elite drama school space who either have attained doctoral qualifications or are in the process of it. Each school is now encouraging staff to publish. I know that through my doctoral studies, I made definite shifts in perception as I delved more deeply into areas of actor training that I had made assumptions about, benefiting from the academic studies of others. The process of staying abreast of current research allows those of us teaching in this space to continue to reflect on our practices and make constant improvements. Embracing research provides the opportunity to place pressure on teachers who are not embracing current trends, especially, I suggest, around the well-being of student actors.

Workload

One of the major indicators for stress and anxiety is the heavy workload experienced by drama school students. At QUT we are looking at how effective the longer hours of engagement are and where we can put in reflection breaks throughout. Assessment tasks are staggered and made clear to not add to anxiety levels. In the first year, the assessment tasks are all aligned to create clarity of progression through acting, voice, movement and acting theory classes. We are looking to determine whether shorter classes could in fact have greater impact and how many hours of practical application are best for knowledge advancement and well-being.

Principles of Teaching Actors

Below is a list of principles that we, at QUT, believe reflect the core beliefs of how we train our actors:

- Include everyone in the room.
- Be alert to any issues: the check-in can help this.
- Pitch the class to the mid range of understanding; acknowledge those needing more challenge and those still comprehending.
- Constantly check for students' understanding of the work.
- Offer the student the opportunity to lead the work and thereby take ownership of it.
- Debrief on each day's work and unit of work, seeking questions and seeking out doubts.

- Seek formal anonymous feedback about the efficacy of the work.
- Refer the work back to the full picture of the training.
- Look for links between the acting classes and the skills classes.
- Have a clear idea of what students are covering in the skills classes.
- Teach by demonstration and practical application – be wary of too much talk and too many anecdotes.
- Use appropriate language: constructive criticism.
- Avoid statements that lead to the actor taking on certain beliefs about their ability – for example, 'that was bad acting', 'you're boring me', and 'I don't believe you'.
- Always offer a solution or search with the group for a solution to any issue.
- Do not assume you have all the answers.
- Be comfortable with not knowing and with discovering with the group.
- Be upfront when the teacher's idea has not worked – admit fault.
- Support teaching with your own teaching philosophy.
- Acknowledge resistance ('The concept of resistance … has been transformed over the years into a not-so-disguised way of blaming the less powerful for unsatisfactory results of change efforts' (Krantz, 1999, p. 42; Wangh, 2013, p. 61).
- Regularly imagine returning to being a student to remember the student–teacher relationship.

The adoption of these principles will hopefully flush out the kind of teaching that we now recognize as detrimental to the mental health and well-being of the actor. Processes that are shaming in nature or that make allegations of the student's ability without concise ways to remedy a problem have no place in a modern drama school.

Summary

By training our trainers to embrace the principles set out above, we will have taken some important steps in achieving greater outcomes in student actor well-being. Further, by instilling habits that encourage autonomy, resilience and empowerment, we hope to help shift the statistics that currently have too many actors experiencing significant mental health issues. WAWPT will hopefully see a new breed of resilient actors with strong indicators in all areas of well-being.

Notes

Ginters, L. (2008). 'Lindy Davies: A Path to a Process, Part 2', *Australasian Drama Studies* 52 (April), pp. 85–96

Hite, B. C. (2015). *Positive Psychological Capital, Need Satisfaction, Performance, and Well-Being in Actors and Stunt People*. Thesis, Minneapolis: Walden University ScholarWorks.

Krantz, James (1999). *Journal of Applied Behavioral Science*, 35, 42 DOI: 10.1177/0021886399351004

Maxwell, I., Seton, M. & Szabó, M. (2015). 'The Australian Actor's Wellbeing Study: A Preliminary Report', *About Performance* 13 pp. 69–113

Prior, R., Maxwell, I., Szabó, M. & Seton, M. (2015). 'Responsible Care in Actor Training: Effective Support for Occupational Health Training in Drama Schools', *Theatre Dance and Performance Training*. Taylor and Francis online

Reeve, J. & Jang, H. (2006). 'What Teachers Say and Do to Support Students' Autonomy during a Learning Activity', *Journal of Educational Psychology* 98(1), 209–218.

Robb., A. E. & Due, C. (2017). 'Exploring Psychological Wellbeing in Acting Training: An Australian Interview Study', in Pitches, J. & L. Worth (eds) *Theatre Dance and Performance Training*. Taylor and Francis online, pp. 297–316

Taylor, S. L. (2016). *Actor Training and Emotions – Finding a Balance*. Thesis, Western Australian Academy of Performing Arts (WAAPA).

Wangh, S. (2013). *The Heart of Teaching: Empowering Students in the Performing Arts*. London: Routledge

3

Being Human

Adrian James

Homo sun, humani nihil a me alienumputo. Over two thousand years ago, the Roman playwright Terence wrote these words, which translate to 'I am human; therefore, nothing human is alien to me.' Having an embodied understanding of this sentence is central to training in behavioural realism; this engagement with the appearance of *truthful* behaviour is essential to an acting student's ability to effectively approach a dramatic text.

When children are allowed to play freely and unselfconsciously, they are hardwired to totally commit to imitating the actions of observed behaviour, and this commitment enables them to develop their imaginations and mimetic sensibilities. In essence, they are creating a relationship between themselves and others and thereby realizing their interconnectedness. The process of socialization and enculturation inevitably narrows our behavioural choices, and our imaginative possibilities are subjected to censure. Moral imperatives and social and personal notions of good and bad, right and wrong, success and failure are internalized and create emotional and psychological blockages to the free-flowing possibilities between our creative impulses and our physical and vocal apparatus. Quite simply, as we grow into adults, we tend to restrict our human potential.

In the United Kingdom, a young person presents for actor training usually between ages 18 and 25; they offer an instrument (themselves) which has to a greater or lesser extent been restricted by their upbringing. The increasingly complex and conflicting demands of our 'connected' society are paradoxically creating more disconnected and anxiety-ridden young adults than ever before. Because these students are often confused and disassociated, their training – which takes place within a carefully disciplined structure – must begin by gently enabling the process of relieving them of their adult enculturation and giving them permission to explore, play and re-find their curiosity and questioning excitement about themselves and the world – an essential prerequisite of the artistic quest.

This process of play and playing has long been recognized in actor training and has taken many forms. However, with the increasing strictures, time pressures, conformities of assessment processes and formal requisites of degrees within the higher education system, dream time – the essential self-discovery process – can be lost. As the demands of increasing social conformity replace genuine human relatedness, it is unsurprising that the ensuing personal anxiety results in entrenched opinions, as a buttress against existential uncertainty. In our efforts to create critically aware artists able to reflect and comment on the world about them, we must create a space for the students to investigate themselves before they attempt to study others. This in no way suggests a 'cure' for personal or psychological conflicts, nor does it look to attempt some form of therapy for the students. Because personal conflicts and neurosis are intimately connected with creativity, it instead suggests that students need practical training in self-awareness, non-judgementalism, narrative structure and the complexity and breadth of human motivation and uniqueness.

The following is an approach to acting training in psychological and behavioural realism which I teach at East 15 Acting School in the United Kingdom. The approach has been developed from the principles of Stanislavski and his European followers, particularly Michael Chekhov, Jacques Copeau, Michel Saint-Denis, Uta Hagen, Joan Littlewood and Margaret Bury Walker, the founder of the East 15 School. The work of the three great mentors who founded The Drama Centre London – John Blatchley, Yat Malmgren and Christopher Fettes – also inform this practice. What follows in this chapter is an indicative process which takes place during the initial training of the actor. Typically, this involves 18–20 hours of acting classes per week over a 12-week term. A further 12–14 hours each week is spent on physical work in movement and dance, alongside voice, speech and singing classes. East 15 students would also be given preparation work, as appropriate.

The three strands of the students' initial acting training are:

1) work on the self
2) object exercises
3) behavioural characteristics.

These are not taught consecutively; rather, they run beside and around and are complementary to each other, each strand exploring ways of approaching the acting process. A general line of development can be easily discerned: 'study first, not the theatre, but the human race … study the human mind, its nature, processes and habits.'[1]

The overall objective of the term is to open up ideas of what it means to be human and to develop a sense of the ensemble. This approach to acting as part of an ensemble is perhaps the essence of East 15 training. The school provides a contemporary conservatoire training, which is now fully embedded within the School of Humanities at Essex University and is one of the largest professional actor training institutions in the United Kingdom. East 15 occupies two campuses and incorporates a number of specialized courses, from the pre-degree certificate in higher education (HE) in theatre arts to master of fine arts (MFA) in acting or directing and a number of bachelor of arts (BA) specialist courses, such as acting and combat and acting and world performance, a degree combining practical performance, acting skills and intellectual scholarship. Despite such a wide and developing remit, the school still retains its founder's original radical objective, based on the ideas of Joan Littlewood's Theatre Workshop, to establish a cooperative and collaborative ensemble training ethos and an international outlook, encouraging its students to create and perform their own work and create their own companies: 'The soul is a vast domain.'[2]

Contemporary acting students often begin their training with little substantial experience of live theatre or performance, and very few have had the opportunity to articulate the artist's job in society, both in terms of craft skills and the role of story-making in relation to memory and social cohesion. In many ways, our culture has downgraded the artist's relationship to society to something akin to consumerist exchange, with the actor existing to entertain or to sell goods and services. This relationship is a far cry from Russian futurist Viktor Schlovsky's claim that art exists to recover the sensation of life; it exists to make one feel things – to make the stone stony. The aim of the initial stages of training must be to reawaken the students' perception of their own aliveness and in so doing recover the authentic sensation of their own lives. The central challenges of learning and teaching behavioural realism are discovering and using the self; self-consciousness; and the appearance of artlessness. To confront and overcome these challenges, students need a non-judgemental space to explore. Such a space is imperative to the practical aims of engaging students in the following:

1. the study of their own biography – examining the self as an actor exploring a character and using the fundamental vocabulary of behavioural realism: Who am I? What do I want? Why do I want it?
2. the study of narrative: What is a story? Whose story is it?
3. the study of character through comparisons and contrasts
4. the study of inner technique through object relations exercises.

The students at East 15 have been auditioned and been invited for training because of their sensitivity, curiosity and open-heartedness; they are aware, albeit not always consciously, of the polarity between what they are told about the world and how they actually experience it. If they are to articulate their personal contradictions and to recognize and embrace their own uniqueness, they need to be given permission, allowance and an enabling scaffolded space within a defined discipline in which to reawaken and rediscover their authentic voice, feelings and sensations.

Margaret Bury Walker would insist that her students go back in order to go forward – that they reassess what the world had made of them. In contrast, my own training during the early days at The Drama Centre London focused on the mimetic sense rather than the biographical, taking the student immediately into an early realist/naturalistic text (Henry Beque's *The Ravens* in my case). My belief is that in our culture we increasingly need, as artists, to begin to rid ourselves of *ideas* about ourselves before studying characters in texts. We need to recover our appetite for life by rediscovering what and if, in fact, we feel rather than to try to feel something. Our present UK school system has for the most part narrowed our children's minds; has taught them 'facts' about the world rather than interpretations; has inculcated the dualities of success and failure, right and wrong and good and bad and given them notions of 'normality'; has taught pupils to mistrust their intuition and the truth of their imagination. Students have been furnished with layers of social masks which conceal their fears, naivety, neuroses, rage and love and every contradictory and affective desire which makes them human and which allows them to express themselves authentically in their chosen artform. Along the way, their human singularity has been subjected to consumer economics, so they arrive at drama school believing in 'progress' and expecting to be 'taught'.

> *Oh, that we had the gift to see ourselves as others see us.*
>
> Robert Burns

'I am/She is' – Poem/Piece & the Study of Self-Model

As preparation, before the commencement of students' first term and before they've been sent out with their equipment list (blacks for movement, practice skirt, etc.), I will often ask members of the incoming cohort to write two short pieces of poetic text: the first one, 'I am', is written from the student's point of view; the second, 'She/He is', is written from a critical stance of a person (real or imaginary) that does not like them. This exercise has nothing to do with literary merit, rhyming or grammar but is instead a portrait in words. During the first few sessions of their course, I ask the students to read out their two pieces to the group. No comments are required. But a palpable sense of a possible shared understanding between the students tends to result, and the personality of the individuals begins to emerge through the writing and reciting.

The study of self-model is their next presentation. The students are asked to create a three-dimensional self-portrait made out of combinations of any materials which they think expresses their nature – for example, wood, cardboard, tissue paper, string, fur, stones, paper or buttons. The resulting object should express aspects of themselves, including their genetic and acquired characteristics. A briefing sheet of biological, psychological, cultural and relationship characteristics is given to help their reflections, and I make clear that the resulting image is not meant to carry an outward resemblance. I also stress that this is a study in self-identification requiring kindly observation, not self-indulgence. It is an observation, recording and describing exercise.

Some students in their presentations will avoid the tender, raw or even gentler aspects of themselves through humour or intellect; others find self-reflection or expression of either themselves or others shocking. It is a revealing and sensitive exercise to which the group almost invariably reacts with empathy and a shared sense of their common identity.

This exercise is followed by their first, more probing biographical investigation.

We live in the shadow of each other.

Traditional Irish saying

My Roadmap – How Did I Get Here?

This investigation demands a considered biographical reflection, and the students are given a week or so to prepare their roadmap. They are asked to look back to their very earliest memories – visual, tactile, aural – and to trace their personal histories which have led them to where they are now and with the people, relationships and possibilities they have now. After reflection, the students are asked to make a mind map and then to produce a visual interpretation of their lives so far in the form of a roadmap with all their biographical details symbolized by the map in terms of destinations, byways, black spots, scenic routes, holdups, dangerous slopes, crashes, freeways, roundabouts, picnic areas, etc. They are asked to consider using colour and shapes and to make it as decorated or as simple as they wish. Robert Frost's 1916 poem 'The Road Not Taken' is offered to them as inspiration.

The students are requested to bring in their roadmaps and to narrate their biographies, referring to the map with the group, explaining how they believe the incidents have formed or affected them as a person. They are not required to reveal traumas or any incidents that they wish to keep private. Mentioning a 'dark tunnel', an 'accident', a 'black spot' or a 'dead end' is perfectly acceptable. That the individuals have considered and reflected on their past is essential; revealing the specifics to others is neither requested nor necessary. Indeed, something apparently trivial may have a defining importance to the individual. This exercise in recall and storytelling may become overextended, and its use as an approach to the elements and construction of narrative and of the process of self-understanding and analysis of how a personality and character is formed needs judicious oversight. Humans are storytelling animals, so a strict time limit needs to be observed.

As cohorts of actors in training have tended to become larger since the conservatoires have been incorporated into the university structures and the ability of students to focus clearly over an extended period of time at the outset of their training is limited, I have tended towards a shorter version of the expressed biographies, asking students to choose from their map four incidents which they feel illustrate their lifeworld, one before puberty, one during puberty, one after puberty and one from the recent past. Editing being an essential element of narrative, a time limit of three minutes is given as a maximum for the relating of any one incident. Students should give a rationale for their choices.

I have found this investigation to have profound and qualitative effects on both individual students and the group as a whole. Individually, students have discovered that their pasts when reflected upon are sometimes vastly different from what they had hitherto believed them to be. As a collective, the students begin to realize with palpable relief that what they believed to be their individual issues, problems or feelings of guilt were actually shared human concerns. Foucault suggests that the enthusiasm to understand human motivation is

> not the curiosity that seeks to assimilate what is proper for one to know, but that which enables one to get free of oneself – there are times in life when the question of knowing if one can think differently than one thinks and perceive differently than one sees, is absolutely necessary if one is to go on looking and reflecting at all.[3]

I suspect that this need to 'think differently' is the driving motivation of many actors and perhaps of all artists. The need to get free of oneself can be seen in the powerful effects that this acting exercise can manifest. Students sometimes for the first time hear another non-intimate contemporary voice their own pain, insecurity and vulnerability, and perhaps most importantly for actors, they may clearly distinguish authenticity from concealment.

These sessions may be powerful, moving or hilarious and sometimes all three at the same time. Certainly, they are draining, and these acting sessions need to be interspersed with introducing the other two strands of the initial pre-textual training: the behavioural characteristics class and object exercises.

> In order to reveal the human soul, we must make the unconscious a conscious technique …. we must learn to see and listen without judgement and to speak without seeking approval.[4]

These classes are concerned with the practical analysis, construction and use of the actor's inner technique; students are required to investigate themselves in order to understand what parts of themselves they require for any particular character they wish to portray.

Behavioural Characteristics: We Know So Much More than We Think We Know

These sessions in observation and transformation rely on the students' willingness/ability to surrender to an experience and to discover or allow their own 'sensation of being' to control them. As Yoshi Oida sees it, this is about the ability to be present inside one's own flesh.[5] The process relies on defining the differences between themselves and others and embodying the axiomatic principle that character is a function of action. In other words, what we do is determined by who we are – the choices we make. It is in these classes that one may clearly observe a student's sensitivity, subtlety, delicacy, courage, boldness and creative risks, their choices directly revealing their ability to understand their position in their physical, psychological and emotional relationships.

Beginning with sessions introducing the vocabulary and physiological and psychological effects of space and gravity (past, present and future and above, on and below), the sessions continue with classes introducing inner and outer characteristics, vocal characteristics, habitual mannerisms, layers of the self, social masks, inner motives, imaginary centres, generic and personal atmospheres, the semiotics of clothes and the close observation of animal behaviour. These sessions develop, adapt, use and critically investigate the observations and methods developed from the work of former mentors and masters, from Michael Chekov and Yat Malmgren to Margaret Bury Walker and Catherine Clouzot. During this period, the students are observing both themselves and other members of their group.

An exercise called a study of another in the group, where over the period of a week, the students are asked to observe, question and imagine the 'being' of another group member, is used to explore the use of the learned techniques. The students come to a specified session as their studied other, wearing the studied person's clothes and adapting themselves as fully as possible. They also venture beyond the studio confines to study 'real' people in an exercise called incidents from the high street, where non-dramatic incidents or relationships are observed and narrated in the studio by using the students' developing understanding of non-judgemental observations. The resulting 'characters' may be developed further and taken into expanded and imagined situations and relationships.

The behavioural characteristics class allows the students considerable creative freedom in interpreting the material offered to them. The object exercises, in contrast, demand rigorous adherence to a creative discipline to investigate the students' individual inner technique.

Any knowledge which is not in your bones is only a rumour.

Traditional African saying

The Object Exercises

I was fortunate enough to have trained under and subsequently assisted Doreen Cannon. The following exercises are a development of the work of Uta Hagen, through and influenced by Cannon. They provide a systematic approach to the development of an inner technique to enable the actor to develop a deeper understanding of themselves so that they may analyse and control their creative ability to exist as a fully functioning, free-flowing, three-dimensional being onstage or in front of a camera. This ability has become vital since rehearsal time and time to prepare oneself and one's relationships within a role has shortened in the highly pressurized industry environment. Over a series of graded training exercises, the student discovers an embodied language of sensation. The sequence of work is focused on an inner-felt 'truth' and the ability to explore this reality to recognize and control their sensations. Focus is related to

1) how a student responds in a variety of circumstances
2) the sensation of a moment-to-moment existence with a free-flowing thought process
3) each student's relationship to themselves, objects, others and the given circumstances of the explored situation.

Preparation and action (want or desire) are viewed as pre-eminent, and the critique to each exercise is a process of the actors' responses to questions on given circumstances, imagination, the magic if, circles of attention, involvement, personalization and specificity, adaptation and relationship to self, objects and others, sensation and emotion memory, through line of physical action, spontaneity and truth, public solitude and the internal monitor. I use a series of four non verbal exercises followed by four verbal exercises:

1. an action with three activities
2. a time-limited action
3. an action with a sleeping partner
4. a life-or-death action with a sleeping partner
5. an action with an outer obstacle
6. an action with an inner obstacle
7. an action with a physical condition
8. a life-or-death action with an awake partner.

I would not expect these exercises to be completed by a group within the initial training; rather, they would be undertaken and developed over an academic year or into a second year of training. Once completed, this work would form the basis of a firm inner technique in behavioural realism, which should become unconscious and automatic with practice. However, during the initial training, where students have not yet incorporated aspects of their work, the vocabulary of behavioural realism is used as they begin to move from an investigation of their reflective biographies into structuring and adapting incidents from their childhood. The intuitive and spontaneous use of what will eventually become craft practice is encouraged, and a reflective understanding of the creation and structure of narrative is brought into focus.

In a two- or three-year course, both of the following projects could be explored during initial training. In a more intensive course, either exercise may stand alone as a further understanding of the importance of knowing oneself. The stages of life project have proven particularly helpful in master of arts (MA) courses.

The stages of life project develops aspects of the road of life project, investigating the development of the self and character through the influences and processes of time, change, motivations, wants, needs and desires in relation to the actors' questions regarding who, what when, where, how and why. The aim of the project is to develop non-judgementalism and phenomenological observation and to investigate the influence of context, history, social mores and values on human desire and action. The project also aims for students to gain a reflective and creative understanding of the development and changes that may affect a person's development throughout their lives.

An introductory session uses Jaques's speech from *As You Like It* (Act 2, scene 7) as a stimulus through which to identify and discuss the constant themes of our existence, such as power, love, shame, self-preservation, death, guilt, loneliness, friendship, memory, etc. This is followed by the influences on these themes: history, ethnicity, gender, class, family, politics, technology, status, etc., as well as the age-related concerns and perspectives on life, such as parents, siblings, fashion, music, money, marriage, career and retirement.

Preparation time is given for each of the following sessions as the students are guided from themselves at ten years old. To do this, the students first need to reflect on their ten-year-old self, construct both an inner and an outer character list for themselves and reflect on their main interests, concerns, worries and wants. They are asked questions regarding their lifeworld. These questions are answered, of course, in character. Students are then put into group improvisations exploring their relationships and actions. Post-improvisational analysis is followed by the students noting in their work journals some of their key reflections and discoveries, particularly their emotions, thought processes, physicality, relationships and how their inner and outer characteristics were manifested in and through their behaviour.

Preparation for the next session, where the students explore themselves at 15 years of age, begins with a discussion of the changes during the five previous years. Improvisations and critique are followed by preparation for the age they are now, including a description of themselves from two contrasting points of view, followed during the next session by individual improvisations addressing their peers on a subject which they feel passionately about (acting and theatre are the only forbidden subjects) and critiquing themselves on what they would like to gain, lose, achieve and change over the next 15 years.

The project now changes from a biographical research project into an imaginative creative exercise where the students imagine a possible future, given their biography. The sessions at 30, 50 and 70 years old are briefed beforehand, and certain externally derived traumas are allowed for, such as death, illness, bankruptcy, alcoholism and other unexpected life-defining changes, such as childbirth and education or occupational changes. A final session would be dedicated to a retrospective analysis of their discoveries, critique and possible further work on devised characters and imagined worlds.

The project covering episodes from family life has been developed to allow the students to engage over a period of time in a developing relationship between collaborative work, experience, memory and imagination and hopefully to begin to engage with an understanding of the profound importance of storytelling to our common humanity. It is an opportunity for the students to embody technical, aesthetic, contextual and sociopolitical awareness in their discovery of the acting process at the same time as they are faced with the dynamics of the group, the struggle with dramatic structure and the methodology of behavioural realism through the use of the actors' basic questions. United structure, through lines of action, improvisational skills and the question of characterization are all inherent in the exercise.

A finalized text is the last aspect to appear in the project. What is being practically explored in the exercise is the essence of the mimetic enterprise – an experience of the basis of what it means to be human – telling *stories* (as opposed to a *narration of events*) and how we use semiotics, essences and symbolism to make sense of ourselves, each other and the world around us. The final text should provide an understanding that it is stories that give us our identity and social cohesion. The students must consider the basis of what makes an 'event', what makes it interesting or compelling and what the very nature of style is. It is an opportunity to consider, even before aesthetics, the nature of family structures, class and education, possessions and property, gender and sexuality, loneliness, peer and social pressures, rebellion, taboos and the possible political danger inherent in any art which authentically considers memory and experience. This exercise can stimulate an awareness of students' own emotional, physical and psychological restrictions and limitations and help them gain a greater openness through transforming their personal experience and fantasies into a more universal form.

A variety of briefing sheets are provided, following a discussion and explanation of the nature of stories, and the following process is carefully scaffolded to nurture a clear developmental process. The students are divided into groups of four to six and share one incident up to when they were eight years old. A group discussion decides which story will be explored and performed. The 'owner' of the story re-narrates and enriches the story, exploring the actor's questions before roles are allocated to the group. The story units are rehearsed, and the process is repeated for different periods in the students' lives, relating to the concerns of childhood and adolescence. At this stage, challenges of group dynamics may appear and need to be resolved by the group in the interests of the work.

When the small groups have begun to form their stories, they are shown to the whole group. After further discussion relating to where the objective of the whole group may be headed, I begin to correlate and shape the material, adding elements of song, movement and dance or short ensemble pieces throughout the iterative rehearsal process, which leads to a late rehearsal showing for the group's skills tutors, where the students are in blacks (close-fitting movement clothing) with minimal props and costume elements.

The next project – the final one before approaching a written play text – further develops aspects introduced in the previous projects and adds the vital skills of actor research. It focuses on the development of the imagination and the great primitive emotions by allowing students to investigate the great primitive desires and needs. Such development also stimulates the enjoyment of enchantment and the power to spellbind and fascinate, through the fairy tale project, which is introduced in the following briefing sheet.

Briefing Sheet: The Fairy Tale Project, Dreams, Longings and the Desire for Love

Our next project is about serial killers, shape-shifters and time travellers. A world of monstrous deformities, mythical creatures, cannibalism, insanity, bestiality, incest, multiple rape, murder, revenge and redemptive love. A world of vicious parents, neglected and abandoned children who are torn apart, burned in ovens and eaten; a world where young girls are forced to surrender their virginity to foul reptiles. It is the world of myth, legend, horror and fairy tales. In every culture and throughout history, our psychic, spiritual life and therefore our personal relationships have been formed by such tales. It is the very heart of the dramatic imagination.

Examples:

The Bible, the Koran, the ancient Greek legends, the Persian tales of 1001 nights, the tales of vampires, Dracula and Frankenstein, the classic Grimms' fairy tales, folk tales of Africa, Doctor Who, James Bond, Harry Potter, Star Wars, The Lord of the Rings, His Dark Materials, Game of Thrones... How many more can you think of?

Reality can be divided into three worlds:

1) The outer world (mundane, commonly accepted, factual reality)
2) The inner world (of personal imagination, between hunger and desire)
3) The secondary world (the other worlds of universal consciousness).

An actor's research for a play, the characters and the context, serves a specific purpose: to enable the actor to more fully understand and inhabit the world of the play and embody the character more truthfully. Any research (e.g. period, history, geography, education, food, furniture, philosophy, music, etc.) must be made transitive; otherwise, it is of no use to the actor, however interesting it may be!

The students are divided into small groups for their research, to investigate and share their discoveries on the history, background and development of fairy/folk tales, the reality of dreams and myths in stereotypes, fashion and advertising, fears, fantasies and the grotesque. The themes and elements of fairy tales, such as prophesies, revelations and rituals, and the contemporary fairy tale makers in written work and in the media are also investigated at this stage to open up a comprehensive possible universe from which choices can be made for closer investigation.

Again, each stage of the project and each group is carefully monitored and scaffolded and the work correlated, rehearsed and scripted as it grows into a unified piece during an extended iterative process. It is during this project, if it has not been realized during the previous work, that behavioural realism can be emphasized as being a methodology of actors' craft practice and that performance does not need to remain naturalistic/realistic in the style of presentation. Mask work and ritualistic, non-Western performance styles may well be integrated or be foregrounded into this project with their attendant discipline demands.

The Quest

The quest is a variation of the fairy tale project which I introduced and substituted recently and is proving popular with East 15 students. It gives the students total freedom to exercise and stretch their narrative imaginations within the disciplined structure of the quest. I have found that the epic nature, clearly defined objectives and strong characterization demanded by the narrative crystallizes the students' comprehension of the through line of action, motivations, relationships and the playing of high stakes. The quest also requires limited but considered (and possibly heightened) text derived from improvisation and also the use of multiple theatrical means and physical skills.

The quest project demands that students research myths and symbols, archetypes, genres and the basic narrative structure of the quest, which will become the main units of action of the students' stories:

1) your created world at peace
2) a disturbance/crisis in your world
3) a demand to act
4) the hero's uncertainty
5) the hero's decision to venture into the unknown
6) the journey (search), where obstacles are faced
7) the overcoming/return/rebirth and/or achievement.

Every character played by the students is based firmly on the archetypes and must have fully embodied the actors' questions (who, what, why, etc.). Each stage of the rehearsal period needs to be monitored to ensure a clear, united structure, through line of plot and character, mythic devices, symbols, archetypal characters and magical transformations.

In a university conservatoire, certainly at East 15, with the first term of training commencing at the start of October, I envisage the fairy tale or quest project being performed to the students' skills tutors before the December vacation. The students' holiday work would include a self-reflective essay on the first term's work, the results of which should give a clear indication of the success or otherwise of the term's objectives and an indication of where and how to progress the acting students' education when written scripts are introduced in the second term, along with the continuation of object exercises and further character classes.

The first 12 weeks of full-time training are designated as the initial pre-text training, in which the emphasis is on establishing first principles – technically, psychologically, professionally and in the establishment of a studio world conducive to the students' self-actualization. Heidegger suggests that an artist 'brings forth into being that which is concealed.'[6] This reaffirms the pre-Socratic notion of *aletheia*: truth always generates more possibilities. All art is created through *techne*, a mode of embodied knowledge: craft knowledge. Learning a craft in order to understand and reveal its essence and attempting to understand more profoundly and deeply what makes us human is for me a fulfilling and endless search.

I believe I have glimpsed in every group of acting students a similar excitement, but so often that powerful drive to explore has been distorted, emasculated or blocked by upbringing, environment or schooling. The initial training must therefore focus on empowering the students' self-belief and encourage self-actualization so that their individual and combined creativity can flourish and so that they can make critically informed choices in their work. Initial training is as concerned with creative and artistic values and behaviour as it is with skill sets. It must be concerned with different ways of seeing and appreciating the world and encouraging curiosity rather than having opinions. This work may bear little coincidence with the professional world of work in the creative industries. However, a connected sense of self, which may be said to identify the central notion of this initial training, enables the students to realize their potential and possibly to survive as an integrated and *authentic* person within the highly competitive professional industry, where commercial casting is based on an actor's suitability for a particular role. Thus, contemporary training for an actor, out of professional necessity (particularly for screen acting, the industry's growth area) becomes more focused on and directed towards the actors' nuanced and psychologically truthful understanding of self. Without a comprehensive self-actualization, actors would be under-equipped to play the delicately honed, measured and truthful versions of themselves and to engage with the myriad varieties of psychological types that they are now required to create for the media.

I am convinced that those of us who wish to teach actor-artists in a non-threatening, anti-discriminatory and creative way need also to have self-actualization as an objective. Our vocation involves close interaction and relationships with our students. We must more fully inhabit ourselves and individuate our work by 'making it present to (our) feelings and imaginations as well as to (our) reason', as Francis Fergusson points out in his seminal work *The Idea of a Theatre*, and resolve to develop a more complete, developed and connected sense of our being in the world.[7] The creation of a studio world, which is a safe creative space, needs to be distinct from the everyday. For me, this means a clear establishment of studio rules: a commitment to the moment of starting (no lateness), no distractions, no food or drink in the studio and the acceptance of a sense of privilege and ensemble. Curtains are drawn over any windows and doors. Inside the acting space, tutors are viewed as involved participants in the creative enterprise, and relationships with peers are based on respect, understanding and shared core values: ownership and validation of the student's felt experience; non-judgemental acceptance of a student's felt truth; and, essentially, a cooperative and non-competitive ethos.

Through a process of being witnessed, listened to without judgement, and presented with personal challenges and a fair discipline, students will gain authentic confidence in themselves and an appreciation of others. Perhaps most importantly for their self-actualization and developed sense of identity, the students' experience may be seen as one that develops the seeing connections between things. This could also be seen as the purpose of the dramatic sensibility and perhaps of art itself.

In this state of heightened awareness and receptivity to others and themselves, students will be more able to approach the riches and qualities of a written script in the next stage of their creative journey, ready to enter and play within a world rather than judge and view with suspicion its unfamiliarity.

Workshop Exercise: Incidents from the High Street

The ability to observe what is around us without a vested interest, or rather with the specific interest of attempting to see the world from another's point of view (putting aside our own concerns), is an essential requirement of an actor. When we are in the high street, we are usually going somewhere or wanting something, and our intention narrows our attention. The objective of this exercise is to develop the student's ability to observe more acutely, specifically, empathetically, contextually and imaginatively.

> **Brief**
>
> The students go out into the high street or shopping centre, in groups of two or three (max) and observe people going about their everyday activities.
>
> They choose a couple of minutes of observed behaviour to bring back to the studio to rehearse and present to the group.
>
> I suggest that the following briefing sheet be fully discussed with the students, (including any possible dangers) before beginning the exercise.

How Actors Should Observe People

The most important aspect of observing is to ensure that you are not the object of other people's attention! In other words, you must not be observed. This entails you fading into the background and becoming anonymous and uninteresting to anyone else. Dress and act appropriately for your context and appear to any observer as interested in something other than them. If you're in a library or bookshop, appear to be reading; if you're in a shop, look at the goods or fiddle with your phone; and if you're in a café, then text, look out a window or anything other than stare at someone or make yourself conspicuous or appear nosy. 'Disappearing' in public takes some practice, but it is a useful ability.

For this exercise, an incident from the high street, take your time to observe what may be actually happening around you. How do you do this?

1. Free yourself from any agenda other than observation.
2. Take your time to free yourself of judgements about what you may be observing. This is called phenomenological observation, or looking with your higher creative consciousness. Such observation involves attempting to look without making a moral judgement about what you are seeing. Avoiding judgements means being aware of and silencing your prejudices and preferences, likes and dislikes and moral scruples. It means being interested in but disinterested in people and not taking an attitude to them, which would put up a barrier to actually observing them.
3. This is not about looking for a dramatic or unusual incident but rather about the acute and specific observation of human interaction, human relationships and how our minds and our bodies are constantly interacting with their environment. It is essentially a training exercise in *observation*. Interpreting what you observe happens at a later stage.
4. At the time, or as soon as you can afterwards, take written and drawn notes, write down everything that you have observed, including the time, place, weather conditions, clothing and any other details and contextual information. These are your given circumstances. If you can hear people talk, then listen in, but it is not essential and can

only be a reminder for yourself later; it is not a substitute for observing at the time.
5. Follow your instinct, your intuition (which is your most essential sense as an actor), when choosing your subject(s) for observation.

After the observation period comes the time for interpretation, using your knowledge of behavioural characteristics and the actors' questions:

1. What are they doing? (What is their desire, want, need?) This is their action.
2. Why do they want it? (What is their motivation?) This is their objective.
3. How are they going about it? (What is their means?) These are their physical and psychological activities.
4. What are the obstacles to their achieving their desire? (What is the problem they have to overcome in order to achieve what they want? Obstacles may be simple, single or many and varied, emanating from inside themselves, another person or object or something in their environment).
5. What surrounds them? (What was the context of their behaviour, their given circumstances?)
6. When you have interpreted your observations, using your knowledge of human behaviour and judgement (not judgementalism), practise your incident, allowing your physicality and psychological and emotional wants to become your subjects', leaving yourself alone to think their thoughts and pursue their desires.

Be prepared to recreate your incident in the studio and discuss your observation process.

Note: The resulting characters may be developed further and taken into expanded and imagined situations and relationships. For example, an elderly couple observed shopping for groceries may be put into an improvisation – having a cup of tea after they arrive home. (What does their home look like? Where is it? What is the furniture like – the pictures on the wall the cups and saucers, etc.?) A whole community may be developed from these observational improvisations.

Notes

1 Bury Walker, M. (1979) *East 15 Acting School, Prospectus*. East 15 Acting School, Archive Collection.
2 Schnizler, A. (1911) *The Soul is a Vast Domain*.
3 Foucault, M. (1985).
4 Stanislavski, K. *Stanislavski Quotes*. www.azquotes.com
5 Oida, Y. (1997) p. 29.
6 Heidegger, M. (1960) *Origins of a Work of Art*. p. 118 insites.harvard.edu.
7 Fergusson, F. (1949) *The Idea of a Theatre*. p. 238.

4

All Those Words: Why Bother with All Those Old Plays?

Annie Tyson

William Hazlitt writes in his essay 'On Actors and Acting' that actors are 'the motley representatives of human nature' and quotes Hamlet – of course – who, in possibly the most celebrated speech about acting, opines that they are 'the abstracts and brief chronicles of the time.' Hazlitt continues:

> Their life is a voluntary dream; a studied madness. The height of their ambition is to be beside themselves .... We see ourselves at second hand in them; they show us all that we are, all that we wish to be, and all that we dread to be. The stage is a bettered likeness of the world with the dull bits left out.[1]

Hazlitt is writing two and a half centuries ago of the theatre, where audiences would go to be thrilled by the likes of a 'splendid gypsy' such as Edmund Kean or John Philip Kemble,[2] and one wonders what he would make of today's diverse and expanding entertainment industry. Declan Donnellan speaks in a similar vein to Hazlitt: 'What theatre can do is present us with ourselves, the unspeakable as well as the charming.'[3]

So, what is the place of the actor in today's world? What does the twenty-first-century actor need in order to sustain a career? How are actors equipped for this radically changed and changing profession? How do we tell stories when communication functions through soundbites, tweets, Snapchat stories, Facebook posts and Skype calls? Where does language that is rich and complex and that works with extended rhetorical structure sit with this? Some of the most potent influences on contemporary theatre have come from the auteurs of Europe such as Thomas Ostermeier and Ivo Van

Hove, who often work with a kind of explosion of the text, where words are just black marks on a page to be manipulated in any way a director sees fit. Fair enough. So they are, and so they can. But does complex, emotional and physical language with the power to persuade and change someone continue to matter?

If one agrees that it might matter more than ever, then how do we help the actor in training take confident ownership of complex text, reach up and out for it and make it sound as if it were written today? One of the guiding principles of training at the Royal Academy of Dramatic Art (RADA) is that of a continued examination of the power of language, particularly complex, poetic and metaphorical text and how this can change us as we both speak it and listen to it: language as persuasion, *how we communicate and respond*, the word in action.

Rather than going to the glorious but obvious example of working with Shakespeare, I intend in this chapter to make a brief exploration of a dramatic genre that is notoriously difficult to crack and has been the Becher's Brook of many an accomplished actor: Restoration comedy.[4] In my experience, it is the material that if embraced fully and confidently, raises one's vocal and physical skill, imagination and intelligence to a level that makes other genres seem infinitely more approachable. It requires, however, the acquisition of a formidable vocal skill/acting technique.

Students occasionally ask, 'Why are we doing this stuff?' They say 'I don't get it, don't understand it, don't think it's relevant. What does it have to do with me? I want to be in films; I want to work with contemporary writing.' I answer them with my own question: What is it that actors do? I then offer Hazlitt's and Donnellan's insights. On a very simple level, acting offers us opportunities to behave very badly or heroically or romantically in the service of an idea, and one might say that all plays are about sex, money and survival.

The Genre and Its Demands

Restoration drama is known for its innate *theatricality*, the complexity of its language and the sheer energy and chutzpah required to deliver it. The plays, comedies in particular, draw laughter and admiration. They also have a dark underbelly and deal with human relationships: difficult marriages, sexual pursuit, infidelity and excess; the need to be 'in'; the lack of inheritance; fortune hunting; the terror of growing old; generational conflict; tensions between urban and rural life and the distrust of the 'foreign'; women and their courageous attempts to take charge of their lives; or their determined pursuit of pleasure as a means of staving off middle/old age. There are glorious chances to seize regarding character archetypes: the rake/sexual opportunist; the fashionable fop; the witty, independent-minded heroine, either stuck in a dreadful marriage or testing her suitor(s) to determine whether they are worth the effort; the clever servants; the impoverished, disinherited younger siblings; the wheedling pimp or bawd; the adventuress; the old men believing they have the attractiveness and libido of youth; the miserly father; the country boys and girls bemused and seduced by the pleasures of the town; etc. Above all, the *word* is a weapon of seduction, power, destruction and joyous celebration. Language tastes like something. It has physical sensations, buoyancy, brilliance and ebullience, requiring actors to be unashamed and open, revealing their human capacities fully and truthfully – some of which might be exposing. In his book *Acting in Restoration Comedy*, Simon Callow identifies the principle challenge in tackling and owning this material:

> Restoration comedies require the most exhausting kind of acting: sustained thinking.... Restoration comedy demands that the brain, as well as the heart and the senses, of the actor are fully engaged. These plays live in the play of ideas.[5]

My first encounters with these plays as an actor led me to experience just how long some of the sentences were within the dialogue, packed with subordinate clauses and diversions before finally landing, hopefully triumphantly, at the full stop. Not only did the text require a prodigious breath capacity but extraordinary intellectual energy and ability to think right down the centre of the thought and keep it buoyant to the end. When one achieved this, it was the most exhilarating thing in the world to play.

Modern actors, in the wake of Stanislavski and the emphasis on screen work are focused on embracing the inner psychological landscape of characters, seemingly at odds with the display of theatricality and the extrovert celebrated in Restoration comedy. If we are to continue to bring these glorious plays to life, we need to marry the inherent demands and sensibilities of the plays with the 'truth and belief' advocated by Stanislavski. When these plays were written, it was believed that one's manners reflected the authentic person. People were not concerned with the ability to express deep psychological conflict; that would have been frowned upon. Rather, to converse in an artful and clever manner was considered a necessary social skill. Emotion was masked or cloaked in beautiful, complex language and the need to be seen as at the top of the heap: words as fencing matches; language as sport; 'artifice' as one's glorious and greatest skill. It is crucial when working on these plays not to confuse 'artifice' with the dreaded word 'artificial' in the contemporary sense of 'inauthentic', fake, or phony. This is how these people are, and this is how they speak. Human desires – sex, money and survival – don't change over the centuries. The expression of *wit* as one's greatest asset means surrendering oneself to unfamiliar sensations and engaging fully and generously with some crucial 'rules' and above all, connecting and committing unapologetically to big, juicy actions. It also means having a vocal instrument that will articulate with energy, muscularity and precision. But it must look *easy*! Easy does not mean sloppy or imprecise: it needs will and effort in rehearsal and in preparation outside the rehearsal room, ultimately, to look effortless.

I engage here in analysis of a section from *The Man of Mode* by George Etherege, a brilliant, diamond-hard courtship comedy. The focus is on Act 2, scene 2. Style notwithstanding, it is essential to ask all the fundamental Stanislavski-based questions: Who and what am I? Where am I? When does it take place? What just happened? What do I want? Why do I want it? How do I get it? What must I overcome? What are my relationships? These form the basis for the script analysis that follows. After this, I offer examples of preparatory workshops for student actors and a guide to demystifying the different kinds of wit encountered in Restoration comedy.

The play's central character is Dorimant, a rich, fashionable man about town and notorious womanizer – the archetype of the rake. The play concerns his ruthless attempts to discard a troublesome mistress, Mrs Loveit, and take up with a new one, Bellinda (Mrs Loveit's so-called friend and confidante) while courting a rich young heiress, Harriet. Harriet has the measure of him and is no pushover; an example of the witty, independent archetype, she is more than his equal in wit and intelligence. Dorimant is fascinating, sexy, witty and energetic but not particularly likeable – very questionable husband material – and the play has a dark, tough satirical edge. It also contains many eccentrics, not least the archetypal fashionable fop, Sir Fopling Flutter. In this scene, students learn how Dorimant provokes Mrs Loveit into a rage so that he looks like the aggrieved party and can throw her over, while also contriving an assignation with Bellinda.

A room in Mrs Loveit's house.

Enter **Dorimant**

Dorimant They taste of death who do at heaven arrive,

But we this paradise approach alive.

(This is from Waller's 'Of Her Chamber Poems' Vol. 1. In quoting this verse, Dorimant indicates that he is well-read and is showing off here to an audience. Being in love is generally thought to be 'heaven' with the sexual innuendo of death as orgasm – but the second line, heavy with sarcasm in its use of the paradise metaphor, suggests that Mrs Loveit's sexual allure is no longer working, as he is 'alive'. The rhyming couplet is full of irony, and the actor needs to relish the metaphor and serve up the rhyme. It's self-conscious and has that sense of 'watch me handle this, everyone.')

Mrs Loveit is pacing furiously.

Dorimant What, dancing the galloping nag without a fiddle? *(Offers to catch her by the hand; she flings away and walks on.)* I fear this restlessness of the body, madam, *(pursuing her)* proceeds from an unquietness of the mind. What unlucky accident puts you out of humour – a point ill-washed, knots spoiled i'the making up, hair shaded awry, or some other little mistake in setting you in order?

Dorimant reduces Mrs Loveit's agitation to a clumsy country dance – and one with no music, thus beginning with an insult. There's a well-placed antithesis immediately following: 'restlessness of the body... unquietness of the mind'. Any possibility of sympathy or concern is scuppered by 'unlucky accident' and then the ladder or list of three, a rhetorical device known as the tricolon that occurs repeatedly in these texts: 'a point ill-washed, knots spoiled i'the making up, hair shaded awry'. These concern small details of dress and appearance – the last one particularly insulting because it suggests that Mrs Loveit has to colour her hair – and are all reduced to 'some other little mistake'. Points and knots are decorative details of dress of the period. Points are ties that link parts of a garment together, and knots are ribbons knotted to form decorative detail at the shoulders or down the front of the bodice.

Pert A trifle, in my opinion, sir, more inconsiderable than any you mention.

Pert, an example of the 'clever servant', puts him down – reducing his relationship with her mistress to a 'trifle' of even less importance than a detail dress.

Dorimant Oh, Mrs Pert! I never knew you sullen enough to be silent. Come let me know the business.

'I might have known you'd have something to say. Come on, as you have a loose tongue, spill the beans'.

Pert The business, sir, is the business that has taken you up these two days. How have I seen you laugh at men of business, and now to become a man of business yourself!

Pert (her name tells us what kind of a servant she is) has a ready reply, punning on the word 'business', giving it a double entendre and nailing his hypocrisy.

Dorimant We are not masters of our own affections; our inclinations daily alter. Now we love pleasure, and anon we shall dote on business. Human frailty will have it so, and who can help it?

Dorimant plays the innocent here and once more uses a clear antithesis to make his point: 'Now we love pleasure, and anon we shall dote on business'. That's life! This exchange between Dorimant and Pert is an excellent example of repartee.

Mrs Loveit Faithless, inhuman, barbarous man -

Mrs Loveit condemns him with a short rant, using the rule of three adjectives all increasing in their emotional violence.

Dorimant *(aside)* Good. Now the alarm strikes -

A quick, direct and self-satisfied connection to the audience, getting them onside. For the actor, the trick with asides is to imbue the audience with the sense of being fellow travellers.

Mrs Loveit Without sense of love, of honour, or of gratitude! Tell me, for I will know, what devil masked she was, you were with at the play yesterday.

Mrs Loveit has to keep the energy going from her previous line to complete the sentence, again using the rule of three to balance the previous line. Her action then changes to a determined interrogation 'for I will know', using the device of personification 'devil' to make her attitude to a supposed rival clear.

Dorimant Faith, I resolved as much as you, but the devil was obstinate and would not tell me.

Dorimant employs a quick bit of repartee to bat the accusation away and turn 'devil' to his advantage by implying 'I wanted to know as much as you, but she was giving nothing away.'

Mrs Loveit False in this as in your vows to me! You do know!

This is another accusation using antithetical balance.

Dorimant The truth is, I did all I could to know.

Mrs Loveit And dare you own it to my face? Hell and furies! *(Tears her fan in pieces)*

Dorimant Spare your fan, madam. You are growing hot and will want it to cool you.

Mrs Loveit Horror and distraction seize you, sorrow and remorse gnaw your soul, and punish all your perjuries to me!

These quick exchanges are an interesting combination of ranting from Mrs Loveit climaxing in the destruction of her fan and repartee from Dorimant, using light oppositions of 'hot' and 'cool' and wittily refusing to be drawn into a row, thus infuriating her further.

Dorimant *(Turning to Bellinda)* 'So thunder breaks the cloud in twain, And makes a passage for the rain.'

This is another quote from Dorimant, Mathew Royden's An Elegie, or Friend's Passion for his Astrophil. Dorimant uses the metaphor of tempestuous weather to make his point to Bellinda: 'Oh, now all that shouting will lead to her bursting into tears'. In doing so, he points out the excessiveness of Mrs Loveit's emotional response.

(To Bellinda) Bellinda, you are the devil that have raised this storm. You were at the play yesterday and have been making discoveries to your dear.

He cleverly accuses Bellinda of causing the trouble – back to 'devil' once more.

Bellinda   You're the most mistaken man i'the world.

An emphatic denial, with alliterative Ms.

Dorimant   It must be so, and here I vow revenge – resolve to persecute you more impertinently than ever any loving fop did his mistress, hunt you i'the Park, trace you i'the Mall, dog you in every visit you make, haunt you at the plays and i'the drawing room, hang my nose in your neck and talk to you whether you will or no, and ever look upon you with such dying eyes till your friends grow jealous of me, send you out of town, and the world suspect your reputation. *(In a lower voice)* At my Lady Townley's when we go from hence - *(He looks kindly on Bellinda)*

The park here refers to St James' Park, a fashionable meeting place near the Court at Whitehall; the mall is Pall Mall, a broad avenue on the St James' Park border.

This is a seduction right under Mrs Loveit's nose. Dorimant plays a dangerous and very sexy game, openly and extravagantly threatening Bellinda with punishment for her supposed betrayal and relentlessly piling on threat after threat in an extremely long sentence that needs each image/threat to top the previous one. The actor needs to build and be kept buoyant to 'suspect your reputation'. The images are a deliberate combination of violent pursuit and obsession, ostensibly to frighten and punish but also to arouse sexually. It is a brilliant example of the list/ladder with a forceful summation (climax) of what will happen to her at its conclusion. There is alliteration in hunt, haunt, hang, nose and neck; assonance in 'dying (with its sexual connotation) eyes'; and double entendre in abundance. In fact, the whole speech is one huge double entendre. Under cover of this seeming rant, Dorimant makes the place of their assignation known.

Bellinda   I'll meet you there.

Dorimant   Enough.

She agrees equally quickly, and he's done it.

Mrs Loveit   *(Pushing Dorimant away)* Stand off! You shan't stare upon her so!

She is immediately suspicious.

Dorimant *(Aside)* Good! There's one made jealous already!

Another display of confidence to the audience – all is going to plan!

Mrs Loveit Is this the constancy you vowed?

She exposes his deceit using 'constancy' as the touchstone.

Dorimant Constancy at my years? 'Tis not a virtue in season; you might as well expect the fruit the autumn ripens i'the spring.

Dorimant turns her idea around again to win the point. He's full of the life and vigour of youth. One comes to embracing constancy only when one is no longer young – again wittily using metaphor to demolish her.

Mrs Loveit Monstrous principle!

Loveit is having none of it – using 'monstrous' not only in the sense that it's a damned lie but also unnatural.

Dorimant Youth has a long journey to go, madam. Should I have set up my rest at the first inn I lodged at, I should never have arrived at the happiness I now enjoy.

He keeps the idea going with the metaphor of a journey with many places to stop, not just the first, and enjoys finishing with a brilliant, complex antithesis.

Mrs Loveit Dissembler, damned dissembler!

She is provoked by his witty argument to further alliterative accusation: all those Ds and the repetition of 'dissembler' further driven home with 'damned'.

Dorimant I am so, I confess. Good nature and good manners corrupt me. I am honest in my inclinations and would not, wer't not to avoid offence, make a lady a little in years believe I think her young, wilfully mistake art for nature, and seem as fond of a thing I am weary of as when I doted on't in earnest.

Nothing seems to faze him. His long sentence 'I am honest.... in earnest' is beautifully flexible, ending in a politely insulting antithesis which in effect says 'Sorry love, you're past your shelf life, and I'm not going to pretend.'

Mrs Loveit False man!

Dorimant True woman.

A short volley of antithetical raillery, which is economically bitter.

Mrs Loveit Now you begin to show yourself!

A triumphant exposure of the real man.

Dorimant Love gilds us over and makes us show fine things to one another for a time, but soon the gold wears off, and then again the native brass appears.

He combines personification, metaphor and antithesis, turning her word 'show' to his advantage. It's a cynical, if realistic, view of what happens when love begins and dies.

Mrs Loveit Think on your oaths, your vows, and protestations, perjured man!

Another desperate rule of three, with alliterative Ps at the end of the line

Dorimant I made them when I was in love.

Mrs Loveit And therefore ought they not to bind? Oh impious!

Dorimant What we swear at such a time may be a certain proof of a present passion; but to say truth, in love there is no security to be given for the future.

Dorimant continues to argue that love cannot be trusted to endure, his point being again well balanced, alliterative ('proof ... present passion') and antithetical.

Mrs Loveit Horrid and ungrateful, begone! And never see me more!

Mrs Loveit is reduced to insulting him; but there is also some implied blackmail in that final command. She's playing a dangerous game.

Dorimant I am not one of those troublesome coxcombs who, because they were once well received, take the privilege to plague a woman with their love ever after. I shall obey you, madam, though I do myself some violence. *(He offers to go, and Mrs Loveit pulls him back.)*

This is exactly what he is after, and he continues his elaborate over-civility with more antithesis. One should assume that there is some kind of physical tussle, which leads him to violently shake her off.

Mrs Loveit   Come back, you shan't go! Could you have the ill nature to offer it?

This translated to, 'Are you going to be so bad-tempered as to be violent?'

Dorimant   When love grows diseased, the best thing we can do is put it to a violent death. I cannot endure the torture of a lingering and consumptive passion.

At this point, Dorimant's tone changes from wittily civilized and provocative to something much more unpleasant and accusing – this is deliberate. He uses images of disease, violence and sickness.

Mrs Loveit   Can you think mine sickly?

Dorimant   Oh, 'tis desperately ill! What worse symptoms are there than your being always uneasy when I visit you, your picking quarrels with me on slight occasions, and in my absence listening to the impertinences of every fashionable fool that talks to you?

He continues the metaphor ruthlessly and in another long sentence uses that rule of three, ending with an extended accusation and more alliteration in 'fashionable fool'.

Mrs Loveit   What fashionable fool can you lay to my charge?

Dorimant   Why, the very cock-fool of all those fools, Sir Fopling Flutter.

Here he repeats 'fool' and more Fs: Fopling Flutter.
For the rest of the scene, Dorimant places the blame fairly and squarely at her door for flirting with Sir Fopling, puts himself in the right and leaves Mrs Loveit, who, after a fruitless attempt to call him back, resorts to a magnificent rant full of assonance, alliteration and hyperbole. It's a gift for the actor to really relish and give rein to the sensuous sensations of the language.

Mrs Loveit   Would I had made a contract to be a witch when first I entertained this greater devil. Monster, barbarian! I could tear myself in pieces. Revenge, nothing but revenge can ease me. Plague, war, famine, fire- all that can bring universal ruin and misery on mankind – with joy I'd perish to have you in my power but this moment!

She says all this in the presence of Pert and Bellinda!

Workshop Exercise

A good sized rehearsal space, preferably with some height, is necessary, together with a sound system.

Confident Command of and Holding the Space

Some research into and examination of the physical space in the Restoration theatre is useful in that it is a stimulus to the imagination and explains the extrovert nature of the playing. Theatres were small (the first was a converted tennis court) and indoors, and the three-sided stage thrust itself out into the auditorium. In front of the stage was the pit and then two or three galleries on three sides – the 'side boxes'. The royal box was in the centre back of the second gallery. The actors performed on the forestage – in close contact with the audience. It was an intimate relationship with the side boxes and the pit, and the actors needed to be able take in the king (and whichever mistress he was with) in his box up at the back too. Entrances were from doors on either side in the new 'proscenium' arch. Behind this, the stage accommodated new 'moving' painted scenery in a series of grooves at the side and various 'flying effects' and stage effects from a trapdoor. Both the auditorium and stage were lit by chandeliers with tallow (sheep fat) candles that were raised and lowered. There was no demarcation between the actors and the audience – no comforting blackness in the auditorium. Everyone was in full view all the time.

Members of the audience were watching themselves as well as the actors and were boisterous, rowdy and not remotely respectful. Whores and orange sellers plied their trades; young men fought each other; and self-styled critics commented on the actors and the play. Seating was available on the stage itself, creating an intimacy and energy that would be hard to match today even at the Globe on the South Bank. The lack of decorum was unimaginable. There is a telling account of the manners of the Restoration gallant in Sam Vincent's *The Young Gallant's Academy* published in 1674 and what might be expected of a fashionable young man.[6] Such behaviour would have him quickly ejected today! The confidence and sheer self-belief of actors to command attention and keep it must have been prodigious.

The confident, assured delivery of these texts requires not only a finely tuned vocal and physical technique but also an unrepentant ego, something which a surprising number of young actors today seem to find hard, or somehow unpalatable, to admit to openly – a kind of odd shyness. It's seemingly not quite nice to exhibit such self-belief, which is not helpful for this kind of work. The following exercises are strategies to unleash the 'star' in everyone. They are simple, fun and releasing. In preparation for the session, ask the actors to come as glamorously dressed as possible – not in period costume but in the smartest, dressiest clothes they have, clothes that make them feel attractive.

Exercise 1: The King/Queen and the Peasants

One actor sits on a chair at one end of the room. They are the king or the queen. (Depending on numbers, both king and queen could be there). The other actors pair up at the other end of the room – male/female pairs as much as possible but male/male and female/female is fine. If you have an odd number, then one actor takes the part of the major domo and heads up the procession. It is important to use music for this exercise, to give a tempo. You could use some of Henry Purcell's theatre music: the Rondo from *Abdelazar* is a useful and well-known example, but also the Air 'The Two Sosias' from *Amphitryon*, and particularly good for this exercise is the overture to the *Music for the Royal Fireworks* suite by Handel. Listen to the music once through to get the tempo inside the body and then, pair-by-pair, process up the room to the king/queen. On arrival at the royal presence, bow or curtsey: period accuracy is not important at this stage, but imagine what you might be saying with this gesture to the royalty. Then split off right and left, and return down each side of the room to the starting position, sustaining the tempo of the music.

This exercise works well when the imagination is fully activated. Go back to the fundamental questions: Who am I? Where am I? When is it? What has just happened? What do I want and why? What are my relationships to the king/queen, to my partner, to everyone in the room individually and collectively? Allow yourself to imagine and fantasize. You could make a collective agreement with your tutor's advice about occasion. What is vital is to admit to an inner life and an outer physicality that says to the world, 'We are it. We are the top of the heap'.

There is a development to this exercise which is useful if the group is large. Divide the group into aristos and peasants. (Make sure that both groups have a turn at each.) The peasants are on either side of the room gazing in through imaginary windows. Each peasant is supplied with a number of bunched-up paper balls, which represent their attitude to the upper classes. This need not be necessarily negative or combative; a mixture of admiration and loathing might be a more creatively potent combination. As the procession proceeds, the gazers throw their balls at the processors *silently*. How easy is it for the aristocrats to maintain their egos and sense of status? Do you get irritated? Do you care? Does it worry you? Is it pleasurable to be 'from the top drawer'? (In our allegedly egalitarian age, some student actors find giving themselves permission to embrace and thoroughly inhabit the notion of entitlement difficult – understandably so.) After you have experimented with the exercise, it is then possible to work with a faster tempo: 'Chasing Sheep Is Best Left To Shepherds' or 'The Disposition of the Linen' from the score to *The Draughtsman's Contract* by Michael Nyman allows for the parade to be more celebratory and 'champagne driven' and the onlookers to be more determined.

Exercise 2: I'm Worth Your Attention

Arrange the actors on three sides of the room, imagining a three-sided auditorium with an entrance centre back. It's useful if upstage centre there is a screen or a flat from behind which one can emerge. Each actor in turn makes an entrance and takes their place onstage at the optimal place to take in all the audience. The actor will be greeted by the audience with loud and approving applause or its opposite – boos, catcalls and generally boisterous disapproval – whichever audience response has been decided collectively before the actor appears. Actors must not know how they will be greeted. It's also useful – and fun – to invent a back story for the actor. For example, 'this is your farewell performance – you have been the audience's favourite and now you are retiring'; 'you are the newcomer to the company and need our support and approbation'; 'you are at the centre of scandal outside the theatre'; or 'you have offended the audience by being drunk and collapsing onstage last week'. The crucial thing is for the actor to enter, take in the response and simply stand there and enjoy it – especially if it is combative. The actor then decides when to exit. Again, it can be challenging for young modern actors to give themselves permission simply to enjoy being the object of admiration or contempt. What one is working for is that sense of 'you are lucky to get me', that ego that will eventually allow actors to offer the text unapologetically, with real confidence and panache.

Exercise 3: Unassailable Opinion – The Epigram

Using the same audience arrangement from the previous exercise, each actor enters, takes their position onstage to maximum advantage and then makes three statements: (1) their name, (2) where they come from and (3) an opinion on something – with the belief that it cannot be argued.

For example: 'My name is Elizabeth Lloyd. I come from Manchester. Facebook is the root of all evil.'

The opinion does not need to be profound, but it must be offered with complete confidence and conviction. The exercise can be developed with the contrary opinion, or some extension of it, offered by audience members.

> Actor: 'Cadbury's Dairy Milk is the best chocolate bar.'
> Audience member 1: 'Melted over ice cream, it is truly delectable.'
> Audience member 2: 'Mars bars melted over ice cream are far superior.'

The point is not to be clever or impressively inventive but rather to offer the opinion with unassailable authority. As the actors get used to the exercise, it can become enjoyably competitive as they use linguistic devices such as alliteration and hyperbole: 'remotely redeeming', 'truly delectable', etc.

Exercises 4, 5 and 6: Relish the Words

4. Partner up, sitting or standing. Agree a subject for an interesting conversation, and have that conversation; the only words you can use are numbers from one to 50. You may speak as many numbers as you like

at once, ensuring that your partner also has the opportunity to speak. You may discover that you like the sound of particular numbers or how they feel in the mouth. This is a good exercise with which to gossip or to imply improper behaviour. The same thing can be tried with letters of the alphabet.
5. Work on similes or similitudes. The group sits in a circle, and one actor begins the first half of the simile: 'The behaviour of those people in the pub was so bad last night that it was as if …' The next actor has to complete the simile: '… a herd of raging bison had rampaged through the bar'. The third actor has to repeat the whole sentence, relishing the cleverness and wit. This sequence is repeated until everyone has participated. As the actors get used to it, they will be able to work imaginatively and come up with exciting first halves and similes. Again, no matter how absurd, everything has to be offered with complete conviction and enjoyment.
6. For verbal battles, partner up or make a trio and decide on a subject with an attitude towards it – critical or admiring. The subject can be anything, such as clothes, food, sport, music, colours, political groups or a particular person. You then create a verbal competition in which each actor attempts to outdo the other using colourful, descriptive and alliterative words .

For example, the subject is dance, with an admiring attitude:

> Actor 1: 'Delightful, delicate, delicious dances'.
> Actor 2: 'Foot-tapping, festive, flowing fiestas'.
> Actor 3: 'Glorious, graceful, giddy gavottes'.

The aim is to explore sound and extravagance and the sensuous connection of the words in the mouth and to compete with each other for the wittiest description. The exercise can be usefully developed when participants take a critical or censorious attitude towards a person or a group of people that leads into character assassination territory that one finds so often in Restoration comedy.

> Actor 1: 'Boring, blustering, barmy braggart.'
> Actor 2: 'Tedious, troublesome, tipsy twerp.'
> Actor 3: 'Malevolent, mean, moth-eaten miscreant.'

The actors should be encouraged to be as colourful and extravagant as possible and not to worry about venturing into surreal and absurd territory. The exercise is about coining the words and scoring points. It might take the actors into protestations of undying love and admiration or violent insults. The important thing is to become comfortable with extravagant expression.

Finish the session with a series of tongue twisters, for example:

In enterprise of martial kind,
When there was any fighting,
He led his regiment from behind -
He found it less exciting.
But when away his regiment ran
His place was at the fore-o.
That celebrated, cultivated, underrated nobleman,
That unaffected, undetected, well-connected warrior,
That very knowing, overflowing, easy-going paladin,
The Duke of Plaza Toro![7]

There is beauty in the bellow of the blast,
There is grandeur in the growling of the gale,
There is eloquence outpouring in the lion when a-roaring,
And the tiger when a-lashing of his tail.
Oh I love to see a tiger, from the Congo or the Niger,
And especially when lashing of his tail!
Are you old enough to marry do you think?
Won't you wait until you're eighty in the shade?
There's a fascination frantic in a ruin that's romantic,
Do you think you are sufficiently decayed?
To the matter that you mention I have given some attention
And I think I am sufficiently decayed.
If that is so, sing derry down derry. It's evident very
Our tastes are one.
Away we'll go and merrily marry, nor tardily tarry
Till day be done![8]

Each of these verses has been adapted from the operettas of Gilbert and Sullivan, a rich mine of witty and alliterative lyrics for tongue twisters that are linked to story, character and action and are not simply mechanical articulation exercises. They can be communicated and inflected. Start slowly and work up speed.

In concluding, I will return to Callow:

> we can never stop asking what words mean, how they are used, what they tell us about the characters and their times. We affirm, in the very act of theatre, the ways in which words transform our whole understanding of life .... That is the theatre's business, the giving and restoring of life.[9]

As well as attempting to prepare actors for the demands of the industry as it has developed and expanded over the last few decades, any actor training should concern itself with the power of language to persuade, provoke, delight and encourage us to *listen*.

Delineating Types of Wit

(My thanks go to Cathleen McCarron, voice coach at the Royal Shakespeare Company.)

- **Repartee** consists of quick back and forth competitive exchanges; badinage or banter which is generally good-humoured and more like ping-pong volleys than tennis. The exchanges between Worth and Berinthia are good examples.
- **Raillery** is similar to repartee, with the same quick tempo and intelligence, aimed at ridiculing another person, group or any topic of conversation. Medley, Dorimant and Young Bellair in *The Man of Mode* provide an example of this.
- **Epigrams** are pronouncements, unassailable opinions and pithy sayings. In the comedies, epigrams are used by characters to sum up their beliefs or sentiments on any subject. Lord Foppington does this in *The Relapse*, where his tortured vowels are deliberate: 'Far once a woman has given you her heart, you can never get rid of the rest of her bady.'
- **Similitudes** would be called 'similes' today, figures of speech where one thing is likened to another, deployed by Berinthia in *The Relapse*: 'There's not a man in town who has a better interest with the women .... He's like a back-stair minister at Court, who, whilst the reputed favourites are sauntering in the bedchamber, is ruling the roost in the closet.'

- **Metaphors** are language devices that use once thing to express another, as Ben to Miss Prue in Congreve's *Love for Love* demonstrates: 'Well, Madam, what think you of a cruising voyage towards the Cape of Matrimony. You father designs me for the pilot. If you'll agree to it, we'll hoist sail immediately.'
- **Antithesis** is the placing in a balanced way of two contrasting ideas. Words, phrases, sentences and whole speeches can be antithetical (see Berinthia above).
- **Double entendres** are words or phrases with more than one meaning, usually to do with sex such as what Pert says to Dorimant in *The Man of Mode*: 'The business, sir, is the business that has taken you up these two days. How have I seen you laugh at men of business, and now to become a man of business yourself!'
- **Rants** are outbursts of emotion, not usually using wit: 'Revenge, nothing but revenge can ease me. Plague, war, famine, fire – all that can bring ruin and universal misery on mankind – with joy I'd perish to have you in my power but this moment' (Mrs Loveit in *The Man of Mode*).
- **Cant** is insincere talk, usually in a so-called declaration of love. Sometimes this can be extremely plausible, such as Worthy to Amanda in *The Relapse*: 'slight your god, if he neglects his angel. With arms of ice receive his cold embraces, and keep your fire for those who come in flames. Behold a burning lover at your feet, his fever raging in his veins! See how he trembles, how he pants! See how he glows, how he consumes! Extend the arms of mercy to his aid; his zeal may give him title to your pity, although his merit cannot claim your love.'
- **Tricolon** is the rule of three in words, phrases and sentences. These can ascend or descend in size, as shown by Mrs Loveit in *The Man of Mode*: 'Faithless, inhuman, barbarous man!'[10]

Acknowledgements

I must thank Edward Kemp, Lucy Skilbeck, Joe Windley, Francine Watson Coleman, Melanie Jessop and John Beschizza at RADA; Ralph Davis, Isobel Della Porta, Sarah Williams, Eleanor de Rohan and the cast of the 2016 RADA project *The Man of Mode*; Professor Vladimir Mirodan, Alex Bingley and Paul Goodwin at Drama Centre London; Neil Swain for many inspiring conversations regarding dramatic language; Joseph Millson and Oengus MacNamara.

Notes

1. Hazlitt's 'On Actors and Acting' was first published in *The Examiner* on 5 January 1817. It was one of the essays picked to go into his first book, *The Round Table* (1815–1817).
2. From Act 3 of *Trelawney of the Wells*, by Arthur Wing Pinero: Sir William Gower speaks to Rose Trelawney of his encounter with the actor Edmund Kean.
3. *Talking Cheek by Jowl*. In conversation with Declan Donnellan. www.culturalised.co.uk with Max Adams, 14 July 2017.
4. Becher's Brook – the most dangerous fence in the Grand National horse race – a metaphor often used to describe any extremely challenging task with a high risk of failure.
5. Callow, S. *Acting in Restoration Comedy*, p. 13.
6. *A Sourcebook in Theatrical History*, pp. 213–214.
7. From *The Gondoliers*, by W. S. Gilbert and Sir Arthur Sullivan.
8. From *The Mikado*, by W. S. Gilbert and Sir Arthur Sullivan.
9. Callow, S. *Acting in Restoration Comedy*, p. 104.
10. There is an extensive and useful examination of the tricolon and its many variations in *Dramatic Adventures in Rhetoric*. See the Bibliography.

5

What Are You Saying? An Approach to Teaching Text in an Era of Language Loss

Laura Wayth

The night before commencing this chapter, I had a read-through for a production that I directed in the School of Theatre and Dance at San Francisco State University (SFSU). I was working with a cast of 20 young actors. It was a fairly simple script. Of those 20 actors, only two at the reading appeared to have any intuitive command of what they were saying. The rest of the actors glazed over language, missing important details, missing nuance, missing wordplay. They bypassed the structure of the language and the visceral nature of words. But even more than that, by treating the language so casually, they missed the intent of the text. They missed the action. They entirely missed the story.

Like one of those apples at a supermarket chain that looks waxy and shiny on the outside but is mealy and flavourless on the inside, text choices for many young American actors these days offer no substance, no nutritional content in terms of the language. This is most certainly not their fault and has little to do with their intelligence. It is a product of their culture and the way they are educated in our school systems. In American schools, we most often teach to the test; language is not something that is valued or revered but a means to an end, something used to impart factual information. In addition, this phenomenon is also a product of their texting and of a watching-rather-than-reading culture. Language feels as though it is being replaced by a kind of shorthand and by an increasingly visual rather than linguistic culture. Consequently, young actors often do not look further or deeper than what is stated on the surface. If words themselves do not carry much weight, why would we even think to look beneath them for an even deeper meaning? Why would actors even think to dig deeper when they cannot even fully command what is lying on the surface?

Encouraging actors to dig deeper has become my challenge as an acting teacher at SFSU. How do I help young actors understand text? How can I help them to go deeper, defining what they are truly saying and uncovering what they are not overtly stating in the text? This has become increasingly problematic. After 16 years in the classroom, I reached a point where I had to look at the changing nature of my student cohorts and recognize that what used to work was simply not working anymore. As the gulf between language and understanding grew wider and wider, I realized that I needed to reinvent my teaching to meet this challenge. What follows is a sense of how I approach this and how it is worked through with students in the room.

Introducing Terminology

As a graduate actor, I spent the equivalent of three years learning the ins and outs of the Stanislavski system. I experienced it viscerally, through études, through exercises and through rehearsals. Non-conservatory undergraduate memes simply do not allow this kind of time and leisure for learning these craft tools. For many years, I tried to replicate my training as a graduate actor in an undergraduate context, offering a Cliff Notes version of my in-depth training. When I was a younger teacher, I thought that this was teaching with integrity and an appropriate reverence for the material. I was mistaken. As undesirable as it may be, the reality, I later realized, is this: you have to work quick and dirty.

This need to work effectively in a condensed and expedient manner is not a need unique to our particular programme but a necessity, I believe, for all BA (bachelor of arts) programmes in the United States. Unlike a BFA (bachelor of fine arts) programme or other conservatory-style programme, BA programmes across the United States do not provide us as much dedicated acting training time with our students as we might like. Regardless of students' ultimate career aspirations (and many of our students do have an interest in working professionally in the field), the nature of BA training is broad and generalized—the philosophy being that a well-rounded, broadly educated person makes for a more complete citizen of the theatre.

Our students take nearly as many units in the general education component of the university as they do in the arts. At the School of Theatre and Dance at SFSU, regardless of an interest in and a commitment to performance, our students are trained equally in other aspects of theatre-making; technical theatre, history and dramaturgy.

Having come from programmes with conservatory models where acting and performance was the main casserole at the meal, and not one of many side dishes, I balked at first, thinking it an inadequate model. After many years of working within a BA programme, I learned that broadly educated students make for more interesting performers. Students who understand history, sociology, anthropology, mathematics, astronomy or other subjects outside of the theatre are better problem solvers and better thinkers in the theatre.

Regardless of the value of the BA model educationally, the model and its somewhat limited contact time does dictate pragmatism and expediency on the part of those who train our actors. Therefore, I developed what I unglamorously and unapologetically term my Quick and Dirty Guide to Acting Terminology, explaining to my students that in an ideal world these concepts would be garnered experientially rather than conceptually and explaining the constraints of our limited time working together. Despite my initial trepidation, it seems to be a model that works. With the terms intellectually spelled out before them (a model that they are comfortable with from all of those years of taking tests in their schools), students later, through scene work and critique, fill in the necessary experiential blanks. It is something of an inverse process from my graduate school training, but it has proven to be the most expedient and effective model under the circumstances.

The following is my crystallized introduction to action-based acting terminology. There are so many ways to explain these terms to students, and each practitioner has a different way of articulating terms and highlighting the salient points of an action-based system of acting. This is mine. It certainly does not cover every aspect of actor training using a Stanislavskian model, but it provides a firm foundation for further craft discussion.

An Introduction to the Craft of Acting

This section details what every actor needs to know when beginning work on a scene or monologue.

The Given Circumstances

For every play that we approach and for every scene or monologue within a play, we need to read the play and carefully gather information to be able to answer the following questions as fully as possible.

1. *Who* is your character?
    In specific detail, what is your name, age, gender, social status, profession and personality? What are your likes, dislikes, insecurities, hopes and aspirations? What do other people say about your character in the play (this is often your best way of getting information about your character)? Who are the other primary characters in the play with whom you interact? What are your relationships with them like, and what is the history or each?

2. *What* is the current situation?
    What is going on? What is the problem that needs to be overcome? What, in a nutshell, is your character's predicament?

3. *Where* are you?
    Literally, physically, what kind of a space is your character in? Are you in a restaurant, are you in a prison, are you in a bedroom, are you in a museum? Your character's location affects their behaviour. Is it hot, cold, raining, snowing? Environment changes behaviour. How does this affect you physically and mentally?

4. *When* is this moment/scene/play taking place?
    What year is it? The time period of the scene will greatly change the character's social behaviour (and what is permissible socially and politically for them). Keep in mind that the play may span different time periods. How does this time period affect your use of language and your physical vocabulary? What season is it? What time of day or night is it? All questions of time, be they big questions (like the era) or smaller questions (like the time of day), profoundly influence your character's behaviour.

5. *Why* is this event happening now?
    Why is this event happening now, at this exact moment? Why didn't this event happen last year, five years ago, five minutes ago, or yesterday? What makes this moment in time unique, and why is it allowing this event to happen?

These questions are called the *given circumstances*—that is, the who, what, where, when and why of a play or scene, given to you by the text. You cannot work on a scene without knowing the given circumstances in full detail.

The Moment Before

The moment before the scene begins, something happened.

Scenes do not begin in a vacuum. Just like in life, you do not magically appear in a place. Something happened before you got here. You got rained on, you ran in late after trying to find a parking spot, you had a fight with someone, or you received a lovely phone call from someone. This is your moment before. The moment before means that you come into the room *with* something—with a previous state of mind, a previous physical tempo and heart rate, and a previous state of being. This prior moment greatly shapes your behaviour in this moment in this scene.

The Character's Objective

The *objective* is what the character needs to get from another character or characters onstage.

No one is ever just onstage talking. Your character is *always* working to get something from someone. Characters do not just 'vent' or 'tell a story'. Theatre deals with the most salient, rich, loaded moments of human experience. Therefore, if it is happening onstage, that means that it is vital. If it's not important, we are unlikely to care about watching it.

Your character is onstage because they desperately need something from another character onstage with them.

Identify what your character wants in the scene from another character or characters. What are you fighting for in the scene?

An objective must be:

- compelling and specific
- tangible and potentially achievable
- positive (state what you want to happen, not what you do not want)
- directed entirely toward another character or characters onstage with you
- consistent with the playwright's intention.

If you choose your objective carefully, you will likely be able to play it for the duration of the scene. The only reason to change your objective in the course of the scene is if you decidedly win it. For example, if your objective is to get the other character onstage with you to put down their gun and on page 27 they do so, you can no longer play this objective. You concretely achieved it and must find a new thing that you need from the other character in the scene in order to continue.

Here are a few examples of strong/playable objectives, which must be concrete and specific and will allow the actor to try to get something from the other person:

Strong objectives:

- to get him to admit that he is being a jerk
- to get her to sleep with me
- to get him to apologize for betraying me
- to get him to sign the papers
- to get her to confess to me.

Why are these strong objectives? They are specific, directed toward the other character, and potentially achievable by your character. They are specific enough to lead the actor toward concrete action onstage and broad enough to allow for a range of tactical possibilities.

Weak objectives are unspecific, inactive and difficult to play. They do not lead the actor to need something strongly from the other person onstage:

Weak objectives:

- to express myself
- to vent
- to tell a story
- to feel sad.

The Character's Obstacle

In every scene in every play, your character has an *obstacle*, something that is preventing you from getting what you want and need and keeping you from achieving your objective. The obstacle provides the conflict in a scene.

If there is no obstacle, there is no conflict. Theatre is about conflict. If there is no conflict, there is no scene or play worth watching.

Obstacles can come from several sources:

- within yourself (you want to let her know that you are attracted to her, but you fear rejection)
- past circumstances (you want to kiss her, but you remember that you ate garlic and onions for lunch)
- present circumstances (you want to kiss him, but your mother is knitting in the next room)
- relationships (you would like to kiss him, but he is your boss)
- the environment (you would like to kiss her, but she is on the balcony)
- the objectives of other characters (you would like to kiss her, but she is flirting with your friend instead).

Identify specifically what is preventing you from getting what you want from the other person. If you cannot name the obstacle specifically, chances are that the scene will not have much conflict and will thus fall flat.

Here are a few examples of naming concrete and specific obstacles. Strong obstacles:

- I cannot get him to apologize to me, because he thinks it is all my fault.
- I cannot get her to agree to marry me, because she is scared of needing someone.
- I cannot get the money from him, because he has a knife.

Tactics

Now that you know what the character wants/needs (what their *objective* is) and what the *obstacle* is that is preventing them from getting what they need, you need to determine by what means they are going to try to get what they need and want from the other character or characters in the scene. These are the character's tactics.

The *tactics* are the specific things that your character does to get what they need from another character (you may hear other theatre practitioners refer to these as 'actions'—both terms work).

There are two ways that I frame a tactic:

1. Name a verb that you are doing to the other person: attacking, seducing, berating, enlightening, enticing, educating, or eviscerating them.
2. Name the way that you are trying to make the other person feel: make her feel ashamed, make her feel afraid, make him feel guilty, make him feel sexy, etc.

A tactic must meet the following criteria:

- conducive to achieving your objective (for instance, if your objective is *to get him to agree to marry me*, it is unlikely that you would want to use a tactic such as *alienating him*, which is likely to move you further away from achieving your objective)
- capable of being concretely done, physically or verbally (i.e. something you can do, rather than just an idea)
- directed entirely toward the other person onstage with you
- consistent with the playwright's intentions.

When a scene falls flat, it is often because the actor has not found a wide range of playable tactics. It is likely that the actor is staying on the same tactic for far too long or playing similar kinds of tactics. Many young actors make the mistake of assuming that a long passage in a text is all played with the same tactic; this leads to colourless, uninteresting acting. Look for variety. If you are not getting what you want in the scene, you need to change your tactic.

Make sure that you concretely name your tactics when you begin your rehearsals. Failure to do this often leads to a generalized scene that does not have a journey.

Beat

The length of time given to the playing of a single tactic is known as a *beat*.

You change to a new tactic at the places in your script where you have marked your beats.

Note your *beats* in the script by drawing a line underneath the text where they occur. This will give you a clearer sense of the dramatic structure and the evolution of the scene.

At the end of every beat, decide whether you won the beat or lost the beat. Did you get closer to achieving your objective in that passage? If so, then you won the beat. Did you get further away from achieving your objective? If so, then you lost the beat. Making a clear decision about whether you won or lost the beat will clarify your next tactical choice and substantially clarify the overall journey of the scene.

Stakes

The *stakes* are what is at risk for your character in the play or at any given moment. What do you have to lose? What would losing your objective cost you?

The higher the stakes, the more interesting and electric the scene. If the scene is boring or uneventful, the stakes need to be raised; that is, what there is for you to lose in the scene must be far more vital.

Audiences are riveted by action movies where the stakes are life or death. It needs to be as important as possible for your character to succeed in their objective in order for the audience to invest and to care.

Conflict

A scene does not work if there is not a strong *conflict* visible. A *conflict* occurs when two opposing forces collide. It is the first element that actors must discover about the story they are telling.

To be certain that you are generating a strong conflict in a scene, look at your objective. What is your objective? Does the objective that you have chosen for the scene 'bump up' against the other actor that you are working with to generate the maximum amount of conflict?

For example, if my character's objective is *to get him to apologize to me* and your character's objective is *to get her to forgive me*, there will be little to no conflict in the scene. We both need the same thing and can easily get it and solve our problem. However, if my character's objective is *to get him to apologize to me* and your character's objective is *to get her to admit that she's wrong*, we will have a lot of conflict in the scene.

While it is not always a great idea to discuss your tactics with your scene partner (often better to surprise them and see how it changes the scene), you may choose to discuss your objective in the scene to make sure that the two of you are creating a scene with the maximum amount of conflict. Be certain to name the conflict in the scene. If you cannot define and name it, chances are your scene does not have a clear conflict.

Discovery

A *discovery* is exactly what it sounds like. Something is uncovered or revealed in the scene that must be acknowledged by the actor.

For example, suppose that in the scene that you are working on, you suspect that your husband, Harold, is having an affair. You come home unexpectedly and find his top shirt button undone and his necktie loose. This is the first discovery in the scene. It is not enough evidence to incriminate him, but it is something that you see that must be acknowledged. The scene continues, and you find underwear on the floor that is not yours. This is the second discovery in the scene (once again, a physical discovery). Next, Harold states that he is too tired to take your planned trip to Venice together. This is the third discovery in the scene (in this case, a verbal discovery).

Next, you hear sneezing coming from the bathroom. As you suspected, you open the door to find Harold's secretary in there wrapped in a towel. This final bit of information creates the event of the scene, which we will now define.

Event

The *event* is the major thing that happens in the scene that changes the scene. It is the moment that marks a complete turning point in the scene.

For example, if someone bursts into a business meeting without his pants, the meeting stops, and everyone turns and stares, this is an event. The course of the meeting will have to change from that point forward. The meeting can never be the same again.

Events can be things that physically happen (as in the above example) or things that are said by a character or characters from which there is no recovery. If, in the scene, you are speaking to your husband and throughout the whole scene he is saying, "I wish you would just come out and say that you don't love me anymore," and after five minutes of dialogue, you finally break down and say, "Fred, I just don't love you anymore," this is an event. The scene is forever changed.

If the actor does not acknowledge physical and textual discoveries and the physical or textual event of the scene, the audience will not understand the story being told. It is surprising how often actors, due to the familiarity of the rehearsal process, begin to gloss over discoveries and events and not give them their proper due. Chart these discoveries and events carefully in your process, and the audience will track the arc of the scene and fully understand and invest in the story that you are telling.

Applying Terminology and Concepts

I find that once student actors have been introduced to these terminologies and concepts, it is crucial to put them into practice right away. If they are left to marinate for too long, they just fall into the abyss of unused facts and terms clogging their overstuffed brains.

What is more, I have discovered that students do not do well applying these terms and concepts directly to the scenes that they are working on in class. They do not appear to be able to take these concepts, learn them and immediately apply them to a script. In the past, I tried this and found that student actors come to class with their work 'prepared' as though they had never been introduced to, let alone mastered, these concepts. Once I discovered this disturbing trend, I determined that I must take these terms and concepts for a spin as a group. I therefore developed a group exercise for text analysis.

The Group Exercise

I always ask student actors the following question before they begin work on a scene. What is the trap of the scene? Another way to frame the question is, how can the scene be bad? Even skilled playwrights write big traps that the actor can fall into if they do not identify the trap early on and navigate around it. What is a trap? A trap is anything that leads the actor into repetitive, one-note, uninteresting behaviour. Almost every scene in every contemporary play has them.

The scene that I most commonly assign the group to work on is from Theresa Rebeck's short play *Train to Brooklyn*. While Rebeck is a skilled and interesting playwright, this play has a large trap for the actor (and a trap that beginning actors are especially susceptible to falling into). The scene is about a strained relationship between two sisters, Stephanie and Julia, and their friend Holly (who is something of a sweet pawn in their sisterly argument). It is easy in the hands of an actor who has not made interesting and nuanced choices for Stephanie to come across as unfeeling and snarky the whole time. In the hands of an untrained actor, this is exactly what happens.

I have the class read the scene out loud, assigning various actors to read the three different roles, switching actors as we go. The initial read-through, invariably, has nothing but snarky tactics for the actor playing Stephanie. I ask the class to identify the trap written for Stephanie in the scene, and they correctly identify that Stephanie could just come off as a one-dimensional character the whole time.

Once the students have identified the trap in the scene, I have them read the scene as a group once again. I ask the whole class to pretend that they are playing the role of Stephanie. I ask them to identify what Stephanie wants in the scene from Julia (her objective). I then ask them what is in the way of Stephanie's achieving her objective (the obstacle). Once we identify Stephanie's objective in the scene and understand the obstacle, we reread the scene, carving it out beat by beat. As a group, we come up with tactics for Stephanie (tactics that are anything but snarky). We identify what Stephanie is really saying underneath the line (her subtext is so much richer than what she is actually saying). We determine for each and every line how she is really trying to affect her sister. How is she trying to make her sister feel? At this point, students write in their tactics for the text. We then discuss where the beat shifts occur and whether Stephanie won or lost the beat. Determining whether she won or lost the beat informs the next set of tactics that we will choose.

I then ask the students to identify the major discoveries in the scene and the scene's turning point (the event). Once the students identify the event of the scene, we determine whether Stephanie won or lost the beat of the event. If we determine that Stephanie won the beat of the event (usually their first inclination), we go back as a group and change the tactics, this time having Stephanie lose the beat of the event. The students see that having Stephanie win the beat often tells a different story and creates a different story arc than when Stephanie loses the beat. I ask the students which choice (both choices are supported fully by the text) makes for a more interesting scene.

While this process is somewhat painstaking, it is a game changer for student actors. The students see the amazing transformation from an uninteresting, one-note, on-the-surface scene to a rich, nuanced family relationship and a funny and moving scene. The night-and-day difference that student actors see as a result of directly applying analytical craft techniques to a script gets them fully on board with the process from the beginning.

The Individual Paperwork

Once the actors have learned the terminology and then been hand-carried, applying it to text through the in-class script analysis group exercise, they are ready to apply this process to the scenes that they are working on.

Before their first read-through of the scene in class, I have actors complete the following paperwork for their selected scenes. In this paperwork, I move past the group exercise of identifying objectives, tactics, beat shifts, discoveries, and events and introduce the student actor to the idea of character biography. I then move further in depth, asking the student actors to experience the language more viscerally and to dig into the subtext of the script. The following is the paperwork that I have them complete.

Scene Analysis

Part 1: What are the given circumstances in your selected scene in full detail?

- *Who* is your character?
- *Who* is the character, or who are the characters, whom you are currently talking to in this scene?

- *What* is the current situation your character is facing?
- *Where* exactly is your character? What kind of an environment is this?
- *When* is this event taking place? Specify year, time of day and season.
- *Why* is this event happening right now?
- What happened the moment before this scene began (explained in one to three sentences)? What did your character experience, or what was said to your character?
- How do you want to change the other person (or people) onstage with you?

My objective is to _____ (in order to)_____.
What is your obstacle? (please explain in one sentence only)
My obstacle is _____.
What is at stake?
If I do not successfully _____, _____ will happen.
Identify the conflict of the scene, using only one sentence.
What discoveries do you make in the scene?
What is the single most critical event in the scene?
What language in the scene do you find moving, beautiful, haunting, violent, etc., and why so? Highlight those places in the script. What is it about the words that affect you? What sounds do you hear, and how do they viscerally feel to you?
What images come to mind when you hear certain phrases or sentences in the script?

Part 2: Detailed biographical questions

Please complete these questions as fully as you can.
Exactly how old am I? How do I feel about my age?
What is my name? What do people call me? Do I like my name?
What is my gender identity? Do I like being this gender? Do I take it for granted? Do I have issues with my masculinity/femininity? Do I use it as power? Do I hide it?
Where did I grow up? How do I feel about where I grew up?
Where do I live now (if it is a different place)? Why do I live here?
What is my home like (if I have one)?
Where did I go to school (if I went to school)?
Do I have a degree? Is education important to me? Is it not? If education is not important to me, what is important to me?
How much money do I have? How important or unimportant is money to me?
Am I single? If I am, am I happy about that?
If I am not single, how do I feel about that?
What do I do for a living? Do I like it? Did I always do this?

> Do I have children? Do I have pets? Am I alone?
> Which people are closest to me?
> What is my religion (if I have one)? How important is religion to me? Do I believe in God, gods, or the divine?
> What makes me feel happy or satisfied?
> What saddens or angers me the most?
> What is my biggest secret?
> What is my biggest fear?
> What is my greatest hope?
> How do I want my life to change?
>
> **Part 3: Scoring**
>
> - Make a photocopy of the scene.
> - Write in the margins of your scene what tactics you intend to use.
> - Draw a line each time you feel that a portion of the scene has ended and there is a clear beat shift.
> - Write down whether you won or lost the beat in the margins.
> - Add subtext: on a separate piece of paper, write what you are really saying through your line. Are you saying exactly what you mean? Are you saying its opposite? If you could speak your thoughts directly and clearly without consequence, what would you say?

Final Thoughts

Script analysis with student actors, in my experience, has always been something of an afterthought. Before I developed this process of teaching, student actors seemed concerned with and focused on everything except the script and the logic of what they were saying. They focused on blocking the scene before they understood what was truly happening in the scene.

This step-by-step process provides them with a concrete foundation to begin their work as an actor. With a practical foundation to build on, they have not only the proper grounding to dive further into language and its nuances, but the awareness that language is power and that language drives action. It is an ongoing battle to equip students to revere language and to explore a text in a culture that grows increasingly disassociated from and dismissive of the written word, but this method, arrived at through much trial and error, has proven to be a step in the right direction. Students walk away from this process empowered, with an increased sensitivity to the meaning of words and the intentions that lie beneath and on top of them; and with a new awareness of the architecture of scripts, students dive into a pond that they once only quickly skated across.

6

Mind the Gap: Gōng Fēng Shuǐ and the Missing Teeth (Ma)

Robert (Draf) Draffin

What is the natural training opiate – those *practices* that sustain a *place/space* of uninterrupted creative processes in the young student actor in that mysterious space/gap/interval between generative input and creative action? What *state* of the body allows the actor to be able to enter with revelation and a specific calmness, into a complex and seemingly tacit dimension, *to descend mindfully into the gap*?

Acting is about processes of creative transformation, and many practitioners over the last century, and more recently backed up by neurological scientists, have explored creativity's somatic nature.[1] Since 1996, the Theatre School at Melbourne University's Faculty of VCA-MCM (Victorian College of the Arts and Melbourne Conservatorium of Music) has been underpinned by a kinaesthetic, corporeal and spatial emphasis on its acting pedagogy and has included many Asian-influenced approaches to performance in its curriculum.[2] As I age and large gaps appear as my teeth disappear, I wish to share some principles and practices about a particular *primary state* in an actor's creative process. These are processes I have gained through Asian artistic interfaces over the past 30 years and employed at the VCA-MCM as an acting teacher, primarily between 1996 and 2010. Over this period, I discovered the most important parts of training are the *foundation practices*. These are the early and repeatable exercises that sustain a creative space of awareness, perception and experience, a gap and in-between space that allows revelation within action – not a spontaneous unaware reaction, not propositions and certainly not a cognitive naming but rather a *knowing doing* rather than a *logo-rational knowing*.

Foundation training offers a platform for the student actor's talent to emerge and grow; it underpins and continually feeds all other aspects of the training, no matter what later method is employed. However, this preliminary phase can become too complicated and over-theorized and not practised deeply or repeatedly enough. Actors in training are too often thrust into methods and approaches before the innate fundamentals of experiencing aliveness in a moment and engaging the imagination have been firmly laid out.[3] Actors need the sustained ability to enter a particular kinaesthetic, corporeal, spatial and temporal place where the imagination and clarity of action can unfold. The Japanese call this *space* or *moment* (*ma*), and the ability or state of the body to enter can be trained by practices underpinned by the Chinese principles of *gōng fēng shuǐ*.[4]

Writing about somatic knowledge and practices is always a challenge. As a practitioner, I am more comfortable in a studio with actors, where like many Asian teachers, the training is as much by touch as by instruction and where instructions are more often metaphorical. However, I will draw on the information, research and experiences of *gōng fēng shuǐ* (*ma*) that I have had, alongside some wonderful artists, before describing some exercises that allow actors to *mind the gap*.

(*Ma*) – Between the Actor and the Tree

In 2017 I asked one of the most famous Indonesia actors, Slamet Rahardjo, what it was in his training that allowed him to become such a fine actor.[5] As a Muslim child living with his grandfather in Yogyakarta, he was influenced by Javanese traditions and Hindu practices, stories and culture before leaving to live on the tough streets of Jakarta. After acting in a student play, he was taken under the wing of the famous Indonesian film director Teguh Karya and was awarded the prize of best actor in Indonesia. Notwithstanding this, he was untrained and eager to understand how to act more deeply. Rahardjo did not go to New York or Europe but returned to Yogyakarta to train with a traditional Dhalang master (master puppeteer of Wayang Kulit). The master told him to do no more than stand in front of a particular tree for weeks. Rahardjo said this was his foundation actor training: a repeated practice. He had to control his body to find ways to control the pain. This for him was a combination of strengthening the body and knowing how to connect, control and balance its energy. This aligns with the traditional Chinese concept of *gōng* (工) energy, which incorporates body awareness and the control of a discursive mind.[6] As Rahardjo stopped questioning why he was doing this, his mind became open and he became aware of the *fēng* (風) energy, the changing energies outside oneself. At this point, he became conscious of encountering the Other: the tree. Finally, he was free to just be in (*ma*), the moment of entering the gap between the actor and the tree. Rahardjo recalls how the tree and he began talking to each other, which gave rise to *shuǐ* (水) energy, a release of imagination and a transformational change through an encounter.

I will focus and expand on the above converging areas: *ma* and the overlapping energy practices of *gōng fēng shuǐ* that hold simple and deep knowledge that I believe should be present in any foundation training.

(*Ma*) – Origins and Meaning

(*Ma*) (間) is a traditional Japanese concept that can be roughly translated as gap, space, the space between two structural parts, interval, blank, room, pause, rest, time, timing or opening.[7] Originally, this character consisted of the pictorial sign for 'moon' (月) (now the present-day 'sun' (日)) between the sign for 'gate' (門). In either way, this is a wonderful metaphorical image where in a threshold or liminal space a light is revealed or a light reveals. Komparu simply defines (*ma*) as being the science of time and space, its apposition and fusion.[8] Nitschke highlights the dual relation of (*ma*) to space and time and all experience of space is a time-structured process, and all experience of time is a space-structured process.[9] For Nitschke, (*ma*) expresses the two simultaneous components of a sense of space: the objective, given aspect and the subjective, felt aspect. (*Ma*) epitomizes the traditional Japanese artistic preoccupation with dynamic balance between object and space, action and inaction, sound and silence, movement and rest. A threshold space and a place of contradictory experiences from multiple inputs that is not static but rather moving and alive. Lorna Marshall brings this into the world of acting by explaining (*ma*) as a space that sustains a tension where some question or impulse is being asked of you: 'An absence of immediate answers which opens up the actor's and the audience's imagination.'[10]

How does entering this complex experiential in-between space or gap (*ma*) allow a lingering question to activate the imagination, thoughts and perceptions in the unfolding creative process?

(*Ma*) – Neurological Application to Creative Process

The neurological understanding of creativity (something newly perceived, imagined and lived) in the body is a complex synthesis involving both right and left hemispheres and the filtering and inhibiting processes of the corpus callosum and the selective processes of the frontal cortex. Richard Kemp explains how cognitive science demonstrates that the imagination is not a discrete or specialized function but a feature of cognition that is woven through much of our mental processes.[11] However, within this complexity the psychiatrist and doctor Iain McGilchrist argues that the process begins in the right hemisphere where embodied experience (through the senses) of the Other (that which exists outside ourselves) is made implicit and then in more complex neurological interactions is made explicit in the left hemisphere (through reductive and conceptual thinking) and taken up again by the right hemisphere in action.[12] McGilchrist expands on Walter Cannon's belief that the major qualities of the creative mind are features displayed in the right hemisphere.[13] Gallese and Lakoff elaborate: 'imagination, like perceiving and doing is embodied and that it is structured by our constant encounter and interaction with the world via our bodies and brains.'[14] The philosopher Alva Noe further explores this recurring theme and importance in the interaction, experience and contact with the external environment/world in suggesting that

> 'perceptual experience is a thoughtful activity. The thoughtfulness of perceptual experience comes out, first and foremost, in the fact that perceiving is a kind of knowledgeable or thoughtful exploration of the environment'.[15]

Zarrilli quotes Noe's belief that perception is 'something we do. … the world makes itself available to the perceiver through physical movement and interaction'.[16] As Ingold argues, 'Imagining is the activity of a being who nevertheless dwells in an actual world … situated in a time and place and therefore in a relational context.'[17]

Regardless of the complexity of the neurological creative process involving perception and imaginings, it is evident that the most important preliminary practice lies in sensorial attention to what exists apart from ourselves: that gap (*Ma*), the living encounter in an embodied and relational space. A state of the body that exists with and allows an experience of the Other.

(*Ma*) – Entering the Gap

The Theatre Training Research Program (TTRP), set up by the late Kuo Pao Kun to investigate contemporary actor training alongside four traditional Asian performing arts, invited local artists to give public lectures on creative practice.[18] Tan Swie Hian (陳瑞獻), a former small-time Singaporean boxer in Chinatown's rough Geylang district and subsequently a famous calligrapher and artist, gave a talk on his artistic process.[19] For Tan Swei Hian, creativity lay in the tension and moment between the paper and the brush, and all his preparation was to provide the greatest awareness and response to that moment. His practice was focused on that gap. He would fast and meditate for many days until it was the correct moment for the brush to play with the paper, informed by the tension of that gap between the brush and paper and the wider encounter or context of that moment. Tan Swie Hian felt in that threshold moment he was only a vehicle for the creative spirit of Kuan Yin (an ancient female Buddhist deity) to guide the brush. He would then paint, and his work would be finished in one sustained unfolding. A threshold space in the artist that was sustained though the entire preparation and creative unfolding.[20]

I became fascinated by the tension that seemed involved in that gap. How the artists find creative clarity where experiences would be presented, initially through the right hemisphere, 'in all their embodied particularity, with all their changeability and impermanence, and their interconnectedness, as part of a whole, which is forever in flux.'[21] What allows the actor to not get overwhelmed or flooded by sensorial rivers in this complex landscape or encounter and allow the light to reveal and the question to be asked of us in that moment? That this ability in Tan Swie and Slamet Rahardjo came from a specific meditative state and practice did not go unnoticed and seemed a key to foundation actor training.

(*Ma*) Mind the Gap

'Mind the gap' has become an international catch cry for transport safety; that is, the threshold between where you are and where you are going needs to be stepped over, safely negotiated and not entered. (*Ma*) is a complex, seemingly unknowing embodied place. Our dominated left-hemisphere, logo-rational culture tends to want to avoid the gap. A place that gives time and space to our somatic intelligence with its potential for 'unfurling meanings and decisions that have their origins in the deeper, darker, more visceral areas of the body and brain.'[22] Better avoid the gap or fill the gap and go to Thailand for teeth implants. Like Slamet and the tree and like Tan Swei with his paper and brush, a particular state of mindfulness seemed key to experiencing (*ma*). However, this involves expanding the concept, definition and experience of *mind*, removing mind from the skull. The Chinese word for mind is xin (心) and actually means heart-mind. In Chinese tradition, the heart is considered the most vital organ due to its importance to any action.

In Tai'ji, xin is the awareness of something (an experience from the Other) not yet expressed; when it resonates and is expressed, it is called yi (thought/perception/imaginings). You must have xin before you can have yi. Xin is the source of yi. They merge to become xin yi (心意) (intention leading to action), but xin is the master of yi.[23] Not every external input will create a resonance, an experience. Professor Gu Yian explains this process as 'the echo in the empty valley' (Kōng (空) Gǔ (谷) Huí (回) Shēng (聲)).[24] The xin will capture the echo or those vibrations that do resonate; all others will pass into silence. However, that capture must come from a particular aware and calm state within the body.[25] Professor Gu Yian explains this meditative process and these practices as first finding kai xin (开心, or open heart/mind to the environment) then grounding it downwards fang xin (放心, or deepen heart/mind focused)[26] to create the calm heart an xin (安心, or open, deepened, focused heart/mind but rested and calm). In this meditative state, an xin, *mind* has become an action; it is a state of the body to mind, to take care of, to experience and become aware of time and space and thus enter (*ma*). Thus *in that gap*, one captures the resonance of many inputs and is not flooded by the numerous complex rivers of a multi-sensorial landscape or encounter.

(*Ma*) – *Gōng Fēng Shuǐ* and Foundation Training[27]

The overlapping somatic practices of *gōng fēng shuǐ*, developed from Tai'ji and its qigong principles, train the state of an xin and provide the experiential space (*ma*). This awareness and connectivity of the body and space holds deep knowledge that I believe should be present in any foundation training.[28]

Gōng (工) is the connection and tension of energy between heaven and earth.[29] The human body is the conduit of this energy and sits between two simultaneous energies. These pass through the body, creating an ongoing game with gravity: the upward and outward *yáng* (陽) energy (playing upwards and outwards against gravity) and inward and downward *yīn* (陰) energy (playing downwards and inwards with gravity). Thus, up is down (when you go up, you feel the resistance of going down) and down is up (when you go down, you feel the resistance of going up). In the same way, out is in and in is out. So every movement and moment (including breathing and especially the hands and feet) has an associated attention to an unfolding tension, a conversation of two energies that releases the energy channels in the body and the 12 cavities where energy gets blocked.[30] This liminal, meditative practice creates a rhythm that is referred to as 'the rise and fall.'[31] In every movement, there is during or at the rise a slowing down of energy before the fall, and at the completion of the fall, a slowing down before the rise.[32] The practice opens the energy pathways, plays with the expansion and contraction of time and space, increases the awareness of the five openings (eyes, ears, nose, mouth and skin – and in Indonesia, the addition of the fontanel and anus), and generates a greater experience of the Other (see *fēng* in two paragraphs below for further explanation).

To retain the interconnectivity and intraconnectivity of the whole body, you must connect to and retain energy in the hands and feet.[33] These connections move through the centre of body to what the Chinese call the *dan tian* (丹田, or the energy centre). The most effective way to connect to this is not to focus on it but to become aware of the extremities: the hands and feet.[34] By focusing on the energy in and between the extremities, the hands and feet, and the dual game with gravity, the actor will become naturally poised in movements.[35] I never use the terms grounded or centred to describe this practice. 'Grounded' implies only a downward static energy, but *gōng* is about movement within two energies. 'Centred' implies an inward attention when actors must instead be poised and attending to what exists outside themselves, and the body's somatic energy that is shifted from that focus.

In practices that involve *gōng*, one recognizes the complexity within a widening horizon of attention. This is to encounter *fēng* (風, or wind – moving air that is continually in flux). If you have *gōng*, you will have *fēng*. Through your heightened senses, you experience the shifting energy in the spaces and the moving air between you and other bodies and hard surfaces that exist in your immediate environment. As my Balinese teacher Ida Bagus Sutarja said to me, 'you are the centre of the universe, but so am I. We are all individual wonderful mountains but connected in one large mountain range.' You become more than just aware of a wider horizon of sensorial elements; you become aware of the energy shifts in the air (wind) between those elements. Some tai'ji practitioners say you are the horizon allowing a greater awareness of the experiences of a moment.[36]

Chinese tradition has it that through the kinaesthetic, spatial, corporeal and rhythmical awareness through *gōng fēng* practices, there is a duplication of ren (人),[37] a duplication of the input of human experience to form wu (巫).[38] These practices create the potential for a powerful transformational energy in the actor and on the viewer of that action. In Bali this is called Taksu[39] – a vital energy/spirit energy that changes and transforms you and those around you.[40] The Balinese say, 'Dancers with Taksu capture the eyes of the audience.'[41]

Gōng fēng practices create (*ma*), the threshold space of increased awareness for potential change, but adding practices in *shuǐ* will allow the energy shifts to move from a potentially formless state to a visible, condensed and focused embodiment – a clear focused light revealed. This is expressed in a traditional Chinese saying: 'Vital energy rides the wind and scatters, but is retained when encountering water'.[42] That is, practices in *shuǐ* will give shape to the experiences created by practices in *gōng fēng*.

To Professor Gu Yain, *shuǐ* (water) is a metaphor for the practices that recognize energy or vibration change, as water can take many forms – solid, liquid or gas – and can be soft or hard. In every spatial and relational moment that the energy experience in the body changes, so too does the nature or quality of the water in the body, or what is potentially recognized.[43] This 'recognition' reminds me of Lindy Davies's impulse training mantra: 'allow yourself to be affected by the stillness and the movement, the light and the shade, and the sounds and the silences.'[44] It is a wonderful threshold exercise that only asks the actor to be affected and does not ask for them to necessarily do anything, not to even know cognitively but to recognize something has shifted. I have lately begun using the word 'infect' and not 'affect'. It implies a slow recognition (allowing expanded time and space) of the dis-ease (in-tension) within experience that ultimately shifts energy, resonates and engages one's perception and imaginings. It means not to react or immediately perform but to allow time for multiple voices to be absorbed and contained and to recognize change within from what is outside oneself. It means to encourage student actors in practices that experience everything around them as an external performance given to them and through *gōng fēng shuǐ* to begin as Noe says 'deploy the skills to bring the *world* into focus'.[45]

(Ma) – *Gōng Fēng Shuǐ* Foundation Exercises

In *Gōng fēng shuǐ* exercises, it is fine to focus on one instruction or one exercise and shift between them all, because they will ultimately converge. The most important focus is not just the movements but the energy pathways and their subtle shifts and ultimately their transformative impact on your body and imagination. Breath should not become a prime focus, but every now and then, it is observed as a physical action that also shifts your energy. You repeat exercises many times for many hours until all elements converge, and in any movement gesture, you will, like *the actor and the tree*, become connected to the many external inputs and experience thoughts, perceptions and imaginings.

Working the Extremities – Hands and Feet

(1a) Standing with one foot slightly in front of the other,[46] touch the middle line of your skull and distinguish the most sensitive area: the fontanel. It will feel the softest and sweetest. It is quite central on the upper skull. Create the image and adjust your body so that a drop of water falls on that spot and then falls through your body and out of your anus. Now, using your thumb, press strongly on the two hand points (勞宮, or láogōng – the palace of energy) and on the two feet points (涌泉, or yǒngquán – the bubbling well).[47] You will feel like the palms of your hands are holding energy and the front pads of your feet are bubbling energy. Now keeping the sensation alive; keep the images of the dropping water and energy in the palm of the hands and the bubbling well in the footpads of the feet.

(1b) Then while just shifting your weight from foot to foot, keep all those points and images alive and breathe freely. Allow your eyes to lead the head, and take in the horizon with your eyes and ears and skin. 'Listen with your eyes and hear with your eyes.'[48] Do not focus too long on the breath, but breathe freely (never deliberately hold your breath).

(1c) Stand with your feet farther apart, one foot slightly forward, and raise your hands over your head so that they are above your corresponding foot. Feel the energy entering your hand points and going through your body and out the opposite foot point. Now feel the energy coming through the foot point and out the opposite hands. Feel the same pathways when you shift your weight between your feet.

The Rise and the Fall – up is down, down is up, in is out, out is in

(2a) Take the same position as (1a), but feel as if a drop of water is falling onto your fontanel through your body and out your anus. It bounces off the ground, enters your anus and moves up though your body and out the fontanel to the heavens. Now allow these movements to happen at the same time – a drop falling and a drop rising at the same time. Breathe freely. Do not concentrate too long on your breath but on the energy shifts. Take in the horizon with your eyes, ears and skin. Do not lose connection to your hands and feet.

(2b) Stand as in (1b), bringing your hands upward to be in line with your belly button (elbows falling – do not engage your shoulders). As you do this, feel like the hands' energy is descending into your feet and the feet energy is ascending into your hands. Raise your hands to shoulder level, with your elbows falling into your knees and your knees ascending to your elbows. Raise your hands above your head to their corresponding feet while feeling the shoulder falling into your hips and your hip ascending into your shoulders, all the while keeping the energy in your hands and feet. Now reverse the movement downwards: shoulders falling into the ascending hips, elbows falling into ascending knees and hands falling into ascending feet. Now with the correct order of feet/hands, elbows/hip and shoulder/hip movements, repeat the upward movement (the rise – the out) and downward movement (the fall – the in). As you rise, feel the fall, and as you fall, feel the rise. Do not let the energy leak from your hands or feet (you will know as soon as you disconnect with one or both hands).

(2c) In free-form movement, start with (2b) and slowly allow yourself to move spatially. With your own movements, keep the connection between your shoulders to hips, elbows and knees, and feet and hands. Each movement becomes a living gesture of outward giving and inward receiving energy. Work with the contradictory energies. Experiencing the rise (upward and outward energy) and the fall (downward and inward energy) in all movements. Take in the horizon and allow your ears, eyes and skin to lead with curiosity and awareness, not reaction. When you lose the connection of the energy in your hand points and feet points, repeat (1b) and (2b). When reconnected, proceed with free form as a 45-minute meditation on all of the above and allow all of the above to merge. Allow your eyes, ears, mouth and skin to be alive.

The Wind between Object, Body and Hard Surfaces[49]

(3) In this spinning exercise, use the following repeatable movement progression make sure you can employ *gōng* in all moments: '*No gōng no fēng shuǐ.*' Standing with one foot slightly in front, do a 180-degree turn/spin led by your hands (make sure that your shoulders, hips and knees

are involved), and your eyes, ears and skin follow. Then do the (2b) progression with equal weight on both feet, and jump in the air (make sure that your hands are engaged). Every movement must have its own rhythm; it cannot become a patterned routine. When this movement progression can be executed, work in a fixed space with other actors and a witness (someone watching). You are now becoming aware and playing with four spatial energies. *I* is your own *gōng*; *we is* the space energies between you and one other (another person, object or hard surface that is more in eye or ear focus – this will change); *us* is your becoming part of everything in the space, the horizon; and *them* is the witness/audience. At any point, the outside witness can clap. At that point, the whole room must converge all movements and contract into exact unison. This will then naturally dissipate into discord. The witness also impacts the exercise with the following mantra: allow yourself to be infected by the stillness and the movement, the sounds and silences, the light and the shade; become infected by the similarities and the differences. When one can begin to become more aware of the energy shifts and retain *gōng*, the exercise can become more complicated by adding movements (walking, running, falling, etc.), objects (props) and text.

You Are the Horizon – Experiencing Spatial, Textual and Temporal Energies

For public mediation, choose a busy public space and conduct a standing meditation based on *gōng fēng shuǐ*.[50] Remember the aforementioned mantra: Allow yourself to be infected by the stillness and the movement, the sounds and silences, the light and the shade; become infected by the similarities and the differences. Because it is a public space and not a performance, your movements must be limited (it is not a happening or a flash mob). You can move and turn, but only slightly. Do nothing to draw attention to yourself; the objective is for you to be attentive to everything happening around you. Everything around you is a visual, spatial, rhythmic and sonic performance for you to experience. You will have many sensations, thoughts and imaginings: allow them to be constantly changing, yet retain a still, calm space in the complexity.

(*Ma*) – Mind the Gap

A colleague at the VCA-MCM once asked me why young acting students seem to lack the ability to engage with their imaginations. Is it a generational, societal or cultural problem? I believed a better question was to ask, what foundation training practices could help train perception and the imagination?

I do understand the importance of actor training that involves spontaneous play, clowning, games, improvisation, etc. However, these experiences *often ride the wind and scatter energy* before foundation practices have been imprinted that generate richer imaginings and perceptions. As actor training institutions move into a university model and away from a conservatoire culture and as class time decreases with increased class sizes, specific foundational training becomes even more critical. It embeds a practice and inquiry that can be applied within any acting method and builds a practice that lives autonomously after the student has departed from their teachers and institutions. Important training practices that the former dean of drama at the VCA Lindy Davies said, 'allow the actor to carve themselves indelibly in the space.'[51]

Simple and detailed foundational training exercises based on the principles of *gōng fēng shuǐ* can deepen and sustain this creative process. Traditional Chinese concepts and somatic practices are aligning with neurological evidence in showing what is necessary in the creative process. The ability to enter a space (*Ma*), encounter external input and capture resonances and experiences more deeply and clearly lays a foundation to build on with later practices involving text speech, language, character, scene and rehearsal processes; to embrace experience; and regardless of the teeth that go missing, to become mindful of and comfortable within the gap.

Notes

1 Somatic practices have been explored by Grotowski, Michael Chekov, Copeau, Suzuki, Marshall Kemp, Zarrilli and Claxton. My interpretation of somatic is where the mind is not separate from body but rather the mind is the body.

2 The Drama School, the once-autonomous institution the Victorian College of Arts (VCA) after the 2010 merger with University of Melbourne, was subsequently called the Theatre School University of Melbourne Faculty of Victorian College of the Arts and Melbourne Conservatorium of Music (VCA-MCM). A more recent change has been to FOFAAM: Faculty of Fine Arts and Music.
3 I would not give the theoretical concepts I explain in this chapter to students until the students had mastered some of the practical exercises introduced in the foundation training. The initial aim is embodied experience.
4 Professor Gu Yian and I undertook research interfacing contemporary acting practices with traditional Chinese martial arts and philosophy at Shanghai Theatre Academy. Gu Yian established the Shanghai International Performing Arts Research Centre (SIPARC). The Chinese references are drawn from a series of interviews and workshops conducted between 2006 and 2014.
5 Slamet Rahardjo Djarot is an Indonesian actor, director and screenwriter.
6 Asian theatre practitioners who follow more traditional philosophies have a different concept of mind than do most Westerners. This concept goes beyond pure mental thought and represents a particular state of the mind/body: an experiential state. It is best described by the Chinese concept of xin yi (heart-mind/heart-spirit) that is discussed elsewhere in this chapter.
7 I have inserted *Ma* within brackets because it is visually close to its Chinese calligraphy of a light in a gateway and because it creates a visual representation of the liminal threshold nature of *Ma*.
8 Komparu (1983), p. 72.
9 Nitschke, C. (1988), p. 3.
10 This comes from a recorded interview conducted with Lorna Marshall in June 2016. I worked with Marshall during 1996 and 1997 at the Victorian College of Art. Marshall is the author of *The Body Speaks* (2001, 2008) and co-author with Yoshi Oida of *The Invisible Actor* (2007). Marshall has taught physical acting to performers in almost every area, from ballet dancers to classical actors and opera singers, and from performance artists to circus acts. She has worked with The Royal Shakespeare Company, Shared Experience and The Royal National Theatre. She runs international workshops and is currently honorary research fellow at The Royal Academy of Dramatic Art, and adviser on actor training at the New National Theatre, Tokyo.
11 Kemp, R. (2012), p. 109.
12 McGilchrist, I. (2009), p. 93. McGilchrist suggests that it is the faculty of the imagination that enables information to be taken back from the left hemisphere to the right hemisphere to make them live as action in the embodied world.
13 Ibid., pp. 85, 468.
14 Gallese, V & Lakoff, G. (2005), p. 455 and cited by Kemp (2010), p. 110.
15 Noe, A. (2008), p. 664.
16 Zarrilli (2015), p. 81.
17 Ingold (2000), p. 418.

18 Kuo Pao Kun was a playwright, theatre director and arts activist in Singapore who wrote and directed both Mandarin and English plays. He formed Theatre Practice with Goh Lay Kuan and has mentored many Singaporean and foreign directors and artists. I was employed as a foundation teacher of TTRP (2001–2003) and was exposed through master teachers from Japan, China, India and Indonesia to the traditional practices of NOH Theatre, Beijing Opera, Bharatanatyam and Wayang Wong. This story about Tan Swie comes from a public talk I witnessed at TTRP in January 2001.
19 Tan Swie Hian is a cultural icon in Singapore. He was conferred *Chavalier de l'Ordre des Arts et des Lettres* and in 1998 was awarded the Marin Sorescu International Poetry Prize from Romania.
20 Tan Swie Hian's drawing *Speed of Light* was painted in 60 seconds, and it sold in Beijing for $4.4 million.
21 McGilchrist, I. (2009), p. 93.
22 Claxton (2015), p. 7. Claxton cites experiments that show our conscious how intellect is often a rather pale reflection or even a crude caricature of the sophisticated operations going on behind the scenes.
23 Dr Yang Jwing Ming (1996), p. 23. This aligns with the underlying thesis in McGilchrist (2009), where the right hemisphere (experience) is the master of the left-hemisphere emissary (cognitive).
24 Professor Gu Yian at Shanghai Theatre Academy set up the SIPARC (Shanghai International Performing Arts Research Centre) to research the integration of traditional Chinese Philosophy and training with contemporary practices. I have been part of this programme since 2006.
25 As in the Indonesian Sabar, this is not a relaxed state but an open, focused and non-reactive state. Even powerful impulses and actions reside in this calm place.
26 Fang xin (放心) also means 'do not worry', which Professor Gu Yian believes is the major block of an actor. That is, the worry and concern generated by the pressure and judgement of outside eyes, personal expectations or any of those projected judgement and thoughts which are actually removed from what is happening at that moment inside and outside oneself.
27 These overlapping principles came from practical and theoretical exploration alongside Professor Gu Yian at SIPARC (2006–2012). They overlap but are dealt with here separately.
28 Tai'ji is a martial art with very specific movements of attack and defence. The bridge to actor training is to use its movement principles and qigong concepts in specific simple movement meditative exercises and to not get caught up in the martial aspect of the forms.
29 It seems similar to the Japanese concept in NOH of *shin-soe-tai* also *ten chi jin*. See Kunio Komparu, p. 23. Gōng also means work energy.
30 A list of the 12 cavities can be found in Olson Stuart Alve (2002, p. 152). Gu Yian believes that blockages are not emotional or postural but rather involve moving energy. By allowing energy to travel through the blocked area, the posture will find its place naturally.

31 Huang Al Chung-Liang (1973), p. 66. This rhythm aligns with the rhythm of breathing, where there is a gap/space, an expansion of time and rhythm between inhalation and exhalation.
32 Huang Al Chung-Liang (1973).
33 Two extremely important Tai'ji and acupuncture points are in the hand (勞宮, or láo gōng – *palace of labour*) and the feet (涌泉, or yǒng quán – *the bubbling well*).
34 There are important connections between hands, feet, speech and gesture. In the Chinese tradition, there is a connection through the energy channel Jīng Luò (经络) of the hands to the heart (xin), and this is connected to gesture. The Chinese word for foot, 足, has two symbols: a foot as a platform, which is connected to an open mouth. The energy of vocal sound is connected to the feet. McGilchrist (2009, p. 111) suggests that there is evidence that referential language may have evolved not from sounds but initially from hand movements.
35 Practices in gōng will naturally shift weight slightly more onto the front pads of the feet and into the hands, creating a state of poised readiness (not static), of balance and of connecting movement to gesture and xin.
36 This is in line with the current discoveries in neuroscience to do with identity, self and the lack of differentiation of inner and outer realities as discussed by Kemp, p. 11, and McGilchrist, p. 87.
37 Ren (人) is the symbol for human.
38 Wu (巫) is the symbol for the shaman or witch – a worker of magic – one who has transformed and who transforms others. Note Ren (人) has doubled.
39 Taksu wields great importance in Balinese culture and is present in performances, healing ceremonies and inspirational speakers. It is sometimes referred to as the Lord of Inspiration (Hobart, p. 93).
40 In China, vital energy (康健) jiàn (downward energy) kāng (upward energy) is associated with or created by a very strong action that has originated from the Dan Tian, like stamping the feet or hitting something. The collision puts transformative energy back into the body. My Balinese teacher made me do a stomping exercise in the pathways in a rice paddy. One is reminded here also of Tashida Suzuki's stomping.
41 Swanson, L. (2011).
42 The *Zangshu*, or *Book of Burial*, by Guo Pu (276–324), Chapter 2, 'Flow of Qi', translated by Stephen L. Field, 9 May 2003.
43 Rick Kemp (2012, p. 17) alerts us to the importance of proprioception, a deeper form of awareness where the nerve endings in our muscles, fascia, tendons, ligaments, joints and skin send signals to the brain about the deformation of tissue. This process is involved in gesture, posture, speech, emotion and sense of self.
44 Lindy Davies is an Australian acting teacher, international acting coach, director and former associate professor and head of the VCA's School of Drama.
45 Noe, A. (2012) *Varieties of Presence*, p. 2.
46 Immediately, I avoid having the actor stand with their feet together but instead have them take a dynamic position. Also, I have observed that we rarely stand with two feet together. We are always shifting weight.

47 The diagram was sourced from AlquimiaInterna V15, October 2013: http://www.alquimiainterna.com/besar-la-tierra-al-caminar-con-yong-quan/.
48 This is an instruction of Slamet Rahardjo, which is very effective in heightening the senses.
49 Tan Swie Hian is a cultural icon in Singapore. He was conferred *Chavalier de l'Ordre des Arts et des Lettres* and in 1998 was awarded the Marin Sorescu International Poetry Prize from Romania.
50 I have been using a busy railway station at peak hour. However, with current security fears, I inform students not to bring bags and to wear public clothing rather than rehearsal clothes.
51 Lindy Davies describes the importance of attaining individual virtuosity in actor training; for Davies, actors should not be bound by the ideological attachment to one method, but should be amplified and alive through a living practice.

Part II

Training and Production

7

The British Tradition in Acting Shakespeare: Challenges to Teaching the Acting of Shakespeare in a UK Conservatoire in the Twenty-First Century

Stephen Simms

The acting department of the Royal Birmingham Conservatoire in the UK came into being in 1936, where much of the curriculum was given over to voice production, public speaking, speech training, verse speaking, choral speaking, singing and even microphone technique. There were also classes offered on period movement and historical deportment and the history of costume, as well as acting technique, dramatic rehearsal and the theory and practice of play production. The strong focus on voice in the school's early curriculum reflects the wider tradition in British acting, especially the acting of Shakespeare, which perseveres until present day. The importance of voice teachers in the establishment of British acting schools, such as Elsie Fogerty, who founded The Central School of Speech and Drama, or Rose Bruford, whose college still bears her name, shows how core voice was in the education of the British actor. The drama schools established in the earlier parts of the twentieth century reflected the British acting they trained their students in and the acceptance of the kind of voice that accompanied it.

Placement of the voice and shape of the vowel has a very English subtext, one not just of class but of intelligence. A geographical triangle of economic wealth between Oxford, Cambridge and London established an accent of privilege, which became embedded in the English public schools and was known as standard English or received pronunciation (RP). Lyn Darnley's thesis, *A History of Voice Teaching in Britain*, traces the work of the earliest professional elocution teachers through to contemporary voice specialists.[1]

As well as promoting RP, the earliest voice teachers used techniques forged by singing teachers; thus the voice was seen as a musical instrument, using vibrato and sustained tone and exploiting all available physical resonators. Early recordings of John Gielgud demonstrate this vibrato and use of chest resonance. His style of speaking dominated Shakespearean acting for a large part of the twentieth century, especially as radio became popular. The BBC advisory committee on spoken English endorsed 'the current usage of educated speakers',[2] by which it meant those with the Oxbridge accent, clearly equating intelligence with RP. In the growth of radio broadcasting, we see the creation and development of a new paradigm of accepted Shakespearean performance, which will influence stage acting as well as the establishment and promotion of the acting tradition. This paradigm focuses on the vocal quality of the actor as the primary indicator of true Shakespearean authority and RP as the signifier of intellectual and cultural esteem.

While the Royal Birmingham Conservatoire continues a tradition of teaching the craft of the voice, contemporary actor training has to deal with a range of uncertainties about what constitutes good acting and good voice work. Actor training for the performance of Shakespeare treads a tightrope in a postmodern, postfeminist, postcolonial and post-dramatic world where previous cultural certainties can no longer be taken for granted. Feeding a mass industry within which anti-establishment waves are tolerated in a wider sea of the conservative mainstream, drama schools are not the natural home of avant-garde challenges. The suspicion that actor training is not far removed from the selling of snake-oil magic remedies further fuels these insecurities.

'Forget RSC Veterans – the best Hamlet I ever saw was a gangling 16-year-old boy in a school play.'[3] Writing in the *Guardian*, Germaine Greer berated the state of acting at the Royal Shakespeare Company (RSC). She contrasts what she sees as the 'highly self-conscious, mannered, even narcissistic performances of today's leading actors' to one seen when she was 16, where a schoolboy Hamlet of the same age illuminated the text with clarity and delight. Greer's complaints are part of an ongoing criticism of the 'current' state of British acting, whenever that 'current' may be. In 2013, RADA graduate Imogen Stubbs complained in the *Guardian* of the quality of the 'current' acting approach: 'Imogen Stubbs hits out at mumbling actors'.[4] The RSC actor was joined by Edward Kemp, Principal at RADA, in her condemnation of the current state of classical acting, Kemp saying in the same article that 'Older actors draw on the subtleties of pitch, timbre and tempo – crucial for big spaces, yet they have gone out of the culture ... with today's actors relying on volume.'

An increasing movement towards naturalism was the reason for Bertram Joseph's belief that 'by the end of the nineteenth century, tragic acting had moved in its techniques and in its fundamental attitudes a long way from the tradition which had existed in Shakespeare's day and for two centuries after.'[5] This meant that 'the majority of actors were no longer able to act these plays satisfactorily.'[6] Joseph spent much time in trying to remedy the failings he saw around him, and he details his theories in his seminal works *Acting Shakespeare* and *Elizabethan Acting*. In Brian Willis's thesis *Text, Subtext, and Vocal Resonance: Speaking Shakespeare on the 20th Century English Stage*, he cites many of the attacks on British Shakespearean acting found in the press, with the bulk of this criticism focusing on actors' use of Shakespeare's written text. Willis's thesis methodically dissects recordings of Shakespearean performance for the stage from the first recording of Shakespeare by Edwin Booth in 1890 through to Simon Russell Beale. Accepting that much of the criticism of contemporary acting is set against a 'past' where it was just done better, Willis's thesis attempts a 'scientific' approach to ascertain the basis of this criticism. Willis attempts to locate the resonators used by various actors and the vocal placements leading to differences of voice quality. He counts the words per minute at which the actors speak and annotates the scripts of performances to illustrate audible breaths, duration of pauses, special emphasis and relative changes in pitch and tempo, among a range of other incidentals or effects.[7]

What we can readily draw from Willis's research is that the use of the voice has clearly been changing over the last century. This is primarily seen in the changes in vowel use and bodily resonators and in an increased use of pause, along with a decrease in vibrato. In the earliest recordings, it is the vibrato which strikes the modern ear first as 'unnatural' or 'performed'.[8] As with singers, it is used to convey and represent emotion with the breakdown of a steady tone into the 'uncontrolled' fluctuations of pitch which signify high emotion in everyday life. In the earlier recordings of actors, we find limited use of the pause, as well as the creation of a sustained tone using elongated vowels, which gives a sense of forward progression, with the long vowels allowing for a transmission of emotional qualities. Generally, in the recordings that Willis reviews, there is a greater use of range or pitch than is found in everyday speech. The introduction by modern actors of pauses in speaking verse, used to signify spontaneity and a subtext behind the verse, from which the actor is seemingly drawing their thoughts, is an approach influenced by Stanislavski.

Much of the blame for the perceived decline in the quality of Shakespearean acting is placed at the door of Stanislavski and interpretations of his method popularized by movie acting. As Stanislavski is at the core of much actor training, this accusation is worrying when it comes to teaching actors to perform Shakespeare. In the conservatoire, our students not only debate and discuss but have to make a choice and stand before an audience to be judged on that choice. As educators, we have to back the horse we are putting into the race: in one form or another, Stanislavski remains at the root of all our actor training. We are therefore constantly balancing modern acting methods, various theories of performance and a slippery British tradition which is frequently under attack.

The approaches used by the RSC have greatly influenced the work that we do at the conservatoire. Lyn Darnley, who became head of voice and artist development at the RSC in 2003, charts the development of training within the RSC in her thesis *Artist Development and Training in the Royal Shakespeare Company*, stating her belief that there are specific skills to improve Shakespearean acting:[9]

> On the most basic level they are rhetoric, verbal expressivity, rhythm, an enjoyment of the textual 'soundscape', clarity and sight reading, all of which can be worked on through exposure to lyrical, narrative and dramatic prose and verse, both classical and contemporary. Without these skills actors wanting to work in classical theatre are disadvantaged. Understanding rhythms and language structure help actors engage the language and use it as an integral part of character. Once they can see how form and content work together classical text ceases to be intimidating.[10]

In her PhD thesis, Darnley discusses the ongoing debates around the quality of Shakespeare and verse speaking, and the training of actors to do this, pointing out that 'Disagreement among professionals is rife. Actors have strong opinions on verse speaking and the degree of attention that should be paid to the form and rhythm';[11] Darnley quotes Alistair Macauley, writing in the *Financial Times*: 'few people claim we live in a golden age of verse speaking now; many people reckon that there was a golden age, two or more decades ago.'[12]

In order to future-proof our actors against ongoing changing tastes and the perpetually shifting 'golden age' of Shakespearean acting, I believe that the best way to approach training is to create transformative actors, who are able to respond to changing requirements and are not tied in time or ideology to any particular method or approach. There is an industry aesthetic which at any given point in time students must be able to meet if they wish to work. However, the Royal Birmingham Conservatoire acknowledges that this is a changing aesthetic and that within the industry, even from one audition to the next, actors can be required to meet a range of cultural expectations. There is no single industry for which students are being trained.

This is something that has to be taught to students, and it does not come easily. Students often want certainty. They want to know what works best and how to do it. Groomed by an educational system to be shown how to pass the test, how to get an A+, they believe that anything other than this is a sign of weak teaching. This is compounded by the current league-table culture in English education and the importance given to the National Student Satisfaction Survey, which takes place each year in the United Kingdom. Under UK law, the student is a customer and needs to feel satisfied in the product they are buying. The best certainty we can offer students is the certainty of change.

At Birmingham we acknowledge the particular challenge that Shakespeare holds for the actor: an extreme of non-naturalistic poetic expression through verse, seemingly true-to-life characters reacting to a range of given circumstances, often based in historical fact, with apparently natural behaviour. These characters exhibit a range of emotion, often at a heightened level and evoke empathy in the audience. They also break out from the imagined situations they are in to directly address the audience, seemingly destroying any suspension of disbelief the audience may hold. Characters reflect upon the situations they find themselves in, explore options for further action with the audience or even divulge secrets to and thus confide in the audience, who become privy to information unknown to other characters. A character might even apologize for the quality of the acting or the poverty of the theatrical experience when compared to the real-life events represented. Academic analysis of these changing theatrical modes can greatly problematize this activity for the actor, whereas in the reality of performance, it is often straightforward to accomplish, effected by a simple turn of the head and instantly accepted by the audience.

However, this approach is rooted in a Stanislavskian interpretation of 'character' and a generally naturalistic performance aesthetic, which has been absorbed into the British tradition. A more postmodern theatre can challenge actors and audiences further, and final-year productions at Birmingham allow students to experience this challenge to their skill-based training. While voice features heavily as part of the training, it is weighted equally with singing and physical skills. These skills are integrated through the training, and the movement of the course trajectory is towards learning through performance. This takes place in studio projects in the first year, seen only by faculty staff; workshops in the second year are seen by an invited audience; and full-scale productions in the third year are seen by a paying public. The journey for the actor is from a space in which it is safe to fail to being unobserved and finally to a public forum where the audience can make judgements as they see fit. All the performance opportunities are tailored to the needs of individuals, and a great deal of time is spent finding the right material as a vehicle for learning. The choosing of material and casting of this aspect of the training cannot be underestimated, and it takes up a great deal of time for the course director and requires a huge resource of artistic creativity and planning ability.

The use of Shakespearean text as a means to create character and emotion is explored in voice and acting classes. This positions the text as primary in the creative process, leading to the creation of character and emotion, rather than character and emotion being formed first. I argue that this is the distinguishing feature of the British tradition in approaching Shakespearean acting. By the end of the students' training, they are required to engage creatively with the performance possibilities of a text or other material used as a source for a production and integrate the skills of acting, voice, movement and singing (where appropriate) to create and communicate a theatrically believable performance with character and emotion appropriate to the demands of a public performance.

The initial focus on RP as an accent reflects the current status quo in British acting: all students are expected to be able to use the RP accent fluently if they had studied acting at a British acting conservatoire. This is a change from previous years, where students might have been expected to completely lose their native accent in favour of RP. RP is now only seen and taught as an accent within the drama school, of equal weight and standing as any other accent. However, it still remains an accent with a definite cultural weight in the United Kingdom, and it continues to contain within it certain class and educational resonances.

All the various artistic directors of the RSC have had an influence on the performance style of the RSC, but the main plumb line from which the company has varied little over the last 50 years was established in the early days of the RSC Studio, an in-house training school organized by Michel St Denis. Colin Chambers gives a detailed sketch of this in his book *Inside the Royal Shakespeare Company*.[13] St Denis believed on the one hand that actors were too heavily influenced by Lee Strasberg's interpretation of Stanislavski, focusing on inner emotion and subtext, and on the other that actors separated movement from speech and acted from the neck upwards. Thus they initiated a programme combining voice and movement and other acting skills, with the aim for an actor to be

> like a glove, open and flexible, but flat. By degrees the text penetrates the actor and brings the actor to life – the text, in other words, animates the glove, which is the actor's blood, nerves, breathing system and voice.[14]

This is as good a description as any of the British approach in the foregrounding of text as the main means to creating character and achieving emotional expression.

However, what constitutes 'text', even Shakespeare's 'text', can be challenged by modern approaches. W. B. Worthen describes a fascinating contemporary production of *Hamlet* by the avant-garde theatre company, The Wooster Group, using as its 'text' a recording of Richard Burton's 1964 *Hamlet*, directed by Gielgud.[15] The performance that Worthen discusses took place in 2007, but it is still at the time of writing part of the group's repertoire.[16] A live performance of *Hamlet* takes place in front of a screening of the Burton *Hamlet*. The live version interacts with the recorded version, re-enacting moments, copying inflections and gestures and sometimes editing the recording at the command of the actors. At times the recording fades out or stops. Elsewhere, other recordings, such as Kenneth Branagh's movie *Hamlet*, replace the Burton recording. The live voices are amplified and electronically manipulated, and sometimes the live is videoed and screened, using freeze-frame and other techniques. Worthen chooses this production to illustrate some of the themes in his 1997 book *Shakespeare and the Authority of Performance*. For Worthen, the Wooster Group *Hamlet* stages the ingoing *subversion of the archive by the repertoire*, suggesting that a dichotomy between writing and performing, the recorded and the live, are inadequate to the critical assessment of performance today, if they ever were really adequate at all.[17]

Worthen argues that in craving authority from Shakespeare to legitimize performance, seeing his work as sacred text, as silent hieroglyphics, we can only scan, interpret, struggle to decode', and 'we impoverish … the work of our own performances, and the work of the plays in our making of the world'.[18] This suggests that for actor training to develop, the implicit ideology of training needs to be made explicit and therefore open to examination. This is a bigger challenge for actor training: Shakespeare has such cultural authority that empowering the actor to be at least an equal partner in the performance of his scripts can meet great opposition.

At Birmingham we offer opportunities to challenge the ideology of the classroom training through the nature of some of the productions our students perform. One such example is my own production of the 1603 quarto version of *Hamlet*, which was the subject of a conference paper I gave at the 7th Annual International Conference on Visual and Performing Arts in Athens in 2016, and from which much of the following description is drawn.[19]

To herald the UK celebrations of the 400th anniversary of Shakespeare's death, I decided to create a production of the 1603 quarto text of Shakespeare's *Hamlet* as a vehicle through which to explore the aesthetic of performing Shakespeare in a postmodern/post-dramatic world. The production would be performed by students studying the master of fine arts (MFA) acting (the British tradition) course, as one of their final productions. Central to the production was whether actors trained in the British tradition could embrace a postmodern approach to production and create a theatrical whole. The challenge of the production was therefore one which tested the flexibility of their training.

The unfamiliarity of the 1603 quarto of *Hamlet* acts almost like a postmodern reflection upon the far better known folio version. In using the 1603 quarto, one gathers a sense of something that we know being subverted; we believe we know what to expect but are suddenly presented with a similar alternative. The text of some of the most famous passages is entirely different. For example, the opening lines of 'to be or not to be' in the 1603 quarto are startlingly unexpected when one is accustomed to the folio:

> To be, or not to be – ay there's the point.
>
> To die, to sleep – is that all? Aye all.[20]

This shocks the audience into an almost Brechtian displacement, out of the world of the play and into a more critical mode of thinking; making us question what we value and the aesthetics of those values. The questioning of these aesthetics was central to the concept of this production. Generally referenced as the 'bad quarto' by academics, the 1603 play-text gives licence to the audience to reject what they see as 'inferior'. However, in directing the play, I believed that this could also be exploited as the fool's licence to question authority figures – in this case, the textural authority in performance of the folio.

The actors in the company were in their second year of ongoing voice training based primarily on the work of Kristin Linklater, alongside a wider understanding of a range of voice and text approaches. As part of the rehearsal process, the cast also had intensive workshops personally delivered by Cicely Berry, Barbara Houseman and Alison Bomber. The MFA group I worked with were all American actors in training who used their own accent in the production.[21] The American voice immediately called into question the hegemony of British RP, which even in the United States still has huge social and cultural cachet. The accents varied depending on where in the United States the actor originated from but had a uniformity of being 'American', and consequently, these accents were clearly removed from any class judgements which might be held in relation to accents in the United Kingdom.

The most extreme deviance from an expected delivery of text within our production was employed by the players in the play within a play (*The Mousetrap*) spoken to a strict metronomic beat composed by James Christopher Oldham, set against a score written for violin and viola. The unflinching delivery and the musical underscoring that combined with physical gestures and movements derived from symbolism used in Chinese opera (choreographed by Andy Yau) created a non-naturalistic approach devoid of any Stanislavski influences. This delivery was echoed in the scenes where Ofelia sings and reveals her unbalanced state of mind. Ofelia in her madness entered as if she were a torch song singer, lit using a follow spot, employing symbolic Chinese opera movements in her expressive use of a large red fan. The same fan was used by the Player Queen, carried by Corambis and used symbolically to represent the arras behind which the character fatefully hides. We referenced Odin Theatre's performance of *JUDITH*, where Roberta Carreri bends forward, fanning out her long hair into an extraordinary display of flowing forms. The external referencing of other theatre forms and productions was purposeful in the refusal to create a self-contained hermetic place of escape for the audience. From the outset, we were acknowledging the ongoing stage history of the play: what Judith Buchanan in her essay on the Wooster Group *Hamlet* has wittily called 'cultural necromancy'.[22] Other aspects of the production had a conventional, naturalistic and character-based approach to speech and character. The scene between Hamlet and his mother (known as the 'closet scene') used pauses and emotional charge in voice and physicality expected in naturalism while allowing the rhyme and rhythm of the verse to heighten the emotional drive of the scene.

Gender expectations were challenged and explored in the multiplicity of casting options used in the production: Leartes was played by a woman in a woman's dress, whereas all text references remained male. This highlighted and challenged the gender preconceptions not just of the audience's expectations of the portrayal of gender but also those expectations as they exist within the play. The only cultural difference between Ofelia and Leartes within the play was the gender assigned to them, and all their treatment and the cultural expectations imposed upon them by other characters could be seen to stem from this. After the death of Ofelia, both Queen Gertred and Leartes wore almost identical 'masculine' black trousers and jacket. Leartes continued to be addressed by the male pronoun, and again, sexual attribution, gender and costume were explored as constructs independent of each other. The inconsistency of gender appropriation within our production was further explored through the character of Corambis (Polonius in the folio). Corambis was played by an African-American female with costume and textual references gender realigned as female. The actor later appeared as the gravedigger in male costume, where she was addressed by the other characters as a male.

Our production was staged in a large black box–style studio space and began by introducing the audience to a pre-show party environment: a wedding or perhaps a wake. The set (designed by Rob Dicks) had two trestle-style tables, used by the cast and at which some spectators could sit. The space was a mixture of a thrust stage and a traverse setting, directly referencing the set for Grotowski's *The Tragical History of Doctor Faustus* and thus employing the 'cultural necromancy' discussed above. The tables would double as walkways, catwalks or battlements, and the space between the two trestle tables could become a grave for Ofelia. The relationship with the audience was intimate and unusual, with spectators perhaps finding themselves sitting next to Hamlet while he speaks directly to them. Hamlet could stand on a table and declaim to the whole audience or speak intimately to individuals. The ghost visibly used a microphone when not on stage. The audience members were seated, some as guests at a banquet, filling and surrounding the acting space rather than being safely hidden behind a fourth wall.

It was purposefully unclear which period this production was set in: at the start, all the characters except for Hamlet wore Elizabethan/Jacobean-period costumes in bright and garish tones. Hamlet was dimly lit and barely visible at the start of the play, barefoot, picking at a banjo, smoking a cherry-scented electronic cigarette, dressed in a contemporary black suit and wearing a mortuary toe tag on his foot. Any audience member close enough could see that this mortuary tag apparently belonged to King Hamlet, his dead father. The space also had the feel of a burial catacombs – an ossuary for the departed. The walls were covered in piles of skulls and bones; platforms were supported by piles of bones; and full-scale skeletons, draped in luxurious fabric and jewels, could be seen in and above the playing area. When Hamlet feigned madness as the play progressed, he stole from one of the skeletons a highly decorated shirt, covered in precious gems, which he then wore with medical hospital paper trousers and Mickey Mouse slippers. The design of the shirt was based on a Chinese opera costume of 'Water Wings' and would later be worn by one of the players taking the role of the poisoner in the play within a play.

The actors at first appeared to be engaged in some naturalistic behaviours as might be found at a party. However, it quickly became clear to the audience that the actors were performing short loops of physical and vocal action, which were repeated and repeated throughout the pre-show opening section as the audience entered the auditorium and which were not in fact naturalistic at all. As the play progresses and Hamlet moves towards action, he becomes more of the traditional Jacobean revenge character. In short, he starts to kill people. This was reflected in our production in his change of costume after he returned from England, having caused the deaths of Rossencraft and Gilderstone as well as Corambis, when he changed from contemporary clothes to Jacobean-period dress.

As each death occurred in the play, more and more of the cast moved into mourning clothes, which were of contemporary style, and gradually they were seen to take up Hamlet's costume style from the beginning of the play. Claudius changed onstage in front of the audience after the death of Corambis, from his Jacobean nightwear to the contemporary clothing of a black suit, white shirt and tie, and Gertred also changed into a black pantsuit. By the time of Ofelia's burial, Hamlet was the only person in Jacobean clothing, and the rest of the cast were in contemporary black mourning garb. The audience did not appear to find any difficulty in accepting this shift of period and time.

The lighting also reflected the non-naturalistic slippage of time and place. It moved between full contemporary use of lighting, with moving lights, follow spots and changing colour wheels, where there was never a fixed lighting state but where the lighting melted and flowed with the action (the show, which ran for one hour and 40 minutes without an interval, contained hundreds of lighting cues). Some scenes were performed in total blackout with only voices heard (e.g. the opening scene of the ghost on the battlements) or were in pure candlelight (the play within a play and the following several scenes). The setting therefore reflected the various unspecified acting forms and challenging production choices that the audience might meet in the course of the performance.

In the RSC's *Flourish Magazine* of autumn 1966, Jerzy Grotowski wrote of the training that he was involved with in his own company:

> In our work everything tends towards the inner ripening of the actor, a ripening expressed by a tension towards the extreme, by an absolute stripping away, by the laying bare of his own intimacy .... when the actor performs he should make a total gift of himself.[23]

In creating this production, I believed that we had in part at least achieved Grotowski's aim. The security and trust that the actors had in the skill base they had created through the traditional conservatoire training, combined with a strong artistic commitment to the values of the production, allowed them to achieve a theatrical whole by using seemingly opposing methods of performance and script interpretation.

In *Acting Shakespeare in a Postcolonial Space*, Denis Salter writes that

> Stage traditions notwithstanding, natural acting is never natural – it is always artificial – a distinctive style or mode of performance that has only been naturalised by traditions, by training practices, by critical standards, and by audience values.[24]

This view of acting is one supported in the curriculum at the Royal Birmingham Conservatoire. However, Salter goes on to state that

> Acting Shakespeare unnaturally is, however, a very dangerous thing to do: actors behaving this way will be routinely censured for not understanding Shakespeare, for not respecting traditions, for not being trained properly. … In brief, they will be censured not just for being unnatural but for being aberrant, perhaps even subversive. Criticisms of this type can of course put an end to an entire career.'[25]

The challenge we face and meet at the Royal Birmingham Conservatoire is to ensure that our graduates have sustainable careers and that they are employable across a range of contemporary practices, with a skill base flexible and adaptable enough to meet the demands of mainstream and non-mainstream productions in what is a constantly shifting professional environment.

Workshop Exercise

Word Statues

Acting Shakespeare: Sonnet 129

- Props required: a drum to beat out rhythm and copies of the sonnet to share with the actors at the end of the exercise. Actors can be barefoot or in soft footwear, such as jazz pumps.
- Time: the time taken for this exercise can vary depending on the stamina of the group, but generally it will take at least 45 minutes, plus discussion and reflection time.

This is an exercise I created to develop a psychophysical relationship for the actor with the word imagery of Shakespeare. It is suitable for actors who have had some training. The aim is to bypass any intellectual or critical understanding of how the language works and experience it as a physical first-instance experience. It can also bring the iambic rhythm as a governing factor into the actor's awareness. The exercise provides a close connection to the sensory/emotional response to each word, to the relationship between words, and to actors' own feelings. When actors put the words together in their original form and speak them at the end of the exercise, they have a visceral connection to the content and tend to express the language in more personal and meaningful ways, communicating the rich content with the audience. They are also directed to relate directly to the words from their own perspective.

The text in this example is Shakespeare's Sonnet 129, but any text could be used. Be aware that this exercise takes an enormous amount of focus and can be tiring for the participants.

I explain that we are going to use our bodies to form a number of imaginary statues. I do not tell the actors that we are working on any particular text. The actors should not worry about what the statue looks like from the outside but simply experience sculpting their statues, making whatever shapes with their bodies which feel right to them in the moment. I suggest they do not look at each other. Ideally, the students do not know the text they are working on. They are presented with seemingly random words.

The actors need to have access to water and the freedom to come out of the work at any time they need to and to sit quietly at the side of the room until they are able to rejoin the exercise.

Actors need to hold each statue pose long enough, around ten seconds, to fully absorb the experience.

1. Begin with a general physical warm-up to avoid injury and prepare the actors for the physical exertion of the workshop.
2. Ask the actors to stand in a relaxed posture with their eyes closed. Ask them to create a pose, without thinking too much, that they could describe as *me today*, expressing how they are feeling at this moment in time. Ask them not to worry about what this statue is saying about them but to just work with whatever they come up with. Ask them to fix this statue in their minds because it will be returned to throughout the exercise, as will with other statues we are going to make.

3. The actors next create a statue called neutral in which they find a *neutral* stance: upright, arms by their sides, head up, feet at a comfortable distance apart and aware of how this *neutral* sculpture feels.
4. While beating out ten beats on the drum (with iambic stress) the actors move gradually from the *neutral* statue, using the full ten beats, to the statue called *me today*, only arriving at the full expression of the *me today* statue on the tenth beat.
5. Repeat this going from *me today* to the *neutral* statue, using the full ten beats to transition one to the other, arriving at neutral on the tenth beat.
6. Next, the actors create a statue called *murderous*. When they have done the transition over ten beats, they go back to *neutral*.
7. Next, they create the sculpture called *savage*, transitioning over ten beats from *savage* to *murderous*, then back to *me today*.
8. Now create the sculpture called *rude*. Transition from *rude* to *neutral*.
9. Ask actors to create *cruel*. Transition from *cruel* to *rude* to *neutral*.
10. Ask actors to create the sculpture *lust*. Transition from *lust* to *murderous*, then back to *lust*, each time using the full ten beats.
11. Create the statue *mad*. Move from *mad* to *cruel* to *me today*.
12. Create the statue *possession*. Move from the statue *possession* to *mad*, then to *murderous* and then to *neutral*.
13. Create the statue *joy*. Move from *joy* to *me today*. Move from *joy* to *mad* to *neutral*.
14. Create *bliss*. Move from *bliss* to *joy*. Move from *joy* to *bliss*. Move to *me today*.
15. Create *heaven*. Move from *heaven* to *savage* and then back to *neutral*.
16. Create *hell*. Move from *hell* to *heaven*. Move from *heaven* to *me today*.
17. Move to *hell*. Move from *hell* to *heaven* but on the fifth beat, call out 'freeze'. They are stuck half way between *heaven* and *hell*. Ask them to experience how this feels. Ask them to continue towards *heaven* with the drum beats, but again pull them to a halt by calling out 'freeze' on the eighth beat. Ask them to hold this. Then ask them to move not to *heaven* but back to *hell* over eight beats and to note how this feels.
18. Move from *hell* to *lust*. From *lust*, go towards *murderous* but again stop the progress at the fifth beat. They are now caught between *lust* and *murderous*. Ask the actors to note the feeling, not to speak or respond. Transition completely over five beats to *murderous*.

19. Ask them to think of what a statue called *hunted* might be like. Move from *murderous* to *hunted*.
20. Move from *hunted* to *lust*. Stop half way, calling out 'freeze', to have them feel this. Then complete the transition to *lust*.
21. Move from *lust* to *me today*.
22. Move from *me today* to *murderous* to *savage* to *rude* to *hunted* to *mad* to *hell* to *heaven* (stopping half way, before completing the last transition).
23. Move from *heaven* to *bliss*.
24. Move from *bliss* to *joy*.
25. Move from *joy* to *me today*.
26. Move from *me today* to *neutral*.
27. Take three calming breaths in *neutral*, then slowly have them open their eyes to look up and around; ask the actors to wiggle their fingers and shake their feet and bodies out.
28. Without any discussion, distribute the sonnet and ask the actors to read it aloud in a circle, each taking one line at a time, and then to read it together in unison.
29. Sit together and discuss with the actors their feelings and observations: how the transitions felt, which statues held resonance for them, which transitions had particular force, how they felt reading the poem at the end of the exercise or how they felt about particular words.
30. End with some gentle physical stretches to ground the group and bring them out of the exercise, transitioning to the rest of their day.

This exercise is particularly tiring for the actors and for the facilitator due to the focus needed, the physical exertion and the intense nature of the imagery involved. The choices of words from the sonnet to work with and the transitions between them are just what have worked for me, but one can choose any words and will find that halting mid transition is useful in evoking a physical sense of emotional involvement with the imagery.

Sonnet 129

The expense of spirit in a waste of shame
Is lust in action; and till action, lust
Is perjured, murderous, bloody, full of blame,

Savage, extreme, rude, cruel, not to trust,
Enjoy'd no sooner but despised straight,
Past reason hunted, and no sooner had
Past reason hated, as a swallow'd bait
On purpose laid to make the taker mad;
Mad in pursuit and in possession so;
Had, having, and in quest to have, extreme;
A bliss in proof, and proved, a very woe;
Before, a joy proposed; behind, a dream.
All this the world well knows; yet none knows well
To shun the heaven that leads men to this hell.

Notes

1. Darnley (1994).
2. Steadman, p. 114.
3. Greer, Germaine, 'Arts Comment', *Guardian,* 20 November 2006, p. 28.
4. Alberge (2013).
5. Joseph (1959), p. xv.
6. Ibid., p. xi.
7. Willis (2008).
8. Recordings are either available commercially on *Great Historical Recordings* (Naxos Audiobooks, CD), in the British Library Sound Archive, or in the Shakespeare Birthplace Trust Archive.
9. Darnley (2013).
10. Ibid., pp. 22–23.
11. Ibid., p. 21.
12. Ibid., p. 20.
13. Chambers, (2004).
14. Ibid., p. 146.
15. Worthen (2008).
16. I saw a performance of this production of *Hamlet* by the Wooster Group at the Edinburgh Festival in 2013.
17. Worthen, *Hamlet at Ground Zero*, p. 308.
18. Worthen, *Shakespeare and the Authority of Performance*, p. 191.
19. *An Examination of Acting Aesthetics in a Reinterpretation of the 1603 Quarto Hamlet in between RSC and Post-Dramatic Theatre*. Panel on the Education and Training of Actors, 30–31 May and 1–2 June 2016, Athens, Greece as part of the 7th Annual International Conference on Visual and Performing Arts hosted by the Athens Institute for Education and Research (ATINER).

20 *Hamlet*, 1603 quarto, lines 115–116.
21 Paul Cartwright (King), Amelia Sciandra (Leartes), Samia La Virgine (Corambis), Morgan Bernhard (Hamlet), Elizabeth Golden (Queen Gertred), A. J. Opp (Horatio), Chris Lyons (Player Queen), Paul Jannise (Ghost), Laryssa Schoeck (Ofelia).
22 Buchanan, J. (2016) 'Look here, upon this picture': Theatrofilm, The Wooster Group Hamlet and the Film Industry. *Shakespeare in Ten Acts*. G. M. a. Z. Wilcox. London, The British Library, p. 213.
23 Grotowski (1966).
24 Salter, D. (1996) 'Acting Shakespeare in Postcolonial Space' in J. C. Bulman (ed.), *Shakespeare, Theory, and Performance*. London, New York: Routledge, p. 113.
25 Ibid., p. 117.

8

An Actor's World: People, Space, Time and Text

Jeff Janisheski

> *The art of the actor, then, will no longer depend, as in previous repertories, on physical qualities or natural gifts; it will gain its life from truth, observation, and the direct study of nature.*[1]
>
> —André Antoine (1890)

> *May Naturalism in the theatre die! The time has come to bring theatricality back to the theatre.*[2]
>
> Evgeny Vakhtangov (1921)

An actor creates a world. With their body, voice and work with the elements surrounding them, they create an imaginary world that draws us into their orbit. The focus of our work as actor teachers and trainers is how to make that world palpable and playful, truthful and theatrical, creative and charged. My own approach to actor training is informed by years of teaching and directing around the world and having trained in a spectrum of styles from the Viewpoints to Stanislavski to *butoh*. In this chapter, I will outline that method and connect it to work carried out with students at the National Institute of Dramatic Art (NIDA) in Sydney, Australia, where I was head of acting.[3]

The curricular changes I made at NIDA meant developing contemporary approaches to actor training; emphasizing group-generated and devised work; increasing training in 'heightened language' plays (from the Greeks to contemporary writers like Suzan-Lori Parks); grounding the pedagogy of the programme in two pillars (Stanislavski's system and Viewpoints); and fusing those two methods into complementary coexistence. The core questions for actors in training at NIDA became: How can an actor be more truthful and transformative? And how can an actor explore and explode the theatrical potential of their work on stage or screen?

One of NIDA's great strengths is openness to innovation, fostering a rigorous and professional environment as a catalyst for personal transformation and excellence. Notwithstanding the fact that subsequent heads of acting inevitably pursue things differently, and even pursue different things, the core of the school's mission remains the same across time: training self-generating artists and strong collaborators who can work across a range of industries. During my time as head of acting, our students have been encouraged to distil all the elements of theatre into four basic building blocks: people, space, time and text. Actors learn how to connect to and/or collaborate with each:

- People: collaborators, scene partners, the audience and characters in the play.
- Space: the rehearsal room, architecture of the theatre, spatial world or environment of the play, production design and engagement with spatial relationships onstage.
- Time: the use (or misuse) of time in the process, the temporal world of the play (which is not just the time period but also the whole sense of time in the play), the rhythm of the production and students' own physical/vocal musicality onstage.
- Text: through detailed script analysis and a deep understanding of con*text* – from the historical context of the play/playwright to current sociopolitical issues that connect to the work.

People. Space. Time. Text. This is the map of an actor's world encountered in training at NIDA, and it forms the basis of this chapter.

People

Two quotes guide the NIDA actor: 'Nature is your teacher', and 'There is no System. There is only nature.' These enigmatic phrases are from two radically different sources: the first was a mantra in the classroom of Japanese *butoh* teacher Kazuo Ohno;[4] the second was advice given to students by Stanislavski.[5] Both cite nature – the natural world for Ohno and human nature for Stanislavski – as the ultimate 'system' for a student to follow. Each implores his students to submit to something larger than what language or logic can pin down – something ineffable and inexhaustible. Both statements are like Zen *koans*:[6] paradoxical, provocative and designed to short-circuit a student's tendency towards wanting fixed or definable pathways.

One of the first steps for an actor is detailed observation and the direct study of nature. Actors must be keen observers of life – of people, the choices they make, their contradictions and complications. Meryl Streep said, 'I'm curious about other people. That's the essence of my acting. I'm interested in what it would be like to be you.'[7] Similarly, the German choreographer Pina Bausch asserted, 'I'm not interested in how people move, but what moves them.'[8] An actor's craft depends on the depth and quality of this curiosity and observation.

Observation Exercises

'Don't act!' That was our first lesson at the St Petersburg State Theatre Arts Academy in Russia. Each year for four years, I travelled with a group of American performers to the academy, where they would train for two weeks in acting, voice and movement.[9] During our first visit in 2009, Sergei Tcherkasski observed the students' Chekhov scenes, which they had rehearsed prior to the trip. Part way through, he stopped the scenes, saying we had 'gotten Chekhov all wrong', before summarizing Stanislavski's philosophy in four sentences: 'Don't act. Don't remember your lines. What is the physical life of the character? What is your own memory [your affective or emotional memory]?'[10] During these intensive training sessions, my own acting pedagogy evolved. Two elements were deeply influential: The first was the teachers' forensic investigation/interrogation of each moment, each choice by the student. The second was their unique system of étude work; students spend their first year of the five-year programme not on scenes from plays but on silent études (focused improvisations or performance sketches) of people, animals and objects. These études have become the bedrock of my work. I grounded NIDA actor training in this practice to help actors to 'not act' but rather focus on the character's 'physical life.'[11]

First-year students at NIDA were all given a simple Stanislavskian observation exercise to prepare before their first class: go to a public place (a café, bus stop or mall) and observe people; choose one person and write detailed notes about them; then create a two-minute nonverbal performance that rigorously replicates that person's physical life, actions and behaviour.[12] These études – performed on the first day of class – challenge students to sharpen their listening and observing skills, aim for specificity and details and use 'nature' as their teacher.[13] During their first month at NIDA, students worked on more challenging études: exploring a wider variety of people, group dynamics and simple arcs with a strong conflict. For example, a person goes to a café to work but realizes that they left a crucial document at home.[14] From the foundation of these études, actors in training learn to analyse and work with four key aspects of any character they perform: physical life, psychological life, patterns and pressures.

Physical Life

Martha Graham declared, 'The body never lies.'[15] The first step towards crafting a character is through the body. Actors steep themselves in their character's physical being: the energy and rhythm of their movement; clothes and personal objects that act as an extension of the body; their 'score' of physical actions and tasks; and their spatial relationship to others and the environment around them. A character's physical life portrays – or betrays – the given circumstances they are enmeshed in: everything from the time of day to their socioeconomic status. Talking about his process, Michael Fassbender remarked, 'For me, sometimes I can express much more of an intention with my body and body language than a page of dialogue.'[16]

Actors must comb through the script for clues to their character's physical life – buried in bits of dialogue or the given circumstances. At the academy, Tcherkasski worked with one of our students on a short étude from the end of Act 2 of *Uncle Vanya*: Yelena leaves her bedroom, where her husband, the professor, is finally sleeping, walks across the living room, opens a window and exclaims, 'The storm is over. Feel how fresh the air is!'[17] Tcherkasski worked on this with the actor for almost an hour, unpacking the minutiae of Yelena's physical life. How does she walk, move, breathe and open a window? How are these influenced by the web of details woven into the scene – the time of day, lack of sleep, atmosphere of the house, sexual/physical relationship with her husband and lack of air in the bedroom, contrasted with the breath of fresh air from the window? Crafting a character's physical life can be technical and detailed. Toby Jones described his process of inhabiting Truman Capote for the film *Infamous* as creating 'a set of physical mnemonics – he breathes like this, his gait is like this – that help me to check in and out of a character.'[18] Or it might be a singular choice that encapsulates the entire character. In one of Anne Bogart's classes at Columbia University, Fiona Shaw revealed her key to performing Medea: she was always standing off-centre, always a bit tilted. It was only after she killed her children and confronted Jason at the end of the play that she stood upright for the first time.[19]

Psychological Life

Another crucial step for an actor is to analyse and internalize the character's psychological life: not only what they are thinking (the words they speak) but also how they think (the quality and style of their language and thought patterns). What are their perceptions of themselves, others and the world around them? What are the scope and quality of their emotions? An actor is a detective decoding clues from the text, like traces of the character's mind.

In the Fundamentals of Acting class at NIDA, students are guided through an hour-long improvisation of a (fictional) day in their lives – from the time they wake up until they go back to sleep. The directions they are given are focused solely on either giving them certain actions to do (going to a class, a date, a party, etc.) or adding details to the given circumstances (you are late for class, you have not had a date in years, you are getting drunker, etc.). Students invariably refer to this as an 'emotional rollercoaster', even though no words about emotions have been given as prompts. Key to the exercise is a simple equation: given circumstances + (physical/psychological) action = emotions.

For an actor to experience emotion in a role, they must be deeply grounded in and committed to their given circumstances and actions. When an actor says that they are 'blocked' or have trouble accessing the emotional life of a character, they are either emotionally blocked in their own life for personal reasons or they are not deeply connected enough to their character's circumstances and actions. Emotions are like a landscape: lush or dry, flat or jagged and difficult for an actor to dig through, excavate and unearth.

The details of a character's psychological life are intimately interwoven into their physical life on a psychophysical continuum. In describing the mind–body connection (our psychophysical continuum), Stanislavski wrote, 'In every physical action, there is something psychological, and in the psychological, something physical.'[20] This holistic approach to human behaviour demands that an actor constantly monitor the complex interplay between the character's thoughts and actions. Stanislavski warned his students, however, to not privilege one area over the other but to have a balance: 'One must give actors various paths. One of these is the path of [physical] action. But there is another path: you can move from feeling to action, arousing feeling first.' The poet Stanley Kunitz wrote,

> What makes the engine go?
> Desire, desire, desire.[21]

Student actors at NIDA are asked the same question: what makes 'the engine' of your characters go – and how does that manifest physically and psychologically?

Patterns

The job of an actor is to observe patterns: their own habitual patterns that help or hinder their performance and the physical, psychological and textual patterns of their character. Acting becomes the art of recognizing and recreating (or removing) patterns.

As actors scour the script, they begin to compile a list of their character's physical, psychological and textual patterns. Out of that list emerges their character's spine or super-objective. A person's anatomical spine is 'the foundation of the body, and the source of human energy and origin of movement for the whole body.'[22] Psychologically, a character's spine or super-objective is the foundation of their psyche; it is the character's overarching action – their dominant objective – that is threaded through everything they do in the play. The importance of this spine work is to unlock the character, unify their activities in the play and give the actor a structure to work with.[23] Our physical spines hold up our body; a super-objective holds up the role.

Students are asked to write down the spine of their character as a spectrum: two contrasting verbs/actions that encapsulate the core tension at the heart of the character. A character will often oscillate between the two. After working on nonverbal études for the first half of the semester, first-year NIDA students then focus in the second half on a rigorous examination of one scene – often the Joe and Edna scene in Clifford Odets' *Waiting for Lefty*, selected for the clarity of those characters and its central conflict. In this scene, Joe journeys from one super-objective (to escape) to another (to fight back). He is escaping for almost the entire scene: blaming the 'palookas' for a phony contract; buttering up or lashing out at his wife Edna but never taking responsibility; excusing his boss's behaviour; or fantasizing, such as 'Jeez, I wish I was a kid again and didn't have to think about the next minute.'[24] Only at the end does he fight back and 'get brass toes on [his] shoes and know where to kick.' Edna's spine is to shut Joe out/down and then to wake him up. Her terse language in the beginning betrays one of the ways she copes with crisis: she shuts down and shuts him out. Quickly, though, her objective changes, at which point she spends most of the scene forcing her husband (and herself) into action: 'I don't care, as long as I can maybe wake you up.'

The NIDA actors explore Joe's and Edna's respective spines on many levels: through a strong commitment to these actions in every beat of the scene and through subtler examinations of their physicality (how does Joe 'escape' or Edna 'wake up' when they walk, talk, relate to each other or handle objects?). If we imagine a spine like a line, it is a line that goes in two directions – two opposite desires, two opposite actions – and the character's internal conflicts are generated by the tension in that line. The dramatic conflict of a play arises from the clash between each of the character's different spines; it is the clash of their overarching actions.

Pressures

Theatre is the art of crisis. Plays are dramaturgically centred on conflicts, and the creative process itself can provoke a personal or artistic impasse. Artists must embrace and lean into these challenges – that is what sparks creativity. When working with actors, focus on the various crises or 'pressures' surrounding a character: from the micro (the furniture being taken away in Joe and Edna's apartment) to the macro (the systems of oppression that Joe and Edna are struggling under) and from specific obstacles in a scene (Joe and Edna not wanting to wake up the children) to larger conflicts in the play (Edna trying to 'wake up' her husband and the world). How does a character react to these pressures? Do they implode or explode, fight or flee? Contemporary psychologists like Paul Tough argue that '[A person's] character is created by encountering and overcoming failure.'[25] The question for an actor is, how has their character been created by the crises and pressures they have encountered?

NIDA students sift through the script to catalogue Joe and Edna's backstory and given circumstances: the who, what, when, where and why of those characters; their socioeconomic background; and how these act as pressures on the characters. Physically, students create études to embody those pressures: How does history (the given circumstances) weigh on Joe or Edna and affect their physicality? How does the ensemble create that chorus of men, with their cigar smoke, that surrounds Joe and Edna in the scene? How does that circle – of men and smoke – imprison and poison Joe and Edna?

Space and Time

'Work with what's in the room,'[26] Bogart would urge in her directing classes. Her provocation can be unpacked on various levels. On one level, actors need to connect to and work with what is *really* in the rehearsal room or onstage: the energy of the ensemble, atmosphere of rehearsals, interpersonal dynamics in the team and personal issues they bring into rehearsal; the opportunities provided by the production design as well as technical obstacles that every production confronts; and the cultural context of the script and any sociopolitical issues in our culture. Clearly, *everything* is in the room, and it is all material for an actor to engage with. On a more fundamental level, actors need to sharpen their skills at working with two basic elements: space and time.

Observation Exercises

NIDA students work through a series of observation exercises to hone their skills at observing and 'reading' space and time.

- Go to a series of public spaces that are radically different (a mall, a bathroom, an alleyway) and write down detailed observations about each space and how space affects people's movements and moods. As Winston Churchill remarked, 'We shape our buildings and afterwards our buildings shape us.'[27]
- Observe one space at radically different times in the day and write down detailed observations about time and how time affects people's movements and moods. Nobel Prize–winning scientist Paul Rich argued that 'Every living organism on this planet responds to the sun. All plant and animal behaviour is determined by the light-dark cycle [i.e. time]. We on this planet are slaves to the sun.'[28]

Although seemingly conceptual, these exercises are a tangible way of analysing space and time. Student actors explore how Joe and Edna are 'slaves' to their space and time: the compression of their apartment and the exhausted rhythms of a late-night argument – and the ways these play out via various elements of the Viewpoints.

Viewpoints

The Viewpoints are a contemporary approach to performance and training that was developed in New York in the late 1970s, first by choreographer Mary Overlie and later by theatre director Anne Bogart.[29] Rather than working with the private/internal realm of psychology, Viewpoints engages solely with the public/external aspects of space and time. Bogart asks, 'How as a performer do you fill time and space – what tools do you have?'[30] Those tools are the nine Viewpoints she devised:

Viewpoints of Time[31]

- Tempo is the rate of speed for any movement or sequence of movements.
- Duration is how long any movement or action continues before it changes.
- Kinesthetic response is the timing of one's responsiveness to external stimuli (e.g. another actor's movement or changes in lights or sound).
- Repetition is repeating a moment in time, either repeating something you have done or someone else has done (in the past) or repeating and synching up with a current moment by the ensemble (in the present).

Viewpoints of Space[32]

- Shape is the contour or outline of the body and the dynamics of those shapes.
- Gesture is specific movements that encapsulate and communicate some meaning – privately, socially or archetypally.
- Architecture includes attunement and responsiveness to the overall physical environment.
- Spatial relationship means one's physical relationship to everything/everyone onstage; like the Japanese term *ma*,[33] this gap or space is not empty but active.
- Floor pattern is the pathway we carve out through movement in space.

In and of itself, the vocabulary of Viewpoints is not revolutionary or new. What is radical is the way it can alter an actor's process. Through weekly training in Viewpoints, NIDA actors evolve into a deeply connected ensemble, able to intuit each other's choices. It empowers them to make bold decisions on their own by grounding them in concrete tools. It allows room for spontaneity because they are responding to the constant flow of moment-to-moment changes. It gives them tools to develop and devise group and solo work. And it focuses on the public realm of time and space instead of the private realm of emotions and psychology.

Like Vakhtangov and Meyerhold, Bogart sees her approach as an intervention against the dominant mode of naturalistic acting and psychological realism in American theatre:

> I feel fairly radical in opposing that sort of theatre, because it creates a kind of solipsism, which I don't believe in, whereby you're thinking about yourself and not others …. I believe that the emotions should be left alone in a rehearsal. What you're looking for in a rehearsal is an action or a shape or a form in which the emotions can always be different. Because the minute you pin down an emotion, you cheapen it. So, I prefer to look at the body, at placement, at arrangement.[34]

The Viewpoints are not a strict method or a style. They function in the same way as scales do for a pianist: as a structure for practice, for keeping specific 'muscles' in shape. They are nine points of awareness that a performer can draw upon to inspire rather than dictate movement, to open rather than limit choices.

Text

In our lives, words are the tip of the iceberg. Psychologist Albert Mehrabian, in his book *Silent Messages*, came up with the famous ratio of personal communication being 55% body language, 38% tone of voice and 7% words.[35] This does not mean that plays – with their 'words, words, words' – are less important or powerful. Those words become the wellspring for the action and ideas of the play. For an actor, Mehrabian's ratio is a reminder that speech onstage springs from an intensely deep reservoir of the character's psychophysical life.

Actors must develop a curiosity and hunger for language. As a clue to how they should approach the text in script analysis, I remind actors of the etymology of that word 'analysis': to break up, loosen, release, set free and unfasten.

World of Play

When analysing, breaking up and releasing a script, a major question I have for any actor is, what is the world of the play? As theatre scholar Elinor Fuchs says, 'A play is not a flat work of literature … but is in itself another world passing before you in time and space. Language is only one part of this world.'³⁶

Using her essay *EF's Visit to a Small Planet* as a guide, students explore the world of the play (how space, time, climate, mood and 'music' operate), the social world of the play (how class rules, social patterns/interactions, power and language operate) and what changes for each. The actors then distil those notes into one sentence that encapsulates the overall world of the play in a potent, poetic image. When working on Strindberg's *Miss Julie* in a second-year acting class at NIDA, students came up with a wide variety of 'worlds': the world of *Miss Julie* is a boxing match between men and women; a birdcage where everyone is trapped and trying to escape; a world of division (of upper class and lower class, men and women, human and animal). The students are asked to bring in ten visual images that portray their 'worlds', and drawing upon their Viewpoints training, they work in groups to create short compositions from those images. The aim is for the ensemble to physicalize the dynamics, energies and atmospheres of these boxing matches, birdcages and divided worlds.

Script Analysis

After physically exploring the world of the play, the actors delve into deeper layers of script analysis of the play and each scene:

- Story: Bogart would often playfully say, 'Never forget the stupid story!'³⁷
- Arc: This is the play or scene's beginning/middle/end, its exposition/conflict/resolution, its structure. The *dramatic conflict* is the engine or motor that moves the play along.
- Event or turning point: This is the climactic moment that everything in the scene or play is driving towards and moving away from.
- Driving/controlling the action: Who is driving or controlling the action? Does it stay the same or shift?
- Beats: A beat is the smallest unit of action/reaction. It is not a change in the dialogue or emotions, although it can lead to these; it is a change in action. When beats change, the body changes: any shift in psychology (actions/objectives) can align with a shift in physicality or blocking.

- Action or objective: What does the character want or want to do? Actions/objectives should be specific, strong and playable.
- Tactics: Tactics are the ways a character goes about achieving their action/objective – the means to an end. There are psychological tactics ('to challenge slyly, aggressively, indirectly') and physical tactics ('to challenge someone by hovering over them, shouting at them, staring at them').

Actors explore these elements through rigorous table work and structured improvisations. The goal of all this text work is to create a foundation for a fully dimensional world on stage.

Application to a Play: *Antigone*

In their 2015 Greek drama class, NIDA's second-year actors staged Anne Carson's bare bones adaptation of *Antigone*. For any play, the first question asked of the actors is, why should we do this play, and why now? *Antigone* is the drama of our time; it speaks to our world of whistle-blowers, leakers and a growing resistance. Thus, the students examined our contemporary Antigones: Edward Snowden, Chelsea Manning, Julian Assange, the Occupy Movement, Black Lives Matter and Nadezhda Tolokonnikova of the Russian punk-rock group Pussy Riot. One of the actors playing Antigone was deeply inspired by her grandfather, who helped create the Aboriginal Tent Embassy, a major site of resistance for Aboriginal Australians in the capital city of Canberra.

For *Antigone*, students incorporated elements of everything outlined above (in the section that covered people, space, time and text) into each stage of our process: choral work, character work and composition work.

Choral Work

The first stage is to make the ensemble cohere into a chorus: a multi-headed storyteller. Each class begins with a series of physical warm-ups, drawing on training in Viewpoints, *butoh* and *noh*:[38]

- Standing silently, without moving, students expand their awareness of the space. Eyes closed, they listen to everything they can hear: sounds near and far, inside or outside the room. Eyes opened, they look at everything they can see: things near and far, inside or outside the room (through the windows). What changes do they hear or see? Composer Pauline Oliveros's deep listening philosophy is our guide: '[deep listening] is listening to everything all the time, and reminding yourself when you're not …. It's an active process. It's not passive.'[39]

- That stillness is the starting point for introducing *butoh*. Just as John Cage insisted that 'there's no such thing as silence,'[40] there is no such thing as stillness. There is always movement. Standing in place, students observe the subtle dance of their bodies – the expansion or contraction with each breath, the tiny tremors of movement throughout the body. This is what *butoh* dancers Eiko and Koma call 'delicious movement'.[41]

- *Butoh* is a paradox: an anti-technique technique, an anti-dance dance, rooted in traditional Japanese aesthetics yet also a global phenomenon. A *butoh* performance might be a grotesque 'dance of darkness'[42] or like a serene Zen rock garden. In working with students, the focus is not on the outer style of *butoh* but the inner energy of that form. Thus, in their warm-ups, students explore extremes of tempo through stillness and slow, geological time. They slowly walk around the room and – drawing on imagery from the world of *Antigone* – they practice transforming from image to image. *Butoh* is the art of transformation from image to image – and that intense imagery can infuse the actor's character work.

- *Noh* is the art of stillness and economy. *Noh* plays and performers are like compressed diamonds of energy and poetry. In warm-ups, students weave in select elements of *noh* to harness the 'animal energy'[43] of the actor and introduce a few key principles:
  - *Kamae* is a position of readiness, relaxed strength and contained energy.
  - *Suri-ashi* means sliding feet. *Noh* is often defined as 'the art of walking', so students learn basic elements of this grounded way of walking – of 'sliding feet (*suri-ashi*)' – to add rigour and focus to their movement.
  - *Jo-ha-kyu* is the lifeblood, the rhythm, of *noh*. It literally means 'beginning, middle, end' or 'slow, fast, faster', but as my teacher Richard Emmert would say, '*Jo-ha-kyu* is really about expansion and contraction of energy.'[44] Through simple walking exercises in their warm-ups, students find a way to have a contained and forceful energy as individual performers and as a chorus.

After warm-ups, the next stage is exploration into the world of the play. Each actor brings in a visual scrapbook of images that capture their vision of the world of *Antigone*, and they share these in small groups. The groups then devise a two- to three-minute étude of the world of the play, drawing upon the dynamics in these images: a world of destruction with chairs and water bottles strewn everywhere; a world of surveillance completely performed on computers and mobile phones; or a world of tension, a tug of war, with a long rope and people pulling on both sides.

Out of this improvisational work, students unearth their vision for the play: a world of opposition, a world divided. There are so many binaries in the play: woman/man, action/stillness, speaking/silence, light/dark, love/hate. The name *Anti*-gone has 'opposite' or 'against' at its etymological root. Antigone sets up this divide when she says, 'I am someone born to share in love not hatred.'[45] The group explores opposition via space and time from the Viewpoints, working in counterpoint to the tempo, duration, shape, gesture, spatial relationship and floor pattern of others on the stage.

The play begins and ends in the dark. The first line is, 'We come out of the dark.'[46] In this world of sharp contrasts – of light versus darkness – a simple rule shaped our design and influenced the staging: the whole presentation was lit by flashlights (torches) and floodlights that the ensemble controlled and moved. This added to the shadowy, expressionistic look of our presentation and built the framework for an actor-driven event. Students explored this concept in various choral moments. When the audience initially enters, the room is pitch black; slowly the actors playing Antigone and Ismene search for each other among the crowd of people (the audience), and the ensemble lights them using only flashlights. Later in the play, the ensemble holds a floodlight over Antigone – and the violence of that bright, brutal light is as strong as Kreon's interrogation.

Character Work

Next, students methodically work on building characters from a series of guided improvisations and Stanislavskian études.

During improvisations, students explore how their character walks, stands, sits or runs, as well as their character's tempo, duration, repetition, shape, gesture, spatial relationship and floor pattern. These are developed further with the introduction of other characters into the improvisation. What changes as a result of the additional characters? For Antigone, how does her tempo, gestural life or floor pattern shift in reaction to Ismene, Kreon or Haemon? How does that improvisation feed into the creation of her physical life and spine?

Students also create a one-minute étude of the character's arc, based on an image from the beginning, middle and end of the play. What does that arc say about their journey in the play? Students then create a one-minute étude of the character's key: a prop, item of clothing or action that unlocks the character for the actor. The actors playing Kreon might use one prop, a coin, as their key to that character; informed by Kreon's repeated mentions of money and bribery in the play, the actors explore how he handles that coin – hiding, flipping, caressing or flinging it. Discovering the right key is like finding the master key to your home: it unlocks doors, allows you to enter deeper into different rooms and helps you feel more settled inside.

Students create a one-minute étude exploring the character's spine. The actors playing Antigone explore her spine, a spectrum wound around her sometimes complementary/sometimes contradictory two main actions: to reject (resist, revolt or not bend) is in tension with to respect (be loyal, be devoted or bend/kneel to a higher power.) The actors explore how that spine manifests physically and vocally. How might she either reject or respect through the movements of her body – her posture, hands, gestures and the 'mask' of her face? How does she revolt or devote herself with each step and every syllable she speaks?

Composition Work

In painter Robert Henri's book *The Art Spirit*, he says, 'Good composition is like a suspension bridge; each line adds strength and takes none away .... Get the art of controlling the observer – that is composition.'[47] My intention is for the work of the ensemble to be like that suspension bridge: to have a tension, rigour and strength; to be a clear pathway for the story and world of the play; to guide the audience in the journey of the performance; and to connect to each other. Students followed a set system when working the scenes in *Antigone*: they developed a rough outline by drafting the arc, dynamics, turning point and 'driver/controller' of each scene. Bogart would often state, 'The director directs the play; the actor directs the role.'[48] NIDA actors learn to be self-directed agents capable of composing or drafting material for the director to shape. Here is an edited version of their process for the opening scene between Antigone and Ismene:

- Arc: The arc consists of two sisters connecting and consoling each other; then fighting with each other over staying alive versus staying loyal; and ending with Antigone rejecting that relationship and any attempts to stay silent. The actors explored that arc through various Viewpoints: tempo (starting slowly, building speed and rapidly running away), spatial relationship (opposite from each other, then intensely close and intertwined and then opposite again) and floor pattern (two lines connecting, spiralling and then splitting off).
- Dynamics: The first scene sets up our world of opposition and contrasts. It starts with whispers and ends with shouting. It goes from the two of them running towards each other to both running away. It begins with both women fearful and ends with one woman unafraid to die. In the middle, during their argument, it is a swirl of energy. My job as director was to orchestrate the 'music' of this dynamic and calibrate the energy of the performance. The actors' task was to discover these dynamics externally and internally, physically and psychologically.
- Turning point: The event of the scene is Antigone's rejection of her sister: 'You know what, Ismene? I wouldn't take your help now if you asked me.'[49] The actors playing Antigone explored the psychophysical life of that moment: What is it like to reject your sister, your only living family member? What is like to reject all safety or solace in the world? What changes in Antigone's mind, body and voice? It is not just a dramaturgical turning point; her whole being is turning towards one irrevocable direction.
- Driving the scene: Antigone clearly drives the scene. She invites Ismene to meet, pleads with her to join in action and bury Polyneikes, and then rejects her and everyone else in her refusal to be silent. In rehearsals for some scenes, the actors improvised by pulling a rope because each scene in *Antigone* is a tug of war over power and control. Who has control of the rope and the relationships? Who resists and pulls back? After the improvisations, the actors need to feel the tension of that invisible rope – the tautness of energy – with their scene partners.

After that general outline, students add more layers of detail: exploring the specific beats, actions and tactics of the characters. The final step is to stitch all the scenes together into one larger composition through transitions. As Gustav Mahler observed, 'The real art of conducting consists in transitions.' The same is true for acting; transitions are key opportunities to orchestrate the energy of one's performance. The transitions that students added between scenes propelled the story forward and created an escalating musicality to the piece. Some of the transitions were the practical choreography of moving floodlights around; some were more surreally poetic images crafted by the ensemble – a wall of 25 bodies pushing Antigone to her death. The purpose of challenging actors to create these transitions is twofold: to become self-generating artists equipped to devise and develop original material and to become proactive, independent leaders in their field, which is a larger philosophical goal that aligns with NIDA's mission. The performance's composition (the blocking, choreography and transitions) is a structure for the actor: a series of rules, limitations and agreements that they inhabit. Bogart has stated, 'I often think of staging as a vehicle that's going somewhere. … It's just a vehicle in which the actors can live.'[50]

Goals

An actor creates a world, one that is truthful, transformational and theatrical.

There are many paths to truth: through external/physical methods or internal/psychological ones; through improvisational exploration or textual analysis; through being 'an athlete of the heart'[51] (Artaud) or an athlete of the mind; through subtle details or dynamic gestures; and through 'finding the mask of that character'[52] (Chekhov) or 'tear[ing] away the masks behind which we hide daily'[53] (Grotowski). Truth is elastic, expansive and elusive – not limited to a specific style, method or form of acting. It is what *fills* that form – through the actor's energy, imagination and action.

Theatre is the art of transformation. An actor must be virtuosic in their ability to transform and immerse themselves in another character. Many actors talk about this. Whether working on *12 Years a Slave* or *Star Wars: The Force Awakens*, Lupita Nyong'o says, 'I like to disappear into character. I like to let go of my ego and just work on the material. I like to be in service of character.'[54] Similarly, an actor is continually changing, from moment to moment, role to role or medium to medium. Actors must also learn how to work with and transform all the elements in the room: how to orchestrate time through their energy or shape space through their actions and how to playfully transform the everyday objects on stage so that books become birds or a table turns into a prison. On a larger scale, the challenge remains: how to create change through our art. As Augusto Boal wrote, 'Theatre is a form of knowledge; it should and can also be a means of transforming society. Theatre can help us build our future, rather than just waiting for it.'[55]

Actors in training are encouraged to exploit and explode the *theatreness* of theatre: its liveness and immediacy, tools and techniques, history and traditions, fictions and artificiality, scale and spectacle. Theatricality is not necessarily about the outward form – expensive stage designs or specific performance styles. The bare roots of theatre can be equally powerful: an actor, a stage, an audience – a communion. Peter Brook's 'empty space' is still an inspiration for all actors: 'A man walks across this empty space whilst someone else is watching him, and this is all that is needed for an act of theatre to be engaged.'[56] The focus of actor training at an institution like NIDA is how to make that connection between performers and audience more magnetic and theatrical.

An actor's world is one that is ultimately inviting, compelling and surprising. It is continually in motion, always moving towards more discoveries.

Notes

1 Drain, Richard. *Twentieth-Century Theatre: A Sourcebook*. Routledge, 1995, p. xvii.
2 Ibid., p. 261.
3 NIDA was founded in 1958 and now offers a range of bachelor of fine arts (BFA) courses (e.g. in acting, design and technical theatre/stage management) and master of arts (MFA) courses (e.g. in design, directing and writing for performance). It should be stressed at the outset that this chapter is focused on the method I practised at NIDA and is not intended to represent the type of work carried out by colleagues currently teaching there.
4 I trained with Kazuo Ohno at his dance studio in Yokohama, Japan, from 1992 to 1994 and again from 1998 to 1999; he often repeated that phrase in his classes.
5 Hodge, Alison. *Twentieth Century Actor Training*. Routledge, 2006, p. 33.
6 Zen Buddhist *koans* are riddles, puzzles and paradoxical statements to be meditated upon; they provoke the meditating monk to abandon their dependence on reason and confront the monk with seemingly impenetrable questions. Famous examples of *koans* are 'what is the sound of one hand clapping?' or 'what is your original face?'

7. Schell, Hester. *Casting Revealed: A Guide for Film Directors*. Michael Wiese Productions, 2011, p. 97.
8. Climenhaga, Royd. *Pina Bausch*. Routledge, 2007, p. 2.
9. I travelled with an ensemble of undergraduate students from the National Theater Institute (NTI), a programme of the Eugene O'Neill Theater Center in Connecticut, while I was artistic director of NTI, from 2008 to 2011.
10. Quote from the classes in spring 2009 with Sergei Tcherkasski at the St Petersburg State Theatre Arts Academy in Russia.
11. I prefer the word 'étude' to 'performances'. Performances imply something final or polished, whereas these are studies and sketches that inform the rehearsal process.
12. I choose to use the word 'nonverbal' as opposed to 'silent' for these études. My experience has been that if I qualify them as silent, then it stifles the students' breath. I would often remind students to breathe and not forget the importance of the character's breath – its quality, dynamics and volume – as an integral part of a character's physical life.
13. For a short description of Stanislavski doing this observation exercise with a student, all NIDA actors read a short excerpt from Nikolai M. Gorchakov's *Stanislavsky Directs*. Minerva Press, 1954, pp. 12–17.
14. This narrative arc/conflict should be something that the student observed or something they imagine that the person would go through.
15. Martha Graham was influenced by her father, a psychiatrist who specialized in nervous disorders and analysed the way people spoke and moved. He would say to her, 'Movement never lies. You will always reveal what you feel in your heart by what you do in your movement.' Later in life, she said, 'This was my first lesson as a dancer.' From Google Arts & Culture website: https://www.google.com/culturalinstitute/.
16. Coyle, Jake. 'Fassbender Fleshes Out Characters with Physicality'. *Backstage*, 30 November 2011: https://www.backstage.com/news/fassbender-fleshes-out-characters-with-physicality/.
17. Chekhov, Anton. *The Plays of Anton Chekhov*. Translated by Paul Schmidt and Harper Perennial, 1998, p. 228.
18. Jones, Toby. 'Toby Jones: "I delve into a character's physicality"'. *Guardian*, May 9, 2009: https://www.theguardian.com/stage/2009/may/09/toby-jones-character-physicality.
19. Shaw was commenting on her performance in the Deborah Warner production of *Medea*, which opened on Broadway in New York in December 2002. This quote comes from an in-class conversation between Bogart and Shaw as part of Bogart's directing classes with her MFA directing students at Columbia University in 2003.
20. Hodge, Alison, p. 17.
21. Kunitz, Stanley. *The Collected Poems*. W. W. Norton & Company, 2002, p. 280.
22. Gutekunst, Christina and John Gillett. *Voice into Acting: Integrating voice and the Stanislavsky approach*. Bloomsbury Methuen Drama, 2014, p. 34.
23. For a thorough analysis of characters' spines, I have my students read Elia Kazan's 'Notebook for *A Streetcar Named Desire*' in *Directors on Directing: A Source Book of the Modern Theatre*, edited by Toby Cole and Helen Krich Chinoy (Bobbs-Merrill, 1963). His copious notes on the super-objectives of the four main characters in that play are a masterclass in script analysis.

24 All quotes are from the play by Clifford Odets, *Waiting for Lefty*. Dramatists Play Service, 1998.
25 Paul, Annie Murphy. 'School of Hard Knocks: "How Children Succeed," by Paul Tough'. *Sunday Book Review: The New York Times*, 23 August 2012, p. 19.
26 This and subsequent quotes by Anne Bogart are from conversations during my training with her at Columbia University during 2002–2005.
27 https://www.parliament.uk/about/living-heritage/building/palace/architecture/palaces-tructure/churchill/ This quote by Winston Churchill comes from a speech in the House of Commons on 28 October 1944.
28 Davis, Nicola and Ian Sample. 'Nobel prize for medicine awarded for insights into internal biological clock', *Guardian*, 2 October 2017: https://www.theguardian.com/science/2017/oct/02/nobel-prize-for-medicine-awarded-for-insights-into-internal-biological-clock.
29 Mary Overlie developed The Six Viewpoints, primarily for dancers and choreographers. Anne Bogart built on that groundwork and changed some of the terminology to create the Viewpoints, her nine points of reference geared for theatre artists.
30 Conversations with Bogart, 2002–2005.
31 I encourage students to explore each of these terms through sources outside Viewpoints too, often from video clips of dance or visual art (e.g. sculpture and installation art). For time, some examples include tempo (La La La Human Steps, *butoh*, *noh*), duration (Pina Bausch, Robert Wilson, Marina Abramović, Tehching Hsieh) and repetition (Pina Bausch, Anne Teresa De Keersmaeker).
32 I encourage students to watch an array of videos by artists exploring spatial elements, such as gesture (DV8, Pina Bausch) and architecture (visual artists James Turrell, Olafur Eliasson, Richard Serra).
33 *Ma* is a Japanese term that can be translated as 'gap,' 'negative space,' 'interval,' or 'pause.'
34 Diamond, David. 'Balancing Acts: An Interview with Anne Bogart and Kristin Linklater'. *The American Theatre Reader: Essays and Conversations from American Theatre Magazine*. Theatre Communications Group, 2009, p. 383.
35 Mehrabian, Albert. *Silent Messages: Implicit Communication of Emotions and Attitudes*. Wadsworth Publishing Company, 1972.
36 Fuchs, Elinor. '*EF's Visit to a Small Planet*: Some Questions to Ask a Play'. *Theater*, 2004, 34 (2), p. 6.
37 Conversations with Bogart, 2002–2005.
38 I have over ten years of experience training in and choreographing *butoh* work, from 1989 to 2000, and it is still a source of inspiration in my teaching. I trained in traditional *noh* theatre in Tokyo from 1992 to 1994 and again from 1998 to 1999.
39 Oteri, Frank. 'Pauline Oliveros Interview: Creating, Performing and Listening'. *New Music Box* website, 1 December 2000: https://nmbx.newmusicusa.org/pauline-oliveros-creating-performing-and-listening/10/.
40 Kostelanetz, Richard. *Conversing with Cage*. Psychology Press, 2003, p. 70.
41 Read about their Delicious Movement Manifesto: http://eikoandkoma.org/deliciousmanifesto.

42 The original term *ankoku butoh* can be roughly translated as 'dance of darkness' or 'darkness (*ankoku*) dance (*butoh*)'.
43 Suzuki, Tadashi. *Culture is the Body: The Theatre Writings of Tadashi Suzuki*. Theatre Communications Group, 2015, p. 140.
44 From conversations with *noh* teacher Richard Emmert during my training in the 1990s in Tokyo.
45 Carson, Anne. *Antigone*. Oberon Books, 2016, p. 29.
46 Ibid., p. 13.
47 Henri, Robert. *The Art Spirit*. J. B. Lippincott Company, 1960, p. 265.
48 Conversations with Bogart, 2002–2005.
49 Carson, Anne, p. 15.
50 Olsberg, Dagne. *Freedom, Structure, Freedom: Anne Bogart's Directing Philosophy*. PhD fine arts dissertation for Texas Tech University, 1994, p. 62.
51 Artaud, Antonin. *The Theater and its Double*. Translated by Mary Caroline Richards, Grove Press, 1958, p. 133.
52 Dalton, Lisa. 'The "Other" Chekhov'. *Backstage West* website, 6 April 2000: http://www.michaelchekhov.net/otherchekhov.html.
53 Grotowski, Jerzy. *Towards a Poor Theatre*. Simon and Schuster, 1968, p. 256.
54 Ulaby, Neda. 'After Very Visible Roles, Lupita Nyong'o Looks to Disappear into Character'. *National Public Radio* website, 23 April 2016: https://www.npr.org/2016/04/23/475263522/after-two-intense-dramas-lupita-nyongo-says-shes-ready-for-a-change.
55 Boal, Augusto. *Theatre of the Oppressed*. Theatre Communications Group, 1992, p. xxx.
56 Brook, Peter. *The Empty Space*. Penguin, 2008, p. 11.

9

Approaches to Acting and Interacting in Immersive and Interactive Performance

Klaus Kruse

Training, Thinking, Doing

In 2008 Dartington College of Arts merged with Falmouth University. The theatre department moved into the purpose-built University Performance Centre, and the provision underwent significant transformation, with the new portfolio building on the defining principles of what was a uniquely innovative approach to training and learning. Founded as the Falmouth School of Art in 1902, with subsequent changes to Falmouth College of Art and Design and Falmouth College of Arts, Falmouth University is a specialist university for the creative industries and one of very few UK institutions with a total focus on creative practice.

A bachelor of arts (BA) honours in acting maintains Dartington's core values of student-centred learning, harnessing these to the challenges and demands of vocational training focused on exploratory practice and strong graduate employability. It is axiomatic that when developing programmes and modules, the teaching team continuously ask themselves what sort of skills, knowledge, abilities and experience graduates need to successfully compete in an ever-fluctuating and constantly progressing industry. The current iteration of BA(Hons) acting was developed by Agnieszka Blonska, Aiden Condron, Misri Dey, Terrie Fender, Richard Gough, Klaus Kruse, Danielle Meunier and Gregg Whelan.

For the acting provision, training in foundational skills has assumed a more central role than in the Dartington model. This centrality is not to replace so much as support a curriculum that promotes creativity, innovation and experimentation. This manifests itself in a reluctance to engage in how-to teaching; another reluctance is to simply work from a set of assumptions, preferring to approach learning as an ongoing enquiry within which all members of staff are as deeply involved as their/our students. To become the pioneers in their profession that the programme intends, students draw on working methods that challenge the status quo in order to help progress and redefine the possibilities of practice.

Each aspect of the acting programme is focused on one of three mutually informing learning strands, coexisting under the following umbrella terms: training, thinking and doing.

Training is learning through doing, incorporating the development of core vocal, psychophysical and textual skills and techniques. Students develop a personal rehearsal process; engage with experimentation within the format of structured play; test and explore ideas through practice; take risks; and embody contextual knowledge.

Thinking amounts to students engaging with theories and histories in the fields of theatre, acting and performance. Modules under this umbrella promote thinking and reflecting; understanding of social and cultural contexts; interrogative and enquiry-based pedagogy; contextual study and research; and industry awareness.

Doing incorporates rehearsals and performances for a range of different contexts and audiences. Within this strand, students integrate theory and practice; approach thinking and doing as combined aspects of a developing acting practice; explore ways of deploying process towards performance; and develop agency and entrepreneurship.

In setting its aims out in this way, the programme positions itself as training with a distinctive and contemporary ethos, offering a holistic approach which emphasizes sustainable skills for the twenty-first-century actor. One of the core objectives is to provide training which prepares students as fully as possible for the diverse challenges and opportunities they face in the job market. Work opportunities increasingly demand that actors be able to contribute to the making process of productions as generative creatives. Consequently, a holistic approach that emphasizes sustainable skills must empower graduates in their ability as interpretive artists, as creators and as entrepreneurs.

It remains critical to the training offered at Falmouth that students are familiar with, comfortable with and competent to work in environments that rely on process-based methods and that they possess the skills and attitudes to actively contribute to a wide range of processes. Graduates need to have the confidence and know-how to make their own work, alongside the skills and agency to network, promote and generate performance opportunities, partnerships and funding. Therefore, an important aspect of learning for our students is the ability to engage with independent projects and interdisciplinary collaborations.

The first year of the course introduces students to three strands of practice: physical, vocal and textual skills and techniques to provide a foundation for acting; acting techniques to develop the craft of character creation and embodied storytelling; and lectures and seminars that engage with theories and practices of acting and performance. The first year focuses primarily on the development of skills and techniques to form the foundations for studio and context-based practice. Students will also receive basic instructions that allow them to use technical facilities.

In the second year of the course, students deepen their physical and vocal engagement with training and develop skills in conceptual research and theories of performance. They develop collaborative productions which afford them opportunities to engage with compositional, dramaturgical and technical aspects of theatre-making applied to devised productions. They also engage with modules that focus techniques and approaches relevant to acting in recorded media, including training for digital media, radio, voice-overs and acting for the camera.

In their third year, students engage in an advanced screen-acting module; develop a solo performance project; and work on a full-scale public performance presented as part of the university's annual end-of-year graduate festival.

An Aesthetics of Interactivity and Immersion

When working with acting students on projects that experiment with audience/performer/spatial relationships and audience performer interaction, most of the cohort will be familiar with the term 'immersive theatre'. Familiarity means they are aware of work by companies such as Punchdrunk, dreamthinkspeak, Secret Cinema, You Me Bum Bum Train or Shunt. The work these companies create is often perceived by students to be an entirely recent, novel development in theatre, and it is useful in classes to look at origins and inspirations that current practitioners draw on, establishing a greater awareness within students of the relationship between tradition and innovation and indeed of the traditions of innovation.

Students look at developments that took place at the turn of the nineteenth century, exploring Wagner's notion of the *Gesamtkunstwerk* that regarded all the arts as significant contributors to a total theatrical experience. Students examine practitioners such as Meyerhold, Piscator and Reinhardt with their reactions against the proscenium stage and the illusionist realism of its backdrops and decor; and of course, they examine Brecht, whose reframing of the relationship between performer and spectator has inspired so much subsequent practice. Students look at how these progressions are connected to movements in other areas of the arts, such as Futurism and Dadaism, inspired in part by Artaud's assertion that

> The spectator who comes to our theatre knows that he is to undergo a real operation in which not only his mind but his senses and his flesh are at stake. Henceforth he will go to the theatre the way he goes to the surgeon or the dentist. In the same state of mind-knowing of course, that he will not die, but that it is a serious thing, and that he will not come out of it unscathed.[1]

The popular use of the term 'immersive theatre' is relatively new, and in terms of what is described by this, it shares much with what Richard Schechner first described as 'environmental theatre'. In his 1968 essay '6 Axioms for Environmental Theatre', he refers to one of his own productions of Ionesco's *Victims of Duty* as well as to a diverse array of examples, such as happenings, street theatre, political demonstrations, ritual performance, the theories of John Cage and the productions of Grotowski.[2] Schechner also directed the infamous production of *Dionysus in 69* with the Performance Group. The work relied heavily on interaction with its audience, with Schechner describing participation as the opening up of a play so that the audience/spectators can enter into the action. Schechner speaks too about the transformation of an aesthetic event into a social event.[3]

As part of *Dionysus in 69*, interaction went as far as audiences and performers engaging intimately with one another; in other instances, actors would start biting and scratching the audience as a means of moving them back from the performance area. Schechner stresses the importance of a rehearsal process through which actors get to know each other intimately and which includes engagement with training at a psychophysical and social level to function as a foundation for actors so that they can deal with the interactive and improvisational nature of the work.[4]

While immersive or interactive work within a university training programme would never be as explicitly controversial as *Dionysus in 69*, the correlation between audience, performers and context is a constantly developing field of research and innovation, usefully pushing the boundaries of theatrical convention. The current popularity of such work with often younger audiences is based on the thrill that can be generated by removing the layer of protection that usually exists between viewer and performer. This makes necessary a re-establishing of a relationship between all participants and roles.

An Ethics of Interactivity and Immersion

Interactivity in the theatre raises a set of problems on an artistic and logistical level and more importantly on an ethical level. The power that performers hold over an audience cannot be underestimated, and thus theatre-makers, producers and performers have a significant responsibility towards their public, a responsibility which is problematized further in the working relationship that tutors have with students. When looking at immersion and interaction, these aspects need to be adequately reflected. When *Dionysus in 69* was restaged by Rude Mechs in 2009, in order to take part in the work, audiences were required to sign disclaimers agreeing not to sue the company over any physical contact.[5] This reflects a shift in social sensitivities since the performance's inception. When we make work, it is necessary to examine ethical concerns and aspects of health, safety and consent.

More recent practitioners whom students might look at are Signa Sörensen and Arthur Koestler. Under the name SIGNA, the pair direct, produce and act as performers in durational projects in which actors inhabit an environment that functions as the setting for a fiction. In their capacity as directors, they create a framework of a backstory. This sets up relations between the different performers and participants. Some SIGNA performances engage performers and audiences over several days, allowing a spectator to stay over or to return to the event at a later point. The SIGNA concept dictates that no performance moment will ever be repeated, and each performance day that passes simply becomes part of the history that informs the actors' subsequent performance and interaction within the fiction.

A question that arises for forms of interactive theatre that heavily rely on improvisation is how these deal with scenes that involve aspects of intimacy and/or confrontation. This is not without complexity. Professional companies, universities and drama schools are increasingly turning to intimacy choreographers to ensure safe working practices. The method of Tonia Sina, the director of Intimacy Directors International, 'borrows from the protocols of fight direction, with the same allegiance to keeping actors safe in potentially dangerous circumstances.'[6] As Sina has it, 'With stage combat, you can get stabbed in the eye or punched in the face …. This is emotional and mental health, which is just as important.'[7]

What are the alternatives to controlled scene studies and clearly established choreographies which can be employed as preventative measures in the context of a prepared play? What sort of framework can simultaneously keep audiences and performers safe and give them sufficient leeway to allow them to engage in immediate and spontaneous interaction?

The rehearsal process is an important way of allowing performers to get to know their fellow actors in terms of the characters they play and to establish a clear sense of the particular trades, capabilities and boundaries of other group members. Student workshops and rehearsals can usefully draw on an aspect of SIGNA's work, where a codeword allows performers to signal to one another if they wish to dissolve a scene. Through this, individuals can take control of a situation without having to drop out of character, and they are able to end a situation that they might for whatever reason feel uncomfortable with.[8]

Giving spectators (and students) the freedom to choose their own route through a performance and letting them influence the proceedings through their interactions foregrounds experience that is at once structured and individual. The former Pina Bausch dancer Felix Ruckert has created the participatory performance *Secret Service*, in which audience members are blindfolded and individually passed through the hands of 12 dancers. Although these sorts of setups give the spectators a significant level of influence over their experience, spectators are also subject to a substantial amount of manipulation.

After the first level of interaction, spectators get to choose whether they wish to progress to the next level. In the second level, they are handcuffed, and the physical experience becomes more extreme. Ruckert speaks about the individual completely submitting to the piece and how the 'visitor's' body becomes the centre of activity in which ultimately the only choice that remains is to continue or to stop.

> I wish to manipulate the audience, so you have the free decision to go into the show and be manipulated or to not go and not be manipulated. As I try to sell my show I have a strong interest that people enjoy this manipulation. As an artist I also try to challenge them. I think the decision to hand yourself over, to trust completely already demands a lot of courage. Trust and abandon is also the most direct way to learn and to get new information. For curious people, there is a lot of joy in learning, for brave people, there is a lot of joy in challenge. Nothing wrong there.'[9]

In relation to the manipulation that takes place in *Secret Service*, Ruckart quotes Susan Sontag: 'Art is seduction, not rape, and art cannot seduce without the complicity of the experiencing subject.'[10] There are of course many examples of interactivity within performance that do not confront us with the same level of ethical dilemma, but when exploring interaction, it is almost inevitable that students in one way or another will come to question the extent to which such interactions might be taken.

We can highlight issues as well as opportunities that lay within interaction through examination and discussion. Schechner and Sörensen mention the particular importance that improvisation has within their work and describe how their way of working requires an intense preparatory process that allows performers to explore each other's boundaries. Working in an educational context, our duty of care requires us to be particularly sensitive. This is balanced against the need to engage in experimentation and risk-taking that comes with the sort of innovative practice that we wish to foster. We therefore have to consider carefully how we might find ways to facilitate challenging ideas so that these can be explored safely rather than just shutting them down.

Within the context of actor training, this involves teachers asking questions of their/our own practice:

- Is participation voluntary, or are students coerced or otherwise incentivized to participate?
- How might student participants withdraw from any given workshop, exercise or project if they feel uncomfortable?

- Are there particular risks or hazards to participants, either physically, mentally or emotionally, and what might teachers do to guard against them?
- To what extent do our working practices recognize and make adjustments for any potential fear, pain, discomfort or distress felt by participants?
- How do we ensure that any physical contact is safe, ethical and permitted – that students do not feel coerced or unnecessarily pressured into work that is imposed rather than agreed upon?

In short, and not least in the wake of #MeToo revelations, how do ethical considerations apply to actor training and practice?

We are training actors, and that training is inevitably taxing, but if our students are actors, they are also themselves, loaning who they are out to the characters and contexts that training demands. A teaching situation that promotes independent learning will rely on the students' active involvement in a making process, and the above questions form a useful platform when moving towards a discussion of the students' own input. Working in an area that explores boundaries can be thrilling. It also increases the danger that personal limits might be overstepped.

Professional Practice

We want to develop students' confidence and sensitivity through their training. Accordingly, modules that foreground immersion and interaction should provide students with opportunities for exploration and experimentation. An important aspect of providing these can be students coming up with their own ideas and taking responsibility for the choices they make.

At Falmouth University, the professional practice of members of staff informs the way we teach, which in turn impacts the student experience. Bringing current professional practice into the teaching space has many advantages. It also necessitates a shift in tutor perspective. While ethical working relationships are central to professional as well as pedagogical worlds, a key difference is that professional actors have more choice over the projects they sign up for. Of course, actors have to make a living, and compromise is a feature of many working lives. Nevertheless, actors can choose, for example, not to work with a particular director; student actors are rarely afforded this choice. Students are often assigned to a project, tutor and director and the demands of cohort size, and modular assessment means that more often than not, students get what they are given. This cuts both ways, with the directors of student productions having some choice over who plays which part but very little over the cohorts they work with.

Despite these issues, my role as artistic director of Living Structures affords opportunities for students to engage with professional practitioners as an assessable part of their training. Living Structures is a collective of international artists of mixed disciplines, using changing spatial reality as a tool to engage audiences in unusual ways. The company (and by definition our students) work with tangible, physical transformations that shift existing spatial boundaries through a variety of theatrical and architectural devices. As part of the acting programme, I lead modules where students engage with participatory performance, immersive theatre and/or aspects of situated or site-specific performance. In the following section, I will provide an outline of an extended foundational workshop that students undertake at Falmouth. The workshop explores performance environments and situations that promote intimate audience–performer interaction. Working with students in such a context is accompanied by a range of complexities, and members of staff need to monitor their own processes and must in a spirit of respectful collaboration maintain constant awareness of any moments that have the potential to cause students any sense of upset.

Workshop

Interacting Eyes

Our eyes can communicate what is going on inside us, both willingly and unwillingly. This is what people mean when they speak of notions such as people's eyes giving them away or the eyes saying something other than words. Eyes can, of course, also be deceiving, and the gaze, for actors in particular, is often used deliberately to put a point across or prompt a reaction in someone else.

While we might not be able to speak of a body language of the eyes, they are nevertheless an important aspect of communication, and for an actor the expressive potential of their gaze is an important area of training. In a great many circumstances, eye contact is also one of the most direct ways through which an actor connects and communicates with other players. Our ability to read another person's eyes as part of their overall facial expression provides a direct way to assess a situation and to evaluate another person's feelings and intentions.

In a setting in which the notion of the fourth wall is maintained and where an audience witnesses the performance from a removed point of observation, actors use eye contact only to establish their connection to other performers. It is predominantly through the eyes that this illusion is maintained, and as soon as the actor's gaze acknowledges the audience, the fourth wall breaks.

When audience and performer are in a setting of close proximity, the way they relate to one another changes. Fundamentally, some of the same principles for establishing and breaking the fourth wall can be relied upon, namely the way a performer acknowledges or ignores the audience's presence through their gaze. Nonetheless, physical intimacy poses a set of additional challenges for an actor. Close physical proximity can create a level of intimacy that would on a stage normally only exist between actors. An unprepared audience will have markedly different origins of expectation than another actor, who would in one way or another have prepared for an anticipated engagement and interaction. Having to interact with spectators – or, for that matter, having to ignore their presence in the space – is different at close proximity and in situations where performer- and audience-space have not been deliberately segregated or clearly defined.

In a setting of intimacy, the audience is likely to remain an unpredictable element, but actors can prepare themselves for a range of eventualities. When performing in an intimate or one-to-one performance environment, the question of how to deal with eye contact will naturally arise. Given the prominent role that eyes play in interaction, it is vital for actors in training to become confident at using their gaze in close proximity.

As part of immersive and interactive performance modules, students explore the way they use their eyes, working both on direct eye contact and through experiments with looking and seeing in general. Each student is directed to have available to them a section of already-learned dramatic text. This could be a monologue or a dramatic poem. If the session is linked to a script-based production, it makes sense to use text from the production; if work is generated by exploring a thematic context, it makes sense to choose material that is relevant to that text. As the workshop develops, the text will be explored with varying inflections, intonations and intentions in a range of different performance situations. In many ways, a workshop such as this is as basic or advanced as the student actors engaging in it. Working with students three years into their training yields responses which are likely to be deeper, more daring and sustained, and while the tutor's questions and prompts remain the same across all years of a programme, the ways in which students react are often markedly different. The most profound insights often emerge from students when tutors offer them opportunities for investigation rather than learning by rote.

Close Range, Mid Range, Long Range, Beyond Range

For this exercise, students are asked to explore and interact with each other and the performing space, using different proximities and modes of focus. Initially, students are invited to move through the space, led by their eyes exploring the following ranges:

- At close range, we get into close proximity with the subject of our observation. We study tiny marks on the floor, speckles of dust on the skirting board, the pores in someone else's skin or the details of the weave of their clothing.
- At mid range, we most commonly interact with one another; it is the distance we would usually perceive as comfortable for face-to-face communication. Also, many day-to-day tasks, including screen-based activity, lead us to interact with our environment at this level.
- At long range, we shift our gaze to the people most distant from us and look to the furthest areas of the space.
- At beyond range, we look into the distance beyond the confines of the room and look through people.

If students are working outside of a studio environment, the definitions for 'long range' and 'beyond range' should be adapted to the specific location.

Students initially investigate different ways of looking, spending time observing and interacting with the space, using the different gazes. Once participants have explored the space at close range, mid range and beyond range, they move on to the next level. For this, students interact and move around each other, using the different gazes. This part of the workshop engages with looking in different ways and leads to shifting physical proximity between the participants. As part of this, students also use their monologues; depending on the material, this text can be looped. As students interact with one another, they are directed to let the way they use their eyes and the proximity of their interaction affect how they deliver the text; in their interactions, students might speak simultaneously or break up the text to create alternating pauses that allow individuals to listen and respond to one another. To make full use of this work, coach students so that they remain as aware as possible of the different options and modes of interaction that are available to them as they engage with the exercise. Coaching here is more akin to suggestion than direction; nevertheless, a number of instructions follow.

Instructions to Students

- Walk through the space.
- Connect to your breath; feel your feet on the floor.
- Keep walking, but now make sure you see the other people around you (while walking, the group should spread out evenly throughout the space).
- Now allow yourselves to acknowledge one another. Although you *may* nod to or smile at each other, this does not necessarily mean that you *will* overtly nod to or smile at one another. Experiment with different levels of subtlety, primarily using your gaze to find ways to recognize everyone else's presence in the space.
- When your eyes meet with another person in the space, allow yourself to slow down and move together while you encounter each other's gaze. As you are doing this, explore the following:
  - being open and receptive
  - staring inwardly
  - projecting a glare outwards
  - looking at someone
  - looking into someone
  - looking through someone
  - using the eyes as lasers to burn a hole first into the wall and then into each other.

Again, coach students so that they remain aware of different ways they can use their eyes as they engage with the exercise.

The next stage of the exercise is to pair up and experiment with different kinds of looking associated with different intentions (and tensions). Participants might stand still or move as part of this. The workshop leader should initially call out a range of stimulating terms to invite participants to explore a wide array of gazes and to ensure that attention is given to the impact that subtle differences in intention can have on how we look at each other. The following are examples of stimuli that a tutor might use for the exercise:

- standing one's ground against the other
- dominating the other
- projecting aggression against the other
- flirting with the other
- establishing trust with the other
- seducing the other
- conveying one's innocence to the other
- conveying one's submission to the other
- caring for the other
- sympathising with the other
- pitying the other
- curiously observing of the other
- engaging in an inquisition of the other.

Initially, one partner observes the gaze of the other, then the partners mirror each other's intentions and eventually engage in an organic dialogue in which each individual lets what the gaze of the other communicates to them trigger a shift in the quality of their own. Run through this exercises in a variety of different pairings to allow participants to work with different partners.

After experimenting with this for some time, participants start integrating their monologue. When speaking to each other, participants let the intention they communicate through their eyes affect the delivery of their lines. They might want to experiment with complementing and contrasting intentions for the way they look at and speak to one another.

During the next exercise, students are asked to partner up and engage in open and receptive eye contact and to hold this for a significant duration. The intention here is for them to reveal and share themselves with the other through their eyes. It is important to establish a prolonged intimate connection before the next stage of this exercise. I like to describe the meeting of the eyes here as an exchange or a negotiation between giving and receiving that creates a feedback loop in which the act of looking will simultaneously generate and receive visual information.

While both students maintain eye contact for the second stage of this exercise, one student starts speaking to the other and reveals to other something intimate about themselves that is not generally known. It does not matter whether what is told is true or fictional; what is important is that whatever is communicated is done so with sincerity and conviction. Students are informed that what they choose to talk about can affect their partner just as much as themselves and thus to be considerate in what they say. The responsive and improvisational nature of the exercise denies the possibility of in-depth ethical approval before any words are spoken, but students are cautioned to exercise care with themselves and their partners.

Students engaged in a workshop are not abandoning who they are; we might say that they are loaning themselves out to us, but this suggests a division between who they *are* and what we are inviting them to *play*. The reality is not so distinct as this, and tutors need to be both attentive and sensitive to the likelihood that relatively inexperienced actors will be affected by the *as if*, particularly in one-on-one and face-to-face encounters.

Exploring Boundaries of Intimacy

Working in close proximity to spectators raises questions in regard to how far an actor can and, more importantly, *should* go in their interactions with them. The following exercise is a practical exploration, and how far students are prepared to take this enquiry in some ways depends on the make-up of individuals in the group. As mentioned earlier, workshop leaders might anticipate that boundaries would be narrower in a group of students on a university course than with a group of professional actors; this is not to suggest, however, that a workshop leader should relax their attentiveness.

Instructions to the students are as follows:

- Walk through the space.
- Connect to your breath; feel your feet on the floor.

- Keep walking, and make sure you see the others around you; while walking, the group should make sure it is spread out evenly throughout the space.
- When your eyes meet with another person in the space, allow yourself to slow down and move together while you encounter each other's gaze.

Following on from this, students guide each other through the space by using eye contact as well as touch. In this interaction, they are encouraged to explore different modes and levels of intensions. Intensions may vary from making a partner feel safe, conjuring a sense of excitement, building up anticipation or giving them a sense of threat or doom. A light touch on a shoulder could become a comfortable or uncomfortable action, depending on the intention with which this is performed. We might also experiment with the firmness that we use when we touch. Proximity in itself might be experienced as comforting or invasive. After guiding each other, pairs should spend a moment reflecting on their experience before swapping.

Following this, students are to come up with ideas for activities and situations that they would not usually think of engaging in with an audience. Each individual proposes an idea, which is added to a list and discussed with everyone. Students then work in smaller groups formed around common interests that emerged from the discussion.

In order for the exercise to achieve its purpose, students need to settle on activities they can actually do with and to one another rather than for them to 'act out' something at a suggestive level. For example, miming the action of washing someone's hair does not reflect the sort of interaction that we are looking for here and that this workshop demands. If the idea is to wash someone's hair, they will have to create a setup that allows them to actually do this.

Students are not working towards the staging of a scene between performers so much as engaging in this exploration with the aim of creating an experience for a participating audience. This means that the interaction can be prepared, but it will not be possible to fully anticipate or choreograph what will happen. Students must constantly observe and read the person they are interacting with. Students should take turns in taking on the role of audience and can interact and challenge the performer in ways that they can imagine an actual audience might do.

Once groups have had time to test and explore their ideas, they can take turns in performing work to one another and so get a sense of how their material works with an unexpecting participant. It needs to be made clear to all participants that any interaction needs to be kept to a level that is both reasonable and safe and that anybody that participates must be able to step away or ask that the exercise be stopped, at any moment and without having to offer any explanation or apology.

Building on previous exercises, the next task is to work in small groups and to devise a range of experiences for a single audience member. As part of this, groups are given the responsibility to come up with the means to bring their audience into the space, to guide them through the experience and to find a way to transition to the next audience member. Again, it is made clear to students that this exercise does not license all types of behaviour. Spectators need to be respected no less than fellow actors, and the onus here is on creating experiences which are the *right kind of provocation*.

As presentations are repeated for each individual, the time that these take can quickly add up. To reduce waiting times, a couple of presenting groups can be scheduled to show work simultaneously in different parts of the space. In this way, spectators can rotate from one event to the other. It is also advisable to limit the duration that each experience can last to no more than a couple of minutes.

This workshop approach is ideally geared towards performance. A recent example of this was a student production based on Dan Farrelly's translation of Goethe's *Urfaust*. In this immersive/promenade production, Farrelly's text was inspired by Brecht's 1952 and 1953 *Urfaust* productions, and a Brechtian approach significantly informed the performance style and overall aesthetic. Another key aspect was location. The production was staged in and around an old fish factory that was situated by the water right next to the River Fal Estuary.

As part of the generative process for this module, students experimented with a wide range of different audience/performer relationships, integrating a variety of these into the finished work. Different scenes placed audiences and performers in varying performative correlations, and through their actions and interactions, the actors animated the environment, facilitating situations in which spectators were able to access and interact with the space in unexpected ways. The scene in which Faust and Mephisto visit Auerbach's

Tavern, for example, located spectators as guests in a bar where they would meet and drink with the different characters of the play; in Gretchen's bedroom scene, on the other hand, spectators took on the role of intruders mirroring the position of Mephisto, who is secretly spying on Gretchen in her room. To frame the viewing experience in the large open space, students needed to find ways to focus the different scenes. Lighting was an obvious device to create visual boundaries, but as soon as spectators entered a space, physical boundaries became a more effective tool for the definition and segregation of space.

As mentioned at the outset of this chapter, all members of staff teaching on BA acting at Falmouth are engaged in ongoing professional practice; a key aspect of my professional work is the manipulation of physical space as it is experienced by audiences. In the spirit of bringing professional practice into student training, this feeds into my directing of student productions. Rather than setting up a fixed installation environment and having an audience determine their own trajectory through this, my approach focuses on augmenting and animating space in ways that initiate a negotiation between the spectator and the physical environment that allows for a set of varying opportunities and limitations.[11] Different spatial relationships require students to engage with the performance situation through different techniques and approaches. In certain instances, they were able to improvize within the parameters of their characters; at other times, they were led by the script. Interaction between audience and actor ranged from intimate and close-up encounters over the presentation of coarsely performed pantomime-style acts to quasi-naturalistic sections of the play in which actors did not acknowledge the presence of the audience. Experiences gained throughout the workshops significantly informed the work process and approach to interaction with the audience.

The Brechtian technique that sees actors and the characters they embody coexist formed the foundation for much of the performative interaction. In particular, the breaking and establishing of the fourth wall became an important device that allowed student actors to integrate the audience as participants in the play, to engage them conversationally at times and elsewhere to regard them as a collection of Peeping Toms, invading the intimate and personal interactions of the actors but remaining ignored and seemingly unseen.

The company of actors needed to be able to establish the sense of the fourth wall with an audience that was in close physical proximity to them at the same time as adopting an attitude suggestive of a more conventionally removed position. Within the project, students were able to explore the fourth wall as something rather more malleable than the term 'wall' might suggest. In so doing, they were constantly constructing, questioning and fragmenting the division between the planes on which audience and actor operate.

It is a given that students are being trained for twenty-first-century theatre. The training that acting students receive at Falmouth does not isolate them from tradition; it equips them with the skills, attitude and fearlessness to reimagine traditions and to operate in contexts that they will do much to invent.

Notes

1 Artaud cited in Plunka, G. A. (1992) *The Rites of Passage of Jean Genet: The Art and Aesthetics of Risk Taking*. Fairleigh Dickinson Associated University Presses, Inc., p. 133.
2 Schechner, R. (1968) '6 Axioms for Environmental Theatre', *The Drama Review: TDR*, 12(3), Architecture/Environment (spring 1968), pp. 41–64.
3 Schechner, R. (1970) *Dionysus in 69*. Performance Group. New York: Farrar, Straus and Giroux.
4 Schechner, R. (2010) on rites and rituals in *Dionysus in 69*: Online Dramaturgy, published on 20 November 2010. Part 3: https://www.youtube.com/watch?v=bcZvjm6fH-qs&t=2s)(This source is the video of a recorded interview published in three parts. The section that I refer to is in part 3. Links to parts 1 and 2 are included here for readers to access the complete interview:Part 1: https://www.youtube.com/watch?v=fZTcdgjSW-c Part 2: https://www.youtube.com/watch?v=UYhxOvCXm5E
5 https://www.timeout.com/newyork/theater/dionysus-in-69 andhttps://bombmagazine.org/articles/rude-mechanicals/.
6 Collins-Hughes, L. (2017) Need to fake an orgasm? There's an intimacy choreographer for that.' *New York Times*, 15 June 2017:https://www.nytimes.com/2017/06/15/theater/need-to-fake-an-orgasm-theres-an-intimacy-choreographer-for-that.html.
7 Ibid.
8 Sörensen, S. (2017) 'Constructed reality or deconstructed fiction – Immersive strategies in the work of SIGNA' Summer Scriptwriting Camp TAM, Velico Tarnovo (https://www.youtube.com/watch?v=5DwUBeT9v8c).
9 Ruckert, F. Interviewed by Natasa Govedic, 'Questions about Secret Service', *Novi List*, Zagreb 3.7. 2004.

10 Susan Sontag quoted in Ben Chaim. Daphna. (1981)*Distance in the Theatre: The Aesthetics of Audience Response*. Ann Arbor, MI: UMI Research Press, p. 43.
11 Living Structure's performances of *Cart Macabre* and *Varyon* can serve here to contextualize the type of aesthetic values that informed student work on *Urfaust*. In *Cart Macabre*, audiences are separated in groups of four and seated in eight fully enclosed, lightproof wooden carts. Once seated, performers move spectators through a multimedia environment in which carts can be docked onto various installations. Peepholes can be opened from the outside, enabling the audience to view and interact with their environment in multiple ways. Carts can also be connected to other carts, allowing audience members of the varying carts to meet each other as dividing walls are slid aside by the performers. The design of *Varyon* consists of stage architecture which places spectators into an animated environment that transforms the volume and shape of the performance space as the structure moves and morphs around them. Performers move 16 interconnected wall panels to create a variety of different geometrical shapes. The space is further animated by a 360-degree projection mapped onto the surrounding screens. This generates an environment of light and shadow and images, patterns and colours that are accompanied by a multidirectional soundscape. Wall panels also function as swivel doors that allow performers to enter and exit the space from any side of the structure. Core members of Living Structures are Ula Dajerling, Dani d'Emilia, Dugald Ferguson, Klaus Kruse and Verity Standen.

10

Yoga in a Circle: Actor Training Across Borders

Diane M. Sadak

Theatre requires community, and to form strong and meaningful communities, a practice must be forged and used repeatedly as reaffirmation of that community throughout the life of the class, the production or the resident theatre. The old adage of 'two boards and a passion' fails to take into account the large community of actors, designers, technicians and audiences. In the past 20 years of my tenure as a professor of acting and directing, I have watched as student actors have seemed to become stiffer physically and shallower mentally. This is not an attack on intelligence but rather an observation of how our culture and society – through technology and other distractions – have permeated the students' ability to sustain a singular and deep thought, through mindfulness and meditation, and to sustain and stretch into a deeper physical relationship to their own increasingly stagnant bodies. Therefore, we find ourselves with a community of people coming together with a common course or production intention but without the skills in which to create, locate and repeat a combined physical and mental practice which will go a long way towards solving the issues of attention and intention, both necessary skills for the actors' ability to focus on themselves and others. Yoga in a circle is an imminently doable and repeatable practice which, when taught and reinforced daily by the facilitator, creates a deeply rich community with the ability to focus the actor's entire instrument on their daily work.

Yoga has enjoyed an enormous resurgence of practice within the United States in the past 15 or so years. Yoga studios are in every strip mall, and a wide array of practices, from Ashtanga to Hatha to Bikram and many more, are available. However, as is true with many such 'workout' styles which enjoy an almost fad-like following with a quick rise in popularity, much of the work by teachers is inconsistent in its integrity, focused on the surface of the practice and expensive. As yoga entered mainstream exercising fads in the United States, it was also finding its way into theatre programmes throughout the country. It is most frequently used as a warm-up for acting classes, and my contention is that when yoga is relegated to designated movement classes and used primarily as a warm-up, the opportunity for deeper exploration into both the eight limbs common to all forms of yoga and a serious engagement into several of those limbs within many performance-driven classes is lost.

Yoga is an ancient art and practice with complicated and varied development. Some forms of yoga are several thousand years old, while new forms are still being developed today. For the purposes of this chapter, I am focusing on a few older and more established practices: Kundalini, Hatha, Ashtanga and Vinyasa. The differences in the primary focus of each make this group of yoga forms relatively broad and inclusive and able to be extrapolated to all of yoga.

By way of broad definition, Kundalini is a rigorous practice involving movement of the spine while using a deep breathing practice. Hatha is a gentle form of yoga. It is focused not on flow but rather in holding poses for prolonged periods of time to work more deeply into the stretches. Ashtanga is several thousand years old and was developed as an exercise practice in India for young male student monks who needed an athletic practice to drain them enough to allow them to work on their studies and meditation practices. It is arguably the most physically difficult form of yoga practice. Vinyasa Power Flow integrates a semi-set series of poses in a constant flow, performed in unison with a deep and unison breathing practice. In Bikram yoga, the room is heated to 40°C (104°F), and humidity is placed up to 33% to allow for a great deal of sweating. The 90-minute class is the same wherever in the world it takes place: two pranayama breathing exercises, bracketing 24 asanas (body poses) done twice in each class.

There are parts of each form of yoga in my study; it can be up to each teacher to find their own practice with whatever community they find themselves working in. It is also important to note that no prior experience is necessary, neither is any particular level of physical capability. No acting students need be excluded from this practice, neither need any teachers. A series of flow-based choreography which may take as little as five or as many as 20 asanas/poses in the set may be found all over social media. With actual, live, daily practices through sites like gaia.com or less formal teaching of a specific series on YouTube or Pinterest, a teacher can teach themselves a wide array of yoga 'salutations' beyond the variations on sun salutations. In this way, a teacher also need not have a background in yoga practice in order to learn a series which they then may impart to the students they are working with.

Yoga is not new to the theatre. Late in Stanislavski's career, he spent time in India and found a piece to his methodological puzzle in terms of how the actor integrates inner life and outer form. This work was buried for a long time, as it was considered a dangerously spiritual promotion within a strictly communist society. But in fact, Stanislavski, while working on *Uncle Vanya*, first came to realize the way attention may easily slip outside of *his* metaphorical circle and found the asanas and pranayama of yoga to be of great benefit when it came to keeping a cast focused. Stanislavski did not limit himself, however, to verbal rules for the teaching of truthfulness on the stage. In 1906, in Hamburg, where he was playing the part of Doctor Astrov, he found his mind wandering to a conversation into which he had fallen between acts. The slip of attention set him to work to discover methods to prevent this dropping out of the cycle of creative imagination on the stage. He found a hint in the practices of the wise men of the Buddhist religion – and thenceforth he required his actors to practise long psychophysical exercises as a means of cultivating concentration.[1]

It has only been in the past 25 years that Stanislavski's writings on his yoga practice have started being translated and the applications to his method widely studied. However, attempts at merely tagging on some yoga stretches – asanas – and perhaps breathing practices – pranayama – tend to be understood only in the most rudimentary ways. In this chapter, I offer a deeper way into the integration of yoga with the acting community, intentionally looking at both the individual actor and the community of practitioners. This community could be a class, a workshop, a cast rehearsing, or even an entire programme-wide academic pedagogy, where this practice could be used in so-called lecture classrooms as well as performance spaces. In fact, yoga in a chair is a widespread practice being used in aging communities, restoration practices and even in some forward-thinking businesses.

Traditional practice is front facing, as are many studio, scene study and lecture courses, with the 'expert' teacher at the front and students lined up on their mats facing front, at times with a mirror and at times without. In better studios, the teacher and assistants walk through the classes making adjustments, or assists, to students as the work continues. While this is efficient in terms of the numbers of people who can practice in one space at one time, it forces the practice into a solo endeavour, the pedagogical approach being 'what happens on your mat is your perfect practice', with little or no awareness of the community of practitioners. An interesting exception to this is in Vinyasa Power Flow classes, where breathing is deep, audible and in unison. Although it is still front facing, by merely walking into a Vinyasa class in progress, the energy of community awareness is palpable in ways that it is not in other trainings. Bikram, for example, the yoga which heats the room to 40°C (104°F) and pushes up the humidity at the same time to encourage sweating, has a unison and identical practice every class in every studio in the world, yet the focus is entirely on deepening your own practice. This consists of 24 asanas framed by two pranayama practices. Students work in front of a mirror, which further pushes the practice towards self-identification and a sense of competition with others in the class who may be further along in their practice than you are.

Through my years of exploration of yoga in a theatre setting, I have turned the room into itself: yoga in a circle. The circle, which in yoga practice creates a living mandala, represents a life cycle and the pattern of the universe. Circles are found throughout the natural world, have been the community form of peoples throughout the world for tens of thousands of years and indeed are believed to symbolize and manifest the unification of body, soul/imagination and mind. In the aboriginal practices of Australia 40,000 years ago – as preserved in dream paintings – and currently in tribal communities as disparate as the Native Americans and contemporary Afghani tribes, circles are the principle layout of the community in meeting.

Whether you are practising in unison – which is the focus in this chapter – or in a less flow-oriented and differentiated set of poses, turning the yoga class into a circle forces an exponentially higher awareness of fellow practitioners; ideally, this encourages a dual focus: on both self and other simultaneously. This addresses the fundamental issue of actors: to focus on a high quality of work which demands the best of the actors' personal practice while asking the actor to work with awareness, deep attention and intention towards the group.

For yoga to work successfully, it must not be considered as merely a warm-up tagged onto the beginning of each class but as an integrated part of the work, whatever the subject of the class may be. When students enter the work space, the space must be heightened and regarded as somehow sacred, a 'temenos' in which we work.[2] From the moment we enter the room, we must turn off our phones, take off our shoes and socks and get our mat, placing it into the circle with fellow classmates. I suggest keeping the between/before class talking to the outside of the classroom door. That way, there is a notable and differentiated energy in the space from the moment it is entered; then there is mindfulness to each stage of the preparation for the yoga practice and not merely a sudden and disconnected beginning on the downbeat of the yoga itself.

Building Unity

In the theatre, there is a lot of discussion about community, teams, groups and casts – many words to describe the same phenomenon: a disparate group of people coming from their own lives and stories and finding enough trust, common ground and shared objective to work to their highest potential as one. In acting classes, through a few ice breakers or theatre games, learning names and finding the laughter in the group, a false sense of community often ensues. There is nothing inherently wrong with this work. But it is shallow, and if truly tested in the fire of differentness, we find that under the easy experience of community, all tested groups will retreat to their own bubble of comfort, culture, political, social and religious norms, and then trust falls apart. Thus, we're left with this question: how do we truly develop a community of learners in which, as educator Parker Palmer says, 'the community of truth is practiced'?[3]

Developing community takes time. There are no quick fixes to developing a community. We sometimes find it in a cast, because a prolonged rehearsal process and a common goal of mounting a specific production provide enough repetitive structure to test and deepen the individual actors into a group of some meaningfulness. It is possible in ensemble theatres, as we have seen repeatedly and historically with companies like the Moscow

Art Theatre, where plays were commonly rehearsed for up to two years. But how do we, as facilitators of actor training and in the short amounts of time provided by classroom constraints, teach community and team building? And why are they important?

They are important because actors are a nomadic people who more frequently than not move from show to show, from theatre to theatre, from cast to cast. It is a truly fortunate actor who finds themselves with more than eight or nine weeks in one place with the same people. It is therefore incumbent upon each actor to learn to enter and trust a community of players so that the process of true team building is given a leg up within the experiences of actors who have practised trust in community. If yoga in a circle has been practised previously in an actor's training, it may serve the actor long after that community has dispersed.

Teachers often point out that they barely have the time to teach their own syllabi, let alone add team building to their curriculum. But it is my contention that even 10–15 minutes at the top of each class can make all the difference in the world in the development of a truly significant classroom or cast community. Yoga in a circle is one time-tested way of building community.

Experience shows that no matter how resistant in the early phases a classroom is to the imposition of the yoga practice, by the end of the semester, student actors have grown in focus, physical strength, flexibility, dual awareness and vocal openness. In fact, many of them will practise on their own or with a smaller group even once the course is over because the value of that work in their lives has taken root. In short, it is worth the time commitment of a few minutes at the top of each class, rehearsal or other community work outside of performance to commit to the practice of yoga as team building. In an acting class, where we ask such vulnerability of our students, this practice has enormous value in shortcutting the honest experience of trust and comfort with their fellow players.

Incremental Development

There is a pragmatic reason to work in a circle. The teacher is part of the circle, simultaneously teaching and practising with their group. It is easier to see everyone working, evaluating abilities and comprehension and teaching at a rate of incremental development that keeps the community together.

This way, the first lesson of otherness is introduced: sensitivity to their community and the knowledge that the work is successful only if everyone is successful at some level. This does *not* mean that everyone is practising with the same core balance, the same level of flexibility or even the same past experience with yoga. It merely means that we don't leave anyone behind to struggle alone. Those students to whom yoga comes naturally must rein themselves in, and those having difficulty have clear incentive to work at their highest present capabilities. This clear balancing act is common to all actors' art. It also allows an incremental development from each part of the teacher's adding yoga beyond the physical forms of the asanas – adding breath and life-force practice of pranayama, adding mantra from the simplest om to a short unison phrase and then adding mindfulness, which I will refer to as attention and intention. Finally for the purposes of classroom work, adding a short period of meditation practice to the beginning of the asanas adds a level of depth and complexity applicable to many aspects of solid actor training.

The Integrity of the Circle

Forming a circle is an act of beauty, awareness and adjustments to others within your circle. It cannot be taken for granted that the simple prompt to get in a circle will create a circle which is perfect, complete and, to use a phrase from Buddhist practise, lacking in nothing. To begin this, ask the students what constitutes a beautiful circle, one with integrity and beauty. A circle is an easy form to attempt, but a true circle is an act of true mindfulness. It's not enough to stand in 'my spot' and expect the circle to form around me. Neither is it acceptable to have people hanging outside the circle or pushing their way in. Students must be equidistant from one another: each person's adjustment and shifting effects the formation of the entire circle. So, time needs to be taken to practise forming the circle. I call these steps making the foreign habitual and the habitual beautiful. Those stages mimic entirely the process of the actors' memorization of their texts. There must be a sense of ownership of the circle. The teacher owns the initial coming to awareness, not letting the students get away with a circle which is merely 'good enough'. After all, what level of performance is 'good enough' for an actor's work? At every moment in this work, the simplest of tasks may be tied to the actor's process. In that way, the teacher shifts the ownership of the circle from themselves as facilitators of a beautiful circle to the students, who, through mindfulness and a sense of pride, create something of value from which to begin the downbeat of the yoga practice that is created without teacher intervention.

This effort in finding the integrity and beauty of the perfect cycle is not preparation for the work to begin; it is an inherent and fully realized part of the work of yoga. There can be no more separation from the attention and intention of forming this circle than there is in practising the asana flow. Although this may seem a random and picky part of the practice, it traces its roots to the very meaning of the word 'yoga', which is to yoke. In this case, yoking the students to the structure of the circle provides a clear anchor that grounds the actor's own freedom. This paraphrases a concept that I learned while training with Anne Bogart and the SITI company – I now use my phrase 'right structure equals freedom'. A solid parallel to the forming and performing of the yoga practice is the conceptualization of actors as athletes. Any actor who has worked their way through five acts of Shakespeare, or a rigorous musical, knows that it takes great physical and vocal stamina to provide an experience to an audience which is as vibrant in Act 1 as it is in Act 5.

There are many parallels between actors and athletes: both require strength and endurance; both require an understanding of the rules of the 'game'; and both must have excellence in their own play as they do in the ensemble play. Indeed, the freedom to breathe into the work and make it alive arrives only if the structure is firmly understood and in place for each member of the team. Although the phrase of choreographed asana flow is relatively short compared to a game, or even a play within a game, it is the practice of a little piece being done deeply through repetition that the value of yoga is found.

Asanas

The first step in the process is asanas, or physical poses. If I am using my yoga in a circle as a warm-up, I use one of a wide array of flow sequences to create something akin to choreography, because it can be memorized, allowing students' minds to become free for future parts of the yoga process. It must also be a self-contained flow, which may be repeated from as little as three to as many as 12 times, depending on the goals of the teacher. It is critical that two things happen: (1) the teacher must begin the work in the circle, with the students learning the work, and (2) the teacher must *leave* the circle once the asana sequence is taught so that the unison work of the students' flow is not practised by leaning on the teacher. This allows the teacher to side coach, make physical adjustments and make sure there is effort at an equivalent level within the community. It generally takes about three to four classes working for 20–30 minutes to put the asanas fully into the students' bodies.

While the students work on asanas, teachers should address the concept of attention. Attention, while a critical part of the actors' process, rarely finds a practice in the daily lives of student performers. I introduce attention as the 'vertical' practice, working from ground to god, encouraging simultaneously both a grounding and a lifting of the body and energy. It demands that within the ground-to-god practice of attention, the objective is the best self. How do students, coming from a wide variety of places and situations just before class, find a quick way to drop into the practice of attention? An asana flow is an excellent way not only to get the individual students to begin focusing attention on their best self but also to balance that singular practice with the unison of the group. If used daily, the students understand their role at the top of class: they get their mats; they form their circle; and they prepare themselves for the start of the practice.

Flock of Birds, School of Fish

To say to a class that we are all leaders and simultaneously all followers usually elicits looks somewhere between the sceptical and the dumbfounded. But this is at the core of what we as actors must come to realize. It's a double-edged sword: you are free in the sense that you *are* empowered to no longer be beholden to a teacher–student or parent–child relationship, but you are responsible for your own work within the unison of the community. At the point, where the teacher has taught and led the asana practice, there will be a moment in time when it is apparent that the practice will not begin unless the teacher begins it. To rectify this, the teacher must remove themselves from the circle and take some rigorous time to practise the aforementioned concept of no leaders, no followers and all leaders, all followers. Think of going to an aquarium and watching schools of fish. Without any evident external cues, the school is able to change direction on a dime, no matter how large or small the number of fish. Similarly, look up into the sky at migrating birds. A flock of birds also is able to change direction without any seeming external cues or prompts, and no one bird begins the change of direction. It is my experience that we, as our animal brothers and sisters, also have these same abilities. The only difference is that it has not been practised or encouraged in the human experiment. Neuron pathways to this instinct die off or lie dormant. For yoga in a circle to be truly effective for the community of acting practitioners, the introduction of a flock of birds or a school of fish must be translated into the practice of unison forms.

Within that unison form, the downbeat – the moment of actual beginning – must be honed and practised. Thus, the teacher watches from outside the circle, and if they can see a single student start the movement, the work is stopped, and the students begin again. This process of practising the downbeat of the work is critical to a true practice of ensemble. Because the student actors genuinely do not believe that what is being asked of them is possible, the teacher is quick to find the students who are fidgety and need to make something happen: the natural leaders and extroverts. Simultaneously, it becomes apparent which students are afraid to be wrong and will therefore never initiate: they are the followers, the introverts. How does one bring these two disparate personalities together? There is no shortcut, only practice, and there are days early in the asana work when all that is practised on a particular day is how to begin with all leaders and all followers working as one. It is slow but critical work, because there comes a time when the teacher catches them being successful and side coaches a resounding 'Yes!' to the group, encouraging this moment to be the definition of community awareness and agreement in how they begin.

This is a breakthrough moment, with students learning the practice of awareness of and responsibility to each other, not to a teacher. Once it occurs one time, it will begin to be the norm for the ensemble. It always begins tentatively and slowly. The teacher, as facilitator, can help the process along by speaking of notions such as awareness of others, a soft focus looking into the circle and both trust and risk. It is only when all of these elements are present that the unison downbeat can become a permanent and critical part of the work of yoga in a circle.

Pranayama

Prana, roughly translated, means both breath and life force. Since energy is difficult to make concrete, using breath practice adds a whole new level to the deepening experience of the yoga flow. Kundalini yoga has many, many prana practices, most involving rigorous work with the spine. One other way into prana is through Vinyasa's unjaii breathing, roughly translated as 'hero's breath' or 'victorious breath'. It is an audible, athletic and unison breath practice which lies well against the asana flow already being explored. Adding to the output and intake of energy being exchanged, we have an awareness of our vertical selves, and we extend now to the horizontal focus of Other. In a circle, you are placed firmly in the sight of your community. Students already have a step 1 awareness of vertical self, so it stands to reason that the next awareness would be the addition of the horizontal practice of Otherness.

While the vertical requires *attention* to the best self within the flow, adding pranayama energizes the room exponentially, encouraging another layer of unison practice and thereby setting an awareness of their *intention* of sending out an objective, a thought, a tangible focus to otherness both within the circle and within the community of the others which each of us bring into any room we enter. Asking students to set a separate intention for each completion of a single pass through the flow asana again deepens and hones the actors' need to find deeper and deeper skills in focus and imagination. At first, prana will hurt the quality of the asanas, but the asanas rapidly catch up as the pranayama becomes internalized. As with any form considered a 'practice', there is no 'mastering yoga', but merely a deepening and heightening of one's own abilities within a framework which has an essentially unreachable ideal form.

Attention and Intention

Here we reach an acting practice crossroads. Every actor knows that to succeed they must memorize their lines; memorize their blocking; find the objectives, tactics and actions for their character; and work to their highest capabilities as a solo artist. This is the vertical/attention practice. Simultaneously, each actor must be trained into a greater awareness of other scene partners, cast members and audience. This is the horizontal/intention practice.

For the actor to be wholly successful onstage, the vertical and horizontal must constantly exist in tandem, each as important as the other. In our yoga practice, we create a situation where the same dual focus must exist. This is a critical point in the yoga practice for the actor. We look at the ground-to-god, vertical and the horizontal lines to otherness and intention, and they intersect in the actors' centre. It is both conceptual and physical; the actor can quite strongly feel the dual, simultaneous occurrence of attention and intention in their core. Strengthening the core, then, becomes the second critical area of acting practice: focus, to be aided and practised through yoga in a circle. Here we also easily identify why the circle is a more successful classroom configuration than the front-facing standard of most yoga classes. To practise intention, having the community turned inwards to itself gives a tangible and close set of other actors towards which intentions may be set. As expected, every time a new aspect is added to the practice, the other already introduced elements will drop back and slightly fall apart. Side coaching from a place of encouragement and awareness is vital to bringing the practitioners through those bumps in the road to a fuller and deeper practice with the new elements added.

Mantra

When the aforementioned elements have had time to settle into each practitioner's instrument, the practice of mantra may be added. Mantra is prayer. Without a denomination or the constraints of religious organization, mantra has the broadest possible ability to be very simple within a much more complex vocal practice. Considering cross-cultural work, it is also possible to identify a pre-verbal sound as mantra, as made evident with the word 'om'. Om is the foundation of mantra. And depending on the class and the objectives of the facilitator, mantras from om through to entire repetitive sentences become possible. The more complicated the mantra, the more challenging the balance of focus and objective. There are countless mantras in the yoga lexicon, many leading back to the roots of each practice, wherever in the world the practice was developed and whatever the intention is at the core of the particular yoga form. How mantra is introduced to a community of performers is delicate. It is not uncommon for a certain percentage of students to bristle at anything which is perceived to be 'spiritual' or in conflict with their own faith. It is for this reason that – with student actors – I keep to the pre-verbal sound 'om'. It opens their vocal instrument, does not require memorization and is user-friendly across cultures. It is widely considered throughout the world to be the first uttered sound of the universe, and it thereby encompasses the vibrations of the universe.

Mantras may be used in a variety of ways. I find an optimal use of mantra is to bracket the asana/pranayama practice. We as a community come to stillness and simultaneously chant a long, extended tone on the syllable om. The work continues as before. At the end of the practice, however, we add a rolling om. The rolling om takes the unison out of the practice, and each student chants three oms as long as they can, breathing when they need to. The result is a powerful and musical statement of presence which begins in unison but ends in a trailing off of voices a few at a time until the community has returned to silence.

Mantra cannot be underestimated in its level of difficulty for the student. The voice is the most vulnerable of our instruments, and many people who are comfortable in their own skins become frozen in the face of even the simplest of sounds. It is delicate to add the voice, and gentleness on the part of the facilitator is key to the successful addition of mantra, even to the point of returning to the circle and leading the group in mantra practice before once again removing oneself from the circle to side coach and assist in deepening and correcting asanas.

It is my experience that starting with a simple pre-verbal sound is the most successful way into mantra, but once that foundation has been established and a level of vocal comfort enshrouds the community, mantra can go in many different directions: short, repeated sentences or a longer, community-specific piece of text. And instead of bracketing the practice, mantra may be an aspect of the yoga which flows along with the asana and pranayama. It is usually at this stage of learning where I let the class settle for a number of days or weeks, depending on how often the group meets and how much commitment the class has to yoga. To reiterate, at this point we have established the following:

1. asana
2. pranayama
3. focus – attention/intention
4. mantra.

Four limbs of yoga is a significant change from the general yoga practice throughout the United States and other countries where getting beyond asana to pranayama is often all that is touched upon. It lays firmly in a parallel track to the actors' process:

1. body and movement strengthening and deepening
2. breath practice and finding the actors' instrument in extending and strengthening breath over time
3. focus, which is a performative combination of the actors' intention and attention to their working objectives
4. text, which develops a comfort with the pre-verbal and verbal voice, the opening sound.

Four components of acting, being daily and simultaneously given a form, a tangible practice and an outlet for the entire community.

Meditation and Mindfulness

Once the teacher senses that the first four elements of the yoga practice have been fully embedded in the community, it is time to add the fifth and final element of the practice: meditation mindfulness. It is astonishing how far away we have gone from the ability to embody Stanislavski's 'art of doing nothing'. Short attention spans, constant attachment to electronics and ever-prevalent outside stimulation are merely some of the factors working against the actor in their ability to feel comfortable in their own skin with the event of an awake and focused stillness. How do we create a practice in the training which guides the actor back to themselves in a way that they are comfortable with over a prolonged period of time in awake and focused stillness? We know the value to the actor. We know it may be a requirement of the actor in the context of performing a play. Yet we spend almost no time on the art of doing nothing. Adding meditation to the yoga-in-a-circle practice creates a daily practice of the art of doing nothing in a mindful and highly awake state.

Doing nothing is a sensitive and difficult practice. In their initial experience, students often find their minds actually more stimulated and active, which is the Zen concept of 'monkey mind'. Sitting in stillness nearly drives students to distraction, and all the actors' habits and patterns will surface in the most uncomfortable of ways. Scratching their noses, playing with their hair, tugging at their shirts, shifting postures and peeking around the circle are all typical early responses to the introduction of meditation mindfulness practice. The teacher, outside the circle, is there to merely bear witness to the meditation process. No side coaching or adjustment need be undertaken. The best response to trouble with meditation mindfulness is the teacher providing patient consistency of experience and the student incrementally building it from a relatively short period of meditation – I start with two minutes – and adding a minute or two at a time to anywhere from five to ten minutes before the yoga asanas, depending on the time at one's disposal. But a mere five minutes at the top of the course before the asana practice will reap enormous benefits for the actor in dropping into a stillness and a quiet, awake mindfulness which many students in this millennium have never experienced before. Many are startled at how their mind quiets, how their body finds stillness and how time drops away. The two minutes that seemed like forever at the beginning of the practice becomes an easy and desired five to ten minutes practised every class or rehearsal.

The introduction of meditation, as with mantra, must be separated from notions of religion or a specific spiritual practice and instead translated to the actors' process. That way, students do not feel as though they are being corralled into a spiritual practice which is at odds with their own. Once that is explained and understood, allow a minute in the circle for the many adjustments, creaks and stretches that students feel they need to make to settle into the meditation posture. Almost any posture is acceptable, except that permission to lie down on their mats may cause students to drift mentally and even fall asleep. Sitting in a posture which is set and identical for every member of the group is ideal, but if there are students with knee problems or weight issues which make crossing the legs distractingly difficult, an alternative of sitting on one's knees with their hands on their laps is possible. The focus of the eyes, which need to remain open (actors don't perform with their eyes closed!) should be at a 45-degree angle to the floor, keeping the desire to peek around the circle to a minimum. To deter fidgeting, hands should remain loosely on their lap; or if the teacher is comfortable with bringing the following exercise into the group, they can use a mudra – hand position – which may be something as simple as having students create an O with their thumbs and fingers and then place that position in the middle of their lap, which is a helpful way to unify the group and make sure that the hands have a set place to be.

Once the minute of preparation has finished, strike a literal tone that marks the beginning of the practice. All is stillness and silence until you strike another tone to release the students from the meditation practice and cue them to stand and prepare for the asana practice. Teachers will find that this short addition of practice goes a long way to placing the mental and physical presence of the students in the same vein at the same moment as the asana practice begins. If a teacher does not have time to add meditation to the beginning of the yoga practice, perhaps add a week-long unit on meditation practice to the calendar. The art of doing nothing is an invaluable skill for an actor, and it must be tended and given space to happen and time to practise.[4]

In conclusion, I suggest that the stronger the psychophysical practice through the lens of yoga as performed on a daily basis, the deeper that the focus, listening, trust, attention and intention will blossom in any given community. Additionally, although the following is not the primary focus, the physical body will grow in strength and flexibility to provide the base for more advanced levels of movement training and a groundwork establishment of the observation of actor as athlete.

With a confident teacher/facilitator at the helm, a community of truth and integrity will grow and provide the sacred space, the *temenos*, from which to propel an accelerated bonding and depth of practice. Yoga, when turned in on itself in the circle of practitioners, takes the healthy practices of asana, pranayama, mantra and meditation mindfulness and builds a community that daily experiences and reinforces each actor as both a leader and a follower, both a learner and a facilitator. Teaching the teacher how and when to enter the circle and then to leave the circle and become a side coach also changes the regular academic or yoga classroom of teacher at the helm and the learners all facing just one 'expert' member of the community.

This work may be successfully applied to many fields outside of acting and ends only at the limits of an educator's imagination and willingness to open themselves to change.

Notes

1 Wegner, Henry W. (1976) 'The Creative Circle: Stanislavski and Yoga', *Educational Theatre Journal*, 28 (1), pp. 85–89.
2 Franck, Frederick (1981) *Art as a Way: A Return to the Spiritual Roots*. New York: Crossroad Publishing Company.
3 Palmer, Parker (2007) *The Courage to Teach: Exploring the Inner Landscape of a Teacher's Life*. San Francisco: Jossey-Bass.
4 Stanislavski, Konstantin (1989) *An Actor Prepares*. London & New York: Routledge.

Part III

The Body and the Word

11

The Architecture of Action: Late Stanislavski in Contemporary Practice

Hugh O'Gorman

Introduction

The mission of the California State University Long Beach (CSULB) acting programme, one with roughly 200 majors, is twofold: (1) train pre-professional students in the art of acting, and (2) train accomplished mid-career professional actors in the pedagogy of performance. The bachelor of arts (BA) and bachelor of fine arts (BFA) teach young students how to act, to demystify and concretize the creative craft of imaginative self-transformation; the master of fine arts (MFA) teaches seasoned actors how to teach others to do this. For each programme, the long-term goal remains the same: ownership of craft. There are two essential foundational requirements to arriving at eventual mastery:

1. Actors need to learn to read a dramatic text for the specific purposes of acting—that is, to divine the dramatic action embedded in the source material.
2. Actors need to know exactly what they are doing when they act—that is, how to play action.

Stanislavski's active analysis is used at CSULB as the vehicle to accomplish these goals. Via this method, actors are taught first how to read a text for the necessary dramatic action on the page and then how to translate that action to a playable action in performance. This multilevel task is achieved via a process known as active analysis. Once students have learned these essential components of the craft, ample opportunity is given for them to practise both. Stanislavski's 'most brilliant student',[1] Michael Chekhov, wrote that 'Repetition is the growing power',[2] meaning that actors practice to build a practice of lifelong learning; therefore a comprehensive, rigorous and repeatable process, one with ample opportunity to exercise the craft, is required to lead students to personal ownership of the work. Accordingly, a production-heavy environment is provided at CSULB via the auspices of our production arm, the California Repertory Company, replete with numerous main-stage productions, smaller studio shows and student-generated laboratory performances, across all ages and experience levels. This chapter describes some of the tools used to accomplish these goals, all of which are grounded in active analysis and its accompanying architecture of action.

I must acknowledge my sources for this material. I am indebted to Viacheslav Dolgachev, currently the artistic director of the New Drama Theatre of Moscow, former producing director of the Moscow Art Theatre and honoured artist of Russia for sharing valuable material with American theatre artists during his workshops at the Actors Center in New York City and in Los Angeles. I also acknowledge J. Michael Miller, the founding director of the Actors Center in New York City and its indispensable and inspiring Teacher Development Program (TDP), currently being offered by the *National Alliance of Acting Teachers*. I wish too to acknowledge the teachers and colleagues with whom I have studied acting and whose teaching has deeply affected my own practice: Jack Clay, Joanna Merlin, Earle Gister, Lloyd Richards, Ron Van Lieu, Mala Powers, Mark Jenkins, David Zinder and Alexandra Billings; my performance faculty colleagues at CSULB, namely Ezra Lebank and Andrea Caban; as well as my cochair of the National Alliance of Acting Teachers, the head of acting at the University of Arkansas Fayetteville, distinguished professor Amy Herzberg. Lastly, I would like to acknowledge associate dean Sharon Marie Carnicke of the University of Southern California's School of Dramatic Arts. Sharon's dedication to Maria Osipovna Knebel's work through scholarship and instruction has been essential to my understanding of active analysis.

Active Analysis

Over the final stretch of Stanislavski's career as artistic director of the Moscow Art Theatre (MAT), he developed a multi-pronged, holistic acting process called active analysis of the play and the role, colloquially known as active analysis.[3] It is composed of two fundamental parts: cognitive analysis, and physical analysis.[4] Stanislavski never formally published on the subject, and little is known outside Russia about either aspect of his actor training system. Active analysis is often mistakenly understood as the method of physical actions. While similar in some ways, these approaches represent very different veins of Stanislavski's final efforts. To this day, certainly in the United States, Stanislavski's later oeuvre remains cloaked in mystery.[5]

For the purposes of this chapter, we can say that the method of physical actions was the component of Stanislavski's experimentations that most suited the demands of Soviet doctrine.[6] After his death, Stanislavski's acolytes at the MAT named this alternative approach the method of physical actions precisely because the highly physical aspect of the technique aligned with Soviet dogma.[7] This physical approach dismissed many of the deeper psychological aspects of acting represented in some of Stanislavski's early work, as well as the use of human 'energy' (or terms such as *prana, chi, ki, spirit* or *life force*) as a component of the actor's craft.

However, artists from an earlier era of the MAT, such as Michael Chekhov and Leopold Sulerzhytski, championed the use of these very aspects and their corresponding nomenclature. Chekhov unapologetically used the term 'energy work' in his approach, and even went so far as to acknowledge the metaphysical and spiritual aspects of acting.[8] After Stanislavski's death, the method of physical actions became the official government-sanctioned approach to acting as professed by the MAT.[9] Active analysis was forced underground. It is only in recent years that this important work has come into greater consciousness and practice, thanks in part to translations of writing by Maria Osipovna Knebel and Boris Zon.

The approach that Stanislavski advocated from 1934 onward was decidedly that of active analysis.[10] This dynamic, practical and imaginative approach leads the actor to profound and inspired ownership over performance; it incorporates the psychophysical approaches of many of Stanislavski's former students and colleagues at the MAT and its respective studios, including Michael Chekhov, Yevgeny Vakhtangov, Vsevolod Meyerhold and perhaps most importantly, Maria Knebel, who coined the term active analysis of the play and the role.[11] Fundamentally, active analysis is a process composed of two steps: cognitive analysis, where the actor reads the texts for its inherent dramatic action and its corresponding events, and physical analysis, where through a process of improvised études, the actor translates the action from page to performance. Although taking different forms at different times, both stages of this process are grounded in action, which lies at the heart of active analysis and all performance.

Acting is Action

The actor's charge is to animate the 'human condition' under imaginary circumstances. Actors are professional human beings, behavioural alchemists breathing life into an author's text through the characters they perform. As far as back as Aristotle, dramatic theorists have understood that character is born out of action. Actors are called 'act-ors' because their work is to lift the text into action. They are not called 'feel-ors', or 'intention-ors', or 'tactic-ors', or any other name, for good reason; the actor's work is steeped in action. How actors discuss what they do—action—is vital; as American acting teacher Earle Gister said, "How you talk about your work, is how your work will happen."[12]

All roads for the actor either originate from, or return to, action. As Hamlet says in his advice to the players: "Suit the action to the word, the word to the action."[13] However, an actor cannot arrive at a particular action if they don't first know how to read a script for the action they must inhabit. Actors need to know how to identify and comprehend the varied dramatic events embedded in the text since it is their job to make those events happen. Actors encounter scripts not as an intellectual exercise but as a dynamic, artistic process that injects palpable life and energy into the text, facilitating the translation from ink into human behaviour. For the actor, action exists on at least two planes: the script and performance. Stanislavski developed a tool for actors to mine the script for action in order to realize their professional and artistic responsibilities in performance.

The Two Actions

There are at least two types of action that an actor must work with: the page and the stage. We can call these two actions: invisible action and visible action.[14] As Stanislavski divided the actor's work into two parts—work on self and work on the role—so too does British theatre director and acting theorist Declan Donnellan split the actor's process into invisible work and visible work.[15] Invisible work is the part of the actor's process that the audience never sees, the preparation. Visible work is the performance the actor gives onstage—or in front of the camera—that the audience observes.

It follows that action for the actor can be divided into the same subcategories: invisible action and visible action. Invisible action is the action that the playwright strategically weaves into the text. The actor's job is to interpret this textual action, to read the blueprint for clues on how to inhabit their role. They must do this *before* they get on their feet. Visible action is that action which the actor performs, either in front of an audience or camera. The first action is the textual manifestation of the author's energy; the second action is the energy generated by the actor to lift the action off the page. It is therefore 'visible' action, because the audience witnesses it. One can say that there are two types of action with which actors must concern themselves:

1. invisible action—the action on the page
2. visible action—the action on the stage

Invisible action is part of the first stage of active analysis and must be dealt with upon initial contact with the source material. The text must be read artistically, thoughtfully and soulfully to make manifest the author's intentions. Stanislavski developed a precise and practicable method to interpret the flow of action from the author's given circumstances. This first part of active analysis empowers actors to become 'action detectives' and is called cognitive analysis.

Visible action is part of the second stage of active analysis and is uncovered in rehearsal with the actors on their feet. This form of action can be discovered only in the studio, as all questions about acting are ultimately answered in the doing.[16] These two actions are different manifestations of the same uber-action: one exists on the page, the other on the stage. The actor's job is to translate one action to the other—to make the invisible visible. In pursuit of a deeper corporeal understanding of action, the seminal twentieth-century American acting teacher Sanford Meisner honed Stanislavski's concept of action, developing a series of exercises to train the actor in visible action. Meisner wrote that "the foundation of acting is the reality of doing."[17] This *doing* is a direct derivative of Stanislavski's *action*. The *doing* an actor must *do* is *play action*. But to what end?

The end of playing action is for the actor to make the 'event' of every scene happen in service of the play.[18] Actors need to read the text to find the exact event in each scene. Without this, there is no subsequent life brought to the dramatic structure. Actors may be moving in space and time onstage, saying words, *living believably* even, but without constructing clear and concrete dramatic events, the acting will be aimless; without creating events, scene by scene, the playwright's original intent will not be realized; without specific actions moving toward specific events, the story cannot be fully told. One cannot *feel* a story to satisfy the precise dramatic demands in the text; nor will simply following random impulses in the moment, no matter how inspired the actor, fulfil the playwright's demands. Stanislavski's process for transferring the action from the architect's blueprint into the actor's body is a called physical analysis.[19] This process of active analysis transforms invisible action into visible action, providing the actor with a map of action with which to orient their performance, allowing the actor to bring the events of the dramatic structure to life in accordance with the playwright's designs. We shall now briefly examine both parts of this process.

Part 1: Cognitive Analysis—Reading Invisible Action

The blueprint of action

Playwrights are architects of dramatic action. Like architects, playwrights are exactingly specific when designing their structures; the text is the playwright's blueprint. If the playwright is the architect, then the actor is the builder. Stanislavski understood that this meant that actors must become accomplished readers of blueprints in order to construct their performances. More precisely, actors need to learn how to read these dramatic schematics for human behaviour, for *action*, as skilfully as possible. It is only via a conscientious and informed reading of the blueprint that the actor can fully identify the details needed to create the behaviour of the world they must inhabit.

The author's text defines the fictional world. It is the map that the actor uses to navigate dramatic action, determining the style of behaviour within that world. There is no such thing as an 'acting style' in and of itself; acting styles don't exist *eo ipso*.[20] Style is, however, embedded in the DNA of the text. Writing itself does have an inherent style to it, as it is the *principium*, the original source. Style is baked into the written creation. As actors are professional human beings, they interpret the text for its corresponding human behaviour. All behaviour for the actor is born from this source material.

The writing and its innate style are the blueprint for the actors' performance—they determine on a foundational level how actors will eventually act. The text, when coupled with the actor's imagination and creative individuality, determines the overall performance. Actors must be able to read the dramatic invisible action that the architect embedded in the blueprint. It is from this detailed plan of action that the actor must spin their imaginary web and interpret what to actually do: what to actually play, what to bring to life, and how.

It follows that if acting is a reproduction of behaviour, actors have to know what influences them from life and what in life makes them do what they do, because acting, ultimately, is doing. As life is composed of an infinite number of circumstances, this feat can be a paralysing proposition; in life, circumstances are constantly changing and overlapping in an unending wave. In order to not drown in this ongoing information onslaught, one needs to organize behavioural indicators into a manageable container. The good news for actors is that in any given dramatic text, the given circumstances are not *infinite*; they are decidedly *finite*. And they can be readily put into a helpful format. Stanislavski developed a process of organizing these behavioural indicators in what he called the three circles of circumstances.

The three circles of circumstances: the major shapers of behaviour

Stanislavski determined that any character's motivating circumstances could be placed in one of three circles. By organizing behaviour, or action, this way, the actor comes to a clear realization of what the event of the scene is, where it is and what to do in order to make the event happen. The resulting composite picture drawn from these circumstances comprises the shapers of a character's behaviour and lays out a specific map for the actor to follow in a performance.[21]

1. The first circle is called the large circle of circumstances, comprised of facts about the character that cannot change. They are always 'with' the character, although they might try to change them in one way or another. Facts from the large circle 'work' on the character in the background, affecting their behaviour at every moment. We bring who we are and where we've been to what we do in every life event, at all times.[22]
2. The middle circle of circumstances comprises any discernible amount of time. Time constantly shapes how we live; our relationship to time drives our behaviour more actively than the circumstances found in the large circle. Playwrights craft time as a sort of pressure cooker in order for the characters to interact. The length and quality of this temporal element shape how they act with one another. This might be the two hours of the play, which correspond to two hours in the lives of the characters in that story, or it might cover many years in the lives of the characters. Time, even more than the large circle, is one of the immediate shapers of how we do what we do and how we behave, which is why it is the middle circle of circumstances. Time is always working on our behaviour, compressing or expanding it. Accordingly, actors must factor this temporal effect into their creative behavioural choices.[23]
3. The last of Stanislavski's organizational circles is called the small circle of circumstances; it is the *moment*, the *now*. It is where we find the primary driver of our behaviour, our *action*. Action can happen only in the moment. The actor's primary craft is articulated moment to moment. Stanislavski determined that the small circle of circumstances is further divisible into the two following parts:[24]
    i. The first part of the small circle is called the leading circumstance.[25] This is the circumstance that defines action at any given moment. Hence it is the 'leading' determinant of our behaviour and the primary shaper of what we do in any event. This leading circumstance is the action that the actor must first interpret from the script and then bring to life in performance. It is always a verb, because it is what the actor will actually *do*. As an actor can play only one action at a time: there is only one leading circumstance per event. Stanislavski stated that to act, the actor must, at a very minimum, recreate the leading circumstance.

The leading circumstance is always present in the text since it is given to the actor by the playwright; it is the actor's job to find it and then make it happen.

ii. Stanislavski called the second part the accompanying circumstances.[26] For the actor, these are the shapers of how the action is played. There may be only one accompanying circumstance, or there may be many. Part of how the actor plays the action also comes from the actor's own imagination, intuition and impulses. Is the character tired, hungry, hot, sick, mentally unstable, or anxious? What accompanying facts about the character's life are working on them as they walk into the scene in pursuit of their objective? These are the facts that *accompany* the action and that colour, affect and shape it. The more gifted the actor, the more accompanying circumstances they bring to their performance.

An event is a noun

The leading circumstance, the *action*, is always a *verb*; the *event* is always a *noun*.[27] For example, it is easy to recognize that a 'class' is an event. All events have an entry and an exit point; correspondingly, all classes have a definite beginning, middle and end. The experience of the event, called a 'class', has temporal boundaries that work on all the characters. Actors must ask themselves, what is the event my character is involved in making happen in this (and every) scene? To elucidate this, simply ask yourself, do I behave the same way at a meal as I do at a funeral, a wedding, a rock concert, a vacation, a date, or doctor's appointment? The answer is no because the nature of the event itself has a leading circumstance, which makes it different from all the others. This brings us to the definition of an event.

Event defined

An event is the change of one leading circumstance to a new leading circumstance. One can also say that an event is the change of one action to a new action.[28] If a leading circumstance changes, there must be a corresponding change of action. New events bring new action; with a new action comes a new objective.

Action is understood as not only what the character is doing physically but, more humanly, what their inner line of action is. In other words, what is the entire being of the character doing psychophysically? The physical action is more attuned to what Stanislavski called 'activities'. The deeper, more profound inner line of action is the current purpose of their life's energy. How are they moving their life forwards in this specific moment?[29] We often think one thing but say another; say one thing and do something else; and do things that we don't want to do. Life is full of behavioural contradictions and paradoxes. Yet that is what makes us human, complex, complicated, and, ultimately, interesting.

On the most fundamental level, life itself is nothing more than a series of events. Yet, this is everything to us. It is the elemental composition of our lives. Samuel Beckett recognized this perhaps better than any playwright in the Western world. Seemingly inconsequential events are the existential fabric of our time. If we think of an average day as a series of quotidian events, then we can see how our behaviour is shaped by the leading circumstance of each of those daily events: sleep, meditation, breakfast, commute, work, lunch, interview, exercise, dinner, concert, stroll, reading, sleep. The actor's first job, then, is to identify in each scene the event in which they are participating and work to *make that event happen*. Actors need a process by which they can determine whether there actually is a change of action. The questions become, was there a change in action, and if so, where did the action actually change? Stanislavski called this means of identification the process of evaluation. This is how an actor discovers and identifies the event designed into the blueprint.

The process of evaluation

Throughout every moment of our lives, at least two things are simultaneously happening to us: we are involved in doing what we are doing, whatever that may be, *and* we are evaluating how it is going. This ongoing evaluation is to determine whether we will continue to do what we are doing, stop doing it, or change it altogether. We are always simultaneously in action *and* evaluating that action as we do it. Stanislavski broke this process of evaluation down into four simple steps:

1. Change of target of attention.
2. Accumulation of information, signs, signals, or attributes.
3. Assignment of highest value.
4. Change of action.[30]

If we go back to the example of the event called a 'class', this process of evaluation will become clear.

The case of the late student

The leading circumstance of an event called a 'class' is to 'learn'. Participants are doing many different physical activities in the class, yet they are all there to learn; it is their main action (verb) for being in an event called a class (noun). If someone comes into the classroom late this changes the flow of the event.

Step 1: Change in target of attention

Students hear the door open and turn their attention to evaluate what is happening. This activates Step 1 of the process of evaluation. Everybody shifts his or her attention to the door in order to accumulate new information. This takes us to Step 2 of the process of evaluation.

Step 2: Accumulation of information, signs, signals attributes

All parties in the event *evaluate* what is going on. They accumulate enough information to tell them that the person arriving is someone they know, a student enrolled in the class, who today is arriving late. As the shift in object of attention is less important than the current leading circumstance of class everyone continues to do what they are doing—learning. The class continues on, as it is not out of the norm in an event called class that students arrive late. There is no Step 3 or Step 4 in the Process of Evaluation as yet, because what the class is currently involved in doing is more important than the new information. Simple enough. However, let's look at another case.

The case of the fireman

Our event is a class. The event is in progress when there is a loud noise, and the door opens abruptly.

Step 1: Change of target of attention

The first thing all participants do is activate Step 1 of the process of evaluation. They hear and see the door open and turn their attention toward it in order to evaluate what is happening. Everybody shifts their attention to evaluate what is going on at the door.

Step 2: Accumulation of information, signs, signals and attributes
Their attention moves to the opening door and they activate Step 2. All parties evaluate what is going on by accumulating information. This time, what they see is a stranger, wearing a reflective hat strapped to their head with a gold badge on it. They now hear this man yell "Fire!"

Step 3: Assignment of the highest value
Because a fireman yelled "Fire!" there must be a fire; because this fact has *higher value* than the class, the characters will go immediately to Step 4.

Step 4: Change of action
Escaping a fire is more important than continuing a class; hence all involved have an immediate shift in their inner line of action. They have a new leading circumstance/action, to escape (verb); a new objective, to save their life; and therefore a corresponding new event (a noun) called fire. The event of 'class' ends; the event of 'fire' begins.[31]

We are all in this constant process of evaluation as we move through our lives from one event to the next, seeking the highest attribute, looking to discover what's the most important piece of information. Is what draws our attention more important than what is currently happening? And this new information provides us with the highest attributed value; it is this to which we react. The introduction of the new information—the fireman's announcement—holds higher behavioural value for the characters than the continuation of a class; consequently, all the characters moved into a new event, with a new inner line of action and objective. When reading a script, the actor must perfect finding this moment, because assigning higher value is what triggers a new action. It is in that moment when we learn the most about the character, how they react to the given stimulus and what they choose to do about it—not *feel* about it, but *do* about it. What they *do* about it forwards the conflict of the rising dramatic action. Watching characters *do* is active, satisfying and ultimately why we go to the theatre.

There is much more to cognitive analysis than this chapter allows. Like everything in an actor's craft, it can be truly understood only through repeated practical application and practice in praxis. Actors learn technique to eventually forget it. As Michael Chekhov wrote,

> First we must know, then we must forget. We must know and then be. For this aim we need a method because without a method it is not possible. To know and then forget. When we reach this point we will be a new type of actor.[32]

Part 2: Physical Analysis—Playing Visible Action and Études

The first part of active analysis is cognitive analysis, where the events and invisible action of the play are identified through an informed reading of the text. The second part of the process, called physical analysis, transforms invisible action to visible action through a series of what Stanislavski called études.[33] Once an actor has read the script and identified all the corresponding events, they must then be able to get on their feet and activate the action through behaviour. Stanislavski developed the process of playing action through études as a means to this end.

Playing action

If "living believably under imaginary circumstances with precise repeatability and complete spontaneity"[34] is an arguable definition of inspired acting and if acting is doing, then one has to ask, what does an actor actually *do* to 'live believably'? Meisner provides solid footing here: "The foundation of acting is the reality of doing."[35] The *doing* is how we live believably. Acting is not the *approximation* of doing, nor the *imitation* of doing, nor the *demonstration* of doing; it is the *reality* of doing—under imaginary circumstances. This raises another question: what is the reality of doing, and how do we teach young actors to *do* that? The answer is *playing action*.[36] The currency of the actor's craft is the *moment*—the now. The actor's work happens in the now as part of the small circle of circumstances. Stanislavski called this work playing action. One must then ask another question: what exactly is playing action?

Action exists as a verb. It is doing. Accordingly, acting classes for beginners appropriately address action as a verb. However, a more detailed and experienced look at action brings us to a deeper, more precise understanding. We come to the realization that a verb is a vehicle of change. It is the 'other' that is changed. If two actors are acting in a scene in which they have identified the event as a 'seduction' (noun), they might rightly assume that their verbs are to 'seduce' one another. But what actually happens when two people seduce each other? There is a cause and effect exchange of energy between those two people that results in a change of feelings. These feelings drive behaviour. In other words, the two actors/people played action (verb: to seduce) onto each other to cause palpable and measurable change in the other. *The result of a verb is a change in the other.* If the feelings of both characters are changed, then the corresponding event (the seduction) is successful. If the feelings are not reciprocal, then the event is not successful. Either way, the resulting emotional shift, due to the exchange of energy, drives the resulting behaviour.

Playing (visible) action is *the exchange of energy between two (or more) actors to make the other actor feel something.*[37] This exchange of energy is not random. The architect/playwright attached a specific purpose to it; they carefully designed it. Stanislavski called this purpose, or motivation, the *objective*. It can also be called the character's 'need': it is what any character immediately needs in any scene. They must use the other character(s) in the scene as a means to obtain that objective, to satisfy that need.

This understanding refines the definition of playing action to *the exchange of energy between two (or more) actors purposefully directed to make the other actor feel an emotion, in pursuit of an objective.* Objectives are in service of the larger event of the scene. If one particular action is inextricably tied to a specific objective and we know that the change of one action to a new action is a new event, then objectives and events are also inextricably intertwined.

This again refines the definition of playing action to *the exchange of energy between two (or more) actors purposefully directed to make the other actor feel an emotion, in pursuit of an objective, to make the event of the scene happen.* Characters are in service of the greater story of the play, the overall arc of action. This is the ultimate goal of the characters, what Stanislavski called the super-objective. These hopes and dreams get characters out of bed in the morning, motivating their behaviour until the end of the play and beyond.

The definition is refined one final time to *the exchange of energy between two (or more) actors purposefully directed to make the other actor feel an emotion, in pursuit of an objective, to make the event of the scene happen, in service of the super-objective.*[38] An actor must be able to 'play action' in pursuit of an objective. If actors are going to live believably under imaginary circumstances with precise repeatability and complete spontaneity, then they must make the event of the scene happen. This is achieved only through playing action, the exchange of energy between two (or more) actors that changes the other actor in pursuit of an objective, in service of the super-objective, which represents the character's hopes and dreams.

Where attention goes, energy flows

Donnellan argues that the target of attention will always be outside of the actor at a measurable distance, ever changing, present before they need it, and the *source* of their action.[39] This is a necessary condition for the actor to play action. The target of their attention must be outside of themselves for their energy (action) to be released. This accords with Meisner's maxim: "Don't do anything until something makes you do it."[40]

Where our attention goes, our energy flows. If we know that playing action is an exchange of energy to change the other actor in pursuit of an objective, it then follows that to play an action the actor must do the following:

1. Direct the target of their attention outside to the scene partner (or an image).
2. 'Source' their scene partner/target.
3. 'Release and receive' the flow of energy between the self and the source/target.

Because energy is action, all the actor has to do at this point is breathe and *allow* the energy to flow between themselves and their 'source', their scene partner, because they will now be in the give and take of energy, the 'releasing and receiving' of action.[41] In this way, acting is as effortless as it is for children, and the actor's work becomes imbued with what Michael Chekhov calls the 'feeling of ease'.[42] Actors then find themselves 'in the river of action' designed by the playwright.

How you talk about the work is how the work will happen

The word 'drama' comes from the ancient Greek meaning 'to do'. Doing is energy, and energy is action. Actors play action, and action is 'action'. Actors do *not* play 'intentions'; they do not play 'tactics'; even worse, they do not play 'objectives' or any other such inaccurate approximation of 'doing'.

'Intention' implies the future. One cannot play the future in the present. If a character 'intends' to do something, they are not actually doing it. It is something they *will* do, and they will do it when they eventually perform it, in action. One hears other inexact terms bandied about with frequency in acting classes such as 'tactics' and 'strategies'. The use of these terms, by actor and teacher alike, has the effect of creating interference in the performer, putting the actor 'in their head', pulling attention back onto the self, and creating self-consciousness. 'Being in one's head' is a metaphor for self-consciousness, for self-targeting; it is anathema to the now. If actors are thinking about what they are doing while they are doing it, then they are self-conscious and unable to be present with their scene partner.

It is not that actors don't know what to do; *it's that they don't do what they know*. When driven by fear, self-consciousness inhibits artistic freedom, keeping talented actors from doing what they know to do. To remedy this, actors must maintain their target of attention on their scene partner. This reduces self-consciousness and is the sole route for the actor to play action in the scene. Acting teachers must consistently, patiently, and kindly redirect the actor's attention back onto their target, reducing the actor's self-consciousness, fear and ego.

To make the action of the story happen, one has to make the other actor(s) on the stage the target of attention and change them in order to achieve their character's objective. Playing action is the 'reality of doing' of any scene. If actors aren't *releasing and receiving* energy with their scene partner, then they are *self-generating* a performance. If actors are self-generating, they are acting independently of one another; if they are acting independently, then nothing is happening between them; if nothing is happening between them, then the events of the story aren't occurring; if the events aren't occurring, the story isn't being told. An actor who isn't playing action isn't doing their job, which is to tell the story.

Feelings arise from action. This is true from the actor's perspective and the audience's. The only people who consciously try to feel are actors in scene work. No one in life is going around 'trying to feel'. And if an actor is trying to generate a feeling, they are by definition 'self-generating'. If their attention is on themselves, they are not playing action. Earle Gister reminds us that "It is not an actor's job to feel, but to make the *other actor feel something*."[43] Feelings are part of the actor's 'state of being'. Actors 'have' a state of being when they enter a scene and then 'play' visible action in that scene. Feelings come along in the doing.

Playwrights put particular characters together in scenes for specific reasons, to change each other in order to ignite the event of the scene. Their reasons for being there are not random or arbitrary; the reasons are inextricably attached to the characters' needs. The process by which actors change other characters to satisfy those needs is called 'playing action'. The action makes the objective happen, which in turn makes the event happen: no action, no objective. No objective, no event. No event, no scene. No scene, no story.

Action and counteraction

In a scene with two characters, there are two independent playable actions, one for each character. For the dynamics of any scene to come to life, there must be at least two competing forces:

1. the action
2. the counteraction.

Stanislavski called the first of the independent forces the action and the second the counteraction. It is the energy of the action against the counteraction that creates the conflict, which results in an event.[44] Coming into the rehearsal room, actors need only have an idea of what the action and the counteraction are, based on their event analysis. They will discover and confirm them 'in the doing'. Initially, they might not even know who is the action and who is the counteraction, just that there are two actions. The action drives the scene, and the counteraction determines, more or less, how the scene will go and how long it will last. This brings us into the rehearsal studio.

Études—work in the rehearsal studio

Actors enter the rehearsal process having completed Part 1 of the active analysis, the cognitive analysis, of their script. This active rehearsal, Part 2 of the active analysis, the physical analysis, comprises two steps: brief table work to arrive at agreement on the fundamental given circumstances of the scene—the event, the action and counteraction—followed by an on-their-feet exploration of that scene, called an étude.

The étude is as an organic and creative process by which actors discover their playable actions in the doing. The word means the study of a subject and is commonly associated in English with instrumental music compositions. In the Stanislavskian context, études are fundamentally improvised explorations of the text for the actor. They take place in the studio before actors have memorized their lines. They have explored the overall text for invisible action, events and other evidentiary given circumstances but have not yet committed the text to memory.

After each improvisation, actors reread the scene, discussing their discoveries, and then improvise the scene/event again. This process is repeated until the architecture of the visible action is clear to the performers and until which character is the driving the action and which has the counteraction are also clear. An ancillary benefit of working in this way is that actors will organically commit their lines to memory in a psychophysical manner that connects the text to the scene's actions and event.

A final word about ownership

Stanislavski wanted to empower his actors, so that they would have 'ownership' over their roles.[45] He understood that when actors are given permission, time, and freedom to explore and discover for themselves what their characters are actually doing in any given scene, their performances are more fully realized and multidimensional. The question for students then becomes, how do actors arrive at ownership?

Performance is the act of doing something, carrying out a task or function, accomplishing an action, where the outcome matters to the agent. A more global, meta-definition of performance is that *performance is potential minus interference.*[46], Understood this way, performance can be boiled down to the following equation:

$$Performance = Potential - Interference$$

'Potential' means the ability of the actor to perform what is asked of them in the here and now. 'Interference' means anything that impedes that ability. A healthy process is one that strengthens and liberates the former (potential) while also minimizing, if not altogether eliminating, the latter (interference).

Stanislavski understood that actors need a creative process that simultaneously empowers their ability and reduces any interference. Paradoxically, one of the great causes of interference is the actor's relationship to their text, inasmuch as *how* and *when* that text is introduced to the actor's process has a direct effect on whether it helps to enhance the actor's potential or becomes a source of interference. This is why the process of études must begin before the actor memorizes the text.

Ultimately, the process of active analysis results in a profound sense of ownership. This is precisely what we hope for our students at CSULB: ownership of a finely honed craft born out of their own creative individuality. This is priceless because it provides an intrepid and inspiring route along the road to mastery.

Notes

1 Stanislavski, K. (1987) *The Stanislavski Technique Russia: A Workbook for Actors*. Applause, pp. 117.
2 Chekhov, M. (1985) "Lessons for the Professional Actor." *Performing Arts Journal*, pp. 65.
3 Knebel, M. O. (2015) *O jejstvennomanalizep'esy I roli*. Translated by James Thomas.
4 Ibid.
5 Carnicke, S. M. (2010) "The Knebel Technique: Active Analysis in Practice." *Actor Training Second Edition*. London and New York: Routledge, pp. 99.
6 Ibid.
7 Ibid.
8 Chekhov, M. (2000) *To the Actor*. London and New York: Routledge, pp. 91; Chekhov Michael, *Lessons for Teachers of His Acting Technique*. Ottawa: Dovehouse Editions, pp. 24.
9 Knebel (1971/2015).
10 Ibid.
11 Carnicke (2017) TDP for the National Alliance of Acting Teachers. O'Gorman's notes from June 2017, University of Southern California School of Dramatic Arts, Los Angeles, CA.
12 Gister, E. TDP at The Actors Center. O'Gorman's notes from June 2003, June 2004, and June 2005. New York.
13 Shakespeare, W. *Hamlet*. Act 3, scene 2.
14 O'Gorman H., copyright.
15 Donnellan, D. (2006) *The Actor and the Target*. London: Nick Hern.

16 Gister. TDP at the Actors Center. O'Gorman's notes from June 2003, June 2004, and June 2005. New York.
17 Meisner, S. (1987) *Sanford Meisner on Acting*. Vintage, pp. 16.
18 Dolgachev, S. TDP for the Actors Center. O'Gorman's notes from June 2003, June 2004, June 2005, June 2006, and June 2008. New York.
19 Knebel (1971/2015).
20 Gister, E. (2003) TDP at the Actors Center. O'Gorman's notes from June 2003. New York.
21 Dolgachev, TDP at the Actors Center. O'Gorman's notes from June 2003, June 2004, June 2005, June 2006, June 2008. New York.
22 Ibid.
23 Ibid.
24 Ibid.
25 Ibid.
26 Ibid.
27 Ibid.
28 Ibid.
29 Van Lieu, R. (2008) TDP at the Actors Center. O'Gorman's notes from June, 2008.
30 Dolgachev, *TDP* at the Actors Center, O'Gorman's notes from June 2003, June 2004, June 2005, June 2006, June 2008. New York.
31 Ibid.
32 Chekhov, M. (2000) *Lessons for Teachers of his Acting Technique*. Ottawa: Dovehouse Editions, p. 28.
33 Knebel (1971/2015).
34 Ibid.
35 Meisner (1987), p. 16.
36 Gister, TDP for the Actors Center. O'Gorman's notes from June 2003 and June 2004. New York.
37 Ibid.
38 Ibid.
39 Donnellan, (2006) *The Actor and the Target*. Nick Hern, chapter 2.
40 Meisner (1987).
41 Chekhov, M. *To the Actor*. London and New York: Routledge, p. 19.
42 Ibid., p. 13.
43 Gister, TDP for the Actors Center. O'Gorman's notes from June 2003 and June 2004.
44 Knebel (1971/2015).
45 Ibid.
46 Sverduk, K. (2010) Instruction in CSULB's Theatre Department. O'Gorman's class notes from May 2010. Long Beach, CA.

12

Standing on the Outside Looking In

Michael McCall

Over the past decade, I have had the opportunity to be a visiting fellow, primarily engaged as a teacher director, to work in various acting and theatre programmes at the tertiary level in Australia. There is no real definition of 'teacher director', other than to note that the principle delivery of a laudable public performance within a relatively short period is an expectation. This sits alongside the imperative to train student actors, those about a year or so into their course, as an itinerant mentor in their larger learning experience. These engagements have been challenging as well as rewarding, and they have allowed me to refine my pedagogy such that it is now shaped to the purposes of actor training within the parameters of a play rehearsal. This chapter considers problems that arise over the course of that early-actor training and how my approach is intended to assist the students' development, from early missteps and sideways glances to an enhanced creativity.

My primary focus in this chapter will be my teacher director experience at the Western Australian Academy of Performing Arts (WAAPA), where I have directed several productions, with the acting and musical theatre students. My approach to actor training is built on techniques that I have developed, adapted and applied over years, influenced by the 'greats' of acting training, such as Stanislavski and the like. Early in my teaching and directing practice, I realized the need to develop a shorthand (albeit not a simplistic) process that would address the pressures I registered that exist between text, movement and voice. That is not to assume that in some way these must harmonize to produce a performance – in many instances, the wrestle between them is potentially where great art resides.

At WAAPA and other institutions, such as the University of Notre Dame, where I currently head the theatre programme, a constant issue is the reduced time of rehearsals compared with professional durations (usually four to five consecutive weeks). This affects the teacher director's ability to gauge individual students' abilities before as well as during the rehearsal process. Arriving in the midst of early-actor training also means that one must quickly surmise how the needs of 18–20 individual acting students must be served and simultaneously moulded into an ensemble for the purposes of the play. This is dealt with better at WAAPA than at many other institutions, which is because WAAPA allows and expects students to prepare extensively beyond their scheduled classes, so they often bring a wealth of prepared work to the rehearsal floor. Student work at WAAPA is innately vocational inasmuch as programmes ensure students graduate industry advised and industry ready, with (at least) eight class contact hours per day expected of the students over their degree. The time does not include many hours of self-preparation, such as line learning, supplementary research, critical analysis and the like. This differs radically from programmes which operate on a schema of 12 class contact hours per week.[1] By the end of the course, this has ensured 'match fitness' for employment in live performance and screen work upon graduation.

The aim of bringing a visiting teacher director into the mix, alongside other specialist permanent staff, is to assist students with the application of the techniques they have learned in class. Problems can arise if students are not open to exploring techniques or if they question the directorial approach as a defence strategy. These can become challenges for the teacher director. Problems also arise if the teacher director does not aim to consolidate and collaborate with student work undertaken as part of the wider programme. Ultimately, staff and students being open is a key part of working in any drama school environment; it is also the gauge that identifies those students with developmental potential who will embrace the pedagogy that the visiting teacher director brings to their brief incursion into the larger course.

First Impressions

After introductions to the cast and crew on the first day of rehearsals for a production at WAAPA, certain aspects of how the rehearsal time will be shaped must be embedded. This begins with a conscious approach to text.

For student actors, a conscious approach is not an innate part of how they work; they are still working out the best way to broach the text. Specific uses of punctuation, for example, have to be relayed at this time. Sometimes students have not been exposed to syntax in the dramatic mode. It becomes crucial for acting students to question what drives a particular playwright to write a play. An answer is vital; something specific must be found which inspires the playwright to commit imagination to paper in the first place. For the student actor, pursuing a character's motivation can be confronting, and it is often connected to their being concerned about their failure. Suffice to say, 'failure', as conceived by Margaret Werry and Róisín O'Gorman, is more useful when viewed as a 'natural condition of collaboration …. In any collective project, some level of failure is inevitable.'[2] As a condition of training, the teacher director must take account of 'failure' as a useful experience for the early actor and offer encouragement: we 'can regulate the level of failure, but we can never eliminate it.'[3] If there is an upside for the student, it is that 'failure's threshold is also an opening. … after the familiar, bleak, heavy vacancy, that bottom-punched-out-of-my-world emptiness recedes, something new happens'.[4] Werry and O'Gorman also point out that if 'failure reveals, it also exposes. And exposure is painful'.[5] Crucially, acceptance of 'failure' implies the need for teacher directors to establish the notion that training is a form of self-reflection, so that the student embraces challenges and obstacles that inevitably arise in practice. The creation of a 'safe' space to fail becomes an integral aspect of an acting programme like WAAPA's.

Stanislavski

Though many Australian university courses have centred their curriculum on devising, as well as on applied and community-based, theatre, much of what is taught at vocational conservatoires, like WAAPA, is Stanislavski based. Alongside the teachings of Adler, Strasberg, Moss, Morris and Donnellan, Stanislavskian techniques underpin the actor training space in Australia. Acting methods seek to assist the actor in inhabiting a psychological and emotional truth, but what is important for the student actor is to clarify the emphasis of what each theorist's methods stress as the indispensable quality that 'good' acting entails. This is something I look to implement in early-actor training.[6]

At the centre of Stanislavski's approach is a respect for the written play and a commitment to realizing the text in a way that gets as close to the playwright's vision as can be imagined. Stanislavskian approaches seem to complement work on narrative plays since he combined literary analysis with the live performance techniques that he developed to support actors. It is no accident that schools like WAAPA exist; the initial vocational organizations that Stanislavski established in the Soviet Union set the institutional framework and were furthered throughout the twentieth century. For a teacher director within current acting courses in Australia, Stanislavski's shadow always looms large. Most realist plays, until recently a staple in Australian theatre companies' repertoires, have the hallmarks of Stanislavski. Even work written before Stanislavski is often approached through the prism of his techniques, and his approach to analysing texts and the application of this close reading have influenced student actors in their search for the meaning in any play.

Consistently used concepts from Stanislavski include the super-objective, the scene objective and the idea of obstacles. These concepts can be broken down in various ways, but over the years I have found that simplifying the explanation of how they work has paid dividends for working with actors in training. First, with the super-objective, the playwright creates for the character a sense of a 'driving force' in life; this is often observed as the character's motivation or goal in life. The super-objective can sometimes be subconscious, but it needs to be revealed in some instance in the play; indeed, for the student actor, it can be initially elusive and difficult to define. Nevertheless, the most important aspect of the super-objective is that it is a robust, continuous idea that shapes the identity of a character and in which they find significant meaning. Whether a play has such an idea can be ascertained only when a student actor has read the whole play, so that they understand the intention of their character in the play.

The super-objective leads to the concept of a scene objective or 'what I want' in the context of the character being played. A scene objective is not fixed; at the start of a rehearsal, that concept is often a problem that must be constantly worked over with the student; there must always be a strong motivation to pursue a character's goal, but it should not be regarded as reductively simplistic. In rehearsals at WAAPA, the scene objective can often be surprising for student actors. Analysis of a character who appears to be Machiavellian in nature may eventually disclose that the motivation for their actions comes from a need for love, which alters the scene objective. Once the character's object has been hypothesized, something tested on the rehearsal floor, discussions with the students around how to achieve that objective ensue. These discussions lead to an exploration of action – tactics to achieve the scene objective, the choice of which is often connected to the overall super-objective that motivates intent to negotiate the obstacles found in the play: other characters, the environment, the inner self.

Punctuating the Text

There is a mantra that accompanies many actors' approaches to punctuation in plays: one thought, one sentence, one breath, one action.[7] Actors communicate by landing thoughts on one another. The preferred communication of these thoughts is via the spoken word. Consequently, these thoughts are communicated on the breath; the actor must expire, breathe out, in order to speak. The sentence is the distillation of the human chaos within us all and will deliver the appropriate choice for the actor in terms of action, in the Stanislavskian sense. It is problematic if actors cannot fully grasp this concept. The longer it takes to comprehend, the worse the actor's ability to mine the meaning from the play's text and subtext. My recommendation to student actors is to always speak the text aloud, to get a sense of how the breath can radically alter their characterization. For instance, if the sentence is long, with no punctuation before the end of the line, the actor will struggle to comfortably complete what they need to say. This would suggest that the playwright wants the character exasperated within the context of the scene – perhaps excitement, frustration, fear or some other emotional state is suggested by this expiration. The opposite might produce a considered character. Again, it depends on the context of the play as a whole. The mantra must eventually become a sensation, an impulse, rather than an intellectual decision. Eventually the student must 'throw the homework away' to embody the characterization in a plausible manner.

The key to understanding when and when not to breathe is wrapped up in the attention given to punctuation by the playwright and actioned by the actor. I should acknowledge here that I was first introduced to this concept by the renowned acting teacher Kevin Jackson while studying acting at the National Institute of Dramatic Art (NIDA), and it has stood me in good stead over many years. Jackson pointed out that a useful way of approaching punctuation in a script is to treat it like a musical score – in fact, studying the playwright's choices in this regard is often called 'scoring' a script.

Approach to Text

Approaches to text provide the acting student with a critical framework through which they can develop an approach to dramaturgy and its relationship to acting. It is difficult for the unaccustomed student to read a play if they are not used to the particular form in which a text is written, such as with Shakespeare's or Chekhov's plays, which is why these texts are often staple parts of these programmes. Peter Brook says in *The Shifting Point*, 'When I begin to work on a play, I start with a deep, formless hunch that is like a smell, a colour, a shadow.'[8] Despite it having been written 30 years ago, experienced actors will undoubtedly understand the ever-present ambiguity of intuitive preparation; for those less familiar with the uncertain craft of acting, Brook's notion may confuse. There are, therefore, certain aspects of a play to try to take on board which are key to training. There is an expectation upon student actors to be able to deconstruct plays, but thankfully for the student, these are usually the 'great' plays, which test the student in a positive sense. These texts will filter back information to the student actor in the dialogue, the diction, the stage directions, the melody and many times the form of the text. Like a detective on a cold case, the actor has the body and now must examine the clues and find out how the events came to pass.

With diligent effort given to exploring how plays are constructed (often a drama school will encourage reading of at least one play per week), the student actor will discover that a playwright has really only one story they wish to tell. Playwrights structure their stories using generic guides as parameters to shape their writing, but not to control or limit them. For example, Shakespeare regularly exposes the reader to the dilemma of action versus inaction, such as in *Hamlet*; Arthur Miller deals with the corporate malevolence and social injustice in *All My Sons*. Through attentiveness to a playwright's motivation to tell their story and familiarization with the genre and style of individuals and movements within the plays of the theatrical 'canon', resonant themes and acting choices that a play can offer come into relief.

By encouraging student actors to read a canon, they are less intimidated when it comes to deciphering characterization and other aspects of plays.[9] While having a canon of plays can sometimes see an academy labelled as reactionary, the short span of a three-year course permits student actors only so much time to fit so many texts into their studies. However, it is also the responsibility of academies, particularly in a multicultural nation like Australia, to ensure that a diversity of texts is front and centre of that theatrical canon. This can enhance the student actor's ability to locate shades of meaning in the literary techniques of many plays. If a character is the sum of their accumulated actions, the student actor cannot logically skip the stage directions, where figurative language will often gift the performer with remarkable given circumstances.

No Such Thing as Character

Following on from initial text work, a focus on characterization is often the next port of call for the student actor. This is partly youthful zeal, tied to the idea that every part is an opportunity for students to present the best in themselves as performers. However, in *True and False*, the iconic American playwright, director and teacher David Mamet puts forward the idea that

> The actor does not need to 'become' the character. The phrase, in fact, has no meaning. There *is* no character. There are only lines on the page. They are lines of dialogue meant to be said by the actor. When he or she says them simply, in an attempt to achieve an object more or less like that suggested by the author, the audience sees an *illusion* of a character upon the stage.[10]

It could be argued that what Mamet's shock to thought suggests is that the text is written to set up a particular way to read the play, which in turn positions the actor to engage with the characterization that the playwright has embedded in the lines of dialogue, as well as in the stage directions, the syntax and even in the silences. The idea of character, then, is based on a reader's ability to construct meaning, which will allow a character to emerge from the page onto the stage. The conventions suggested by the playwright are based on the reader's knowledge and expectations of plays that fit familiar categories, such as realism.

Dramaturgically, student actors will connect more readily with the text when they can recognize the conventions in a play – which can be more or less obvious but which usually depend on form – along with the student actors' opportunity to *familiarize* themselves with the text. That is to say, the more exposure and knowledge of particular texts (and their place in the canon), the more comfortable and confident they will be when it comes time to work on that play. If nothing else, what can be assumed by the student actor is that every key needed to unlock the text is within the play itself. However, unlocking will only occur if one takes the time to learn how to research and interpret the meanings in the play, which should deliver the playwright's intent and suggest an appropriate characterization.

First Approaches

Having said that, a standardized approach is needed in order to research the foundations of any character. In the initial stages of rehearsals, sometimes beforehand if the opportunity arises, simple dramaturgical propositions might be asked to stimulate the actor: What is this work? What happens? What do I want the audience to leave the theatre feeling? Why do I want to do this play? Where am *I* in the play? To get to the point where these questions can be asked, the first thing for the student actor to do is, simply, read the play. This may appear inherent in the idea of actor preparation, but it is a necessary directive for some student actors, who might regard 'their part' as the central focus of time. This same directive applies to individual words. Ideally, the student should look up every word to really understand a text; definitions mean more to some than others, but each effort taken to go to the origin of a word will pay dividends. For example, what does the word 'exhausted' mean to an individual? Thinking on the word, how does it make you feel? The answers will produce something individual when each student actor performs 'exhausted'. So often, student actors have been exposed to little more than a cursory study of a play in a high school literature class; encouragement of further recommended readings must be an imperative of the academy. Nonetheless, it is the responsibility of the student to take the necessary steps to increase their breadth of reading.

At the time of a first read-through with an ensemble, students can be offered particular directives around the play – what we call their 'table work'.

They are asked to read the play once, then write down their initial impressions of the text: what worked for them, what did not work for them and the simple consideration of whether they found some joy in the work. Joy in so much of modern life is derided as indulgent. However, student actors must be honest with themselves: if there is no joy in the initial read, it may be that they are about to embark on six weeks of tedious rehearsal and then public performance. Sometimes a recalcitrance can be a subjective response to a particular type of play ('Shakespeare sucks'), sometimes it is connected to the part they land. A mature actor will recognize their ambivalence to the play, but temper it accordingly over the course of rehearsals to never go below a fine standard of acting, despite any inherently negative feelings about the written work.

After a second read of the play, completed in isolation outside the rehearsals, students are asked to write down what they think of the play.–Tthis includes plot structure, stage directions, craft aspects implied by the playwright about lighting or sound and so on. The purpose of a second read is to enable students to reduce the preliminary emotional response that a first read nearly always brings and to temper it with more objectivity. The student actors (who have been tasked to complete in groups a research project before the first read) are then asked to deliver their research to the rest of the ensemble. Research often involves looking at the socioeconomic and political background to the play, as well as the cultural zeitgeist of the time of the play; the world of the playwright; important conceptual ideas that run through the text; and any other topical area that could enchance their understanding of the play. Other tasks assigned to the student actor include looking at other works of the writer; this will often reveal, as mentioned, that a playwright composes similar plays that will suggest a unity of characters or themes. Analysing the playwright's biography is also essential – discoveries of what motivates the playwright can regularly expose the significance of a scene to a student actor. Once this table work is complete, then individually or in small groups, the ensemble will convey what they have learned to their colleagues. This can sometimes take a couple of days. Composing biographies of characters in the play and exploring what is significant to their character's circumstances also assists the student actor in imagining how their character might relate to others, along with the development of their character's status compared to other characters in the play.

Serving the Text

What becomes clear to the student actor through this process is that it is rare for a playwright to approach writing with an arbitrary hand. From punctuation to plot, every detail is designated to advance the narrative. Knowing how to effectively read a text will help student actors decipher performance suggestions in the work. The principle of playwriting is that the written sentence in naturalistic or realist works is customarily a falsehood (of varying proportion) which will, if we continue to watch the play, permit a subtext to establish 'true' meaning, revealed in the outward actions of the character, which will construct their self-identity. This ties in with Mamet's idea of 'no such thing as character'. Another way to encapsulate this in a neat phrase is that a character's inner life will be betrayed by their outer life. That is, an audience can interpret better what the character is thinking/feeling by what they do and how they respond physically to precise stimuli and the various antagonists in the world of the play. At WAAPA, the desire to sustain a precise and alive inner process is implicit in the growth of each student actor.

Patsy Rodenburg discusses in *Speaking Shakespeare* the need for and application of an imaginative exploration of text in relation to voice which is fundamental to any actor, not just in relation to Shakespeare.[11] Rodenburg observes that 'It as though speech reflects the amount of clutter surrounding a person: the more in touch people are with themselves and their surroundings, the more direct and simple the language.'[12] This search for economy in relation to speech, as well as a cognisant appreciation of the imaginative world produced by the play, is vital and pertains also to an actor's physicality. At WAAPA, there is continual attention to the need for student actors to be *changed*, to operate in an altered state within the imaginative world of the play. Paring back of what I term 'white noise', anything vocally or physically that does not serve the text or any other aspect of the play is vital, whether in regard to speech, thought or action. If the student actor is able to absorb this early in their development, they will find reflexivity that allows them to elicit and advance meaning within the play's language, delivering dramatic complexity to their audiences. Students at WAAPA are continuously encouraged in their practice to create and sustain characters' imaginary world, using their *instrument*: themselves.

I Can't See Where I'm Going

In many ways, my approach to training students through directing emerged from the consideration I had given to mine and others' imperfect approaches to blocking, both of which I had experienced and observed in my practice. I developed awareness that blocking was intrinsic to the realization of any play. Blocking was also integral to acting choices; in particular, the technique proves most useful in the early stages of an acting student's development. I have often noticed student actors who find it difficult to deal with the practice of blocking or how we place characters on a stage and move them around with purpose. Students need to be able to imagine how characters move within the imaginative world of a play. As an emerging actor, as a director and then as a teacher director, blocking was one of the main problems. My intuition told me that movement had to occur at certain points – 'open the window, on that line, after that pause' – but what that generally took the shape of was asking actors to sit, stand and go over there because it felt right to me. As I progressed, I realized this was unspecific and not helpful to myself or any performer I directed; I developed a system to assist with this, which I now abbreviate to T/A/S (towards/away/stay). I use T/A/S each time I work at WAAPA with student actors, and I believe its simplicity is one of its strengths.

My premise is that there are generally three distinct ways of motivating blocking. You can move towards either someone or something (T), move away from someone or something (A) or stay still (S). Moving towards conveys a need to intimately ascertain the attention of the other or to get closer to an object for some reason. This can be a movement that reads either positively or negatively: the extreme positive, to kiss someone; or the extreme negative, to stab someone. Within these two polarities, the student actor can consider myriad other choices. The arbiter of the choice will always be the line or stage direction and would be negotiated with the director and other actors regarding whether it was appropriate.

In the second part of T/A/S, the character can also move away, to convey a need to be apart from the scene for some reason. The extreme positive of this would be in the realm of avoiding what might seem at first a healthy scenario: perhaps the love of your life wants to kiss you, but you are not ready, so you must depart. The negative of away sees a character repulsed to the extent that the only course of action is to exit. Again, these moves away can be graded based on appropriateness to the scene: the away could see a character storm out of a room, or they may just move their body back slightly from another character, perhaps in response to something they don't like.

In the last part of T/A/S, a character can stand still. This suggests either that they need to stand their ground (positive) or that they are unsure about their subsequent course of action (negative). The nature and challenge of stillness for the student actor forces them to consider how they might change their breathing to suggest emotional change; stillness also sets up the parameters around larger movements which might feel more secure because the student feels they are doing something. By imagining the physical proximities and mise en scene surrounding the characters onstage from the reading of the play, the student actor can then make a clear assessment of what is going on, enabling them to contextualize what the playwright suggests would be the most appropriate choice of movement. This will also reveal clues that will help the student actor validate the construct of self that they have exposed through a close reading of the text. It may also hint at how the character's verbal communication sounds, but this depends a lot on the setup of an offstage world.

T/A/S has also found a place in the screen acting toolkit of actors because it permits the individual to give attention to their acting choices within the various frames that are used by cinematographers. An actor will find T/A/S transformative by playing with the angle and orientation of their body, as well as the gaze upon the characters in the mise en scene. The duration of a movement and the space between characters add more nuances to T/A/S. If there is a limitation to T/A/S, it comes from student actors treating it as a 'paint by numbers' approach to acting; there is still room for discernment in the choices offered. Discussion in rehearsals should not end the same day that the first decision is made – around whether a sentence suggests to move towards, move away, or stay still – for fear that the outcome is generalized acting. T/A/S allows student actors to consider a multiplicity of physical choices, whether large or small gestures, determined by the pressures and stakes on the character discovered during table work or on the rehearsal room floor, which will assist in the formation of cohesion between speech, thought and action. In the end, as the playwright Richard Nelson believes, the relationship is the 'truth' – not the 'I'[13] – and all training must finally bare the 'reality' of the story which unfolds on the stage. In the current

Australian context, where a culture of perennial development is to be reasonably expected of actors throughout their practices, it is vital that a drama school honours the three-year investment of students by exposing them to the most useful toolkits, in relation to industry expectations, that they can. T/A/S can assist as one of these training tools, not as a solo technique but as part of a wider kit, and it is a valuable approach within conservatoires and other courses.

Conclusion

Over the several years that I have been associated with WAAPA, I continuously see pressures during the early training of student actors. Ardour – as they necessarily engage with text, movement and voice – is not an inefficacy of a fragmented programme; rather, it is evidence of the rigour required to compress complexities of training into a unified body of practice. This problem is not exclusive to WAAPA, but it is apparent as a sustained characteristic of training schools. This might otherwise take an individual a great many years to experience outside of the conservatoire environment. When text, movement and voice are supported by newly harnessed skills, the ability of students to work towards the development of their overall craft is increased. These three areas account for the basic tenets of the acting programme. When it comes to training the student actor, academies must expose their students, as much as possible, to many different viewpoints; for the student actor, the imperative then becomes to embrace uncertainty. Openness helps encapsulate a wider perspective on how to approach acting, which may be the breakthrough in the training that a student requires. Through a diversity of pedagogy and practice, WAAPA has become an outstanding drama academy, with its graduates applauded both nationally and internationally onstage and on-screen.

The sum of these insights make up a personal method, which might seem to some like a haberdashery of approaches, some old and some new. Nevertheless, over the years it has stood actors in good stead as they undertake their initial training. Through performance practice, student actors grow in both confidence and competence, making clear and specific choices over all areas of their craft. This is the basic aim of training, and illuminating this for the student is vital. As students proceed to gather various techniques from different tutors over the duration of their studies, keep in mind that over their three years of training, they will seek to accumulate what they believe is needed to best inform their acting practice. Teacher directors must assist in this development, through creating a rehearsal experience that allows students to not only apply their learning but also be challenged, enlightened and nurtured while realizing the play in production. Most importantly, the student must find the rehearsal room a safe place to fail gloriously, without fear of retribution for the creative risks they take. Ultimately, it is the students' selection of these techniques which will assist their acting method as they enter the profession upon graduation.

Workshop

Towards/Away/Stay Exercises

As outlined above, apply T/A/S to any scene or part of a scene, and start to familiarize yourself with potential choices that you can make. When you play the scene, include the various facets mentioned thus far in thuis chapter. The more T/A/S is practiced, the easier it becomes to apply to play texts.

Character Exercises: The 'Who' in You

These exercises are considerations for examining the 'who' in you and the text. Actors write down a dot point biography of themselves in the rehearsal space – everything that they believe shapes them and that has made them who they are up until this point in their life (e.g. you might point to parents, education, health, etc.). The ensemble has around ten minutes to complete that task. They then consider what and why certain events have been left out. What did people think might happen if they wrote down particular incidents (e.g. first sexual experience, most embarrassing moment, people they hate)? What is it about these events that disturbs them or makes them essentially dear to an individual? Do they reveal something profound about the nature of *your character*?

Once this has been floated in the minds of the actors, the tutor should make clear that these pieces of writing were never intended to be read aloud. However, it should be pointed out that the events that students would never commit to paper, sometimes due to the risk of re-traumatization or embarrassment, can be applied to characters encountered in scripts. Private moments onstage are where the drama really happens. Actor trainers, like audiences, want to see what happens in people's intimate moments; the rest is, in a word, boring.

After the 'who' task, actors are invited to think about three major turning points that they perceive as affecting their life in the greatest ways – it could be a death, a birth, a migration, a cup of coffee, an accident, a promotion, a war and so on – the possibilities are endless and always unique to the individual. As above, they also become unique to any character an actor takes on. Students can try applying the idea of one or two turning points to the play. They may be self-evident, or they may exist prior to the play's temporality. It is important for actors to also focus on others, to understand and reveal the way you are, which can be done by asking the following questions of your character:

- What do other characters do around you?
- What do they say about you when you're there?
- What do they say when you are not there?

Improvisatory Exercises

Mike Leigh Hands is a technique to explore gradual intimacy with actors. The actors begin by touching fingertips. Then once they have endowed the others' hands with a value or character, they begin to explore the relationship that the two have. The tutor can then encourage the actors to respond to discoveries they make while touching. Once this has been achieved and the actors seem reasonably comfortable, pairs might move onto gradients of intimacy, depending on the script, but they must be in line with the actors' levels of comfort and consent. This exercise takes away tension and allows the actors to expose their intimate selves at a pace which can be advanced or diminished depending on the dynamic. It is a particularly useful tool for younger performers to use. Adding T/A/S to the exercise creates the play as the site of arbitration about what takes place between the actors in the scene.

She Went to Sea in a Sieve is a line given to two or three actors and is the only dialogue that they may use. A high-stakes improvization is established (e.g. there is a bomb planted somewhere). One character is an interrogator, and the other is the bomber that knows where the bomb is located. With only the line 'she went to sea in a sieve' to work with, the actors first try to make sense of the line, then inflect it in different ways, then generate more emotion, before they finally dismiss language altogether and accept that they can communicate what they need to only physically. Physical violence is not the preferred outcome, but frustrations will often run high in this scene. Therefore, it is worth keeping this exercise down to a few minutes only. 'She went to sea in a sieve' is an arbitrary line which could be replaced just as easily with 'Jack and Jill went up the hill'. What is important is that the line is unconnected to the event taking place within the improvisation. Often T/A/S will appear inherently as the interrogator struggles to ascertain the location of the bomb.

The Status Game is another exercise which reveals the use of T/A/S. Any situation can be thought of; for this example, we can use flatmates. There are three flatmates: a couple and a boarder. One of the couple has decided the boarder has to go for some reason or another. The task is given to the other member of the couple. The boarder arrives home once this has been established, and the improvisation ensues. Over the course of the improvisation, the status of each character is by turns powerful, indecisive and lowly. These are shuffled to see what happens. It's important here that actors are not allowed to quickly end the scene, and the tutor should keep negotiating offers. This is a good exercise to do to highlight status in a turbulent world where dominance is fleeting.

Objective/Action Exercise

Hackey Sack Tag a simple game which can be used to highlight the main points of Stanislavskian work. The game sets up conflict: you must risk what you have in order to gain what you want. One person has a hackey sack: they are 'it'. They have a partner who is also 'it'. Between them, the task is to chase and tag as many of the class as possible. They can only tag a classmate when they have the hackey sack in their hand. If they succeed in tagging, that classmate becomes 'it' too and so on; eventually, there will be only one classmate left who is not 'it'. This exercise is more than a warm-up. It is used to demonstrate the focus of an objective; the different actions required to achieve that objective; the obstacles; the changing tactics that don't work and therefore emphasize the need to do the same with actions; the hazards of taking your eyes off the objective and of indulgent playing; and the acceptance of failure in order to generate the characters' stories. Any teaching artist will be able to use this exercise to highlight what they need to communicate. The way to win is to watch their eyes and let intuitive awareness function.

Notes

1. Where other Australian institutions continue to punch above their weight, this is invariably thanks to the calibre and commitment of their permanent and sessional staff.
2. Margaret Werry and Róisín O'Gorman (2012) *The Anatomy of Failure: An inventory*, Performance Research, 17(1), 105–110, doi: 10.1080/13528165.2012.651872
3. Ibid.
4. Ibid.
5. Ibid.
6. It needs to be acknowledged here that WAAPA runs an equally successful contemporary performance stream. While this is beyond the scope of my experience as a teacher director at WAAPA and beyond the remit of this chapter, I believe that it is creating an exciting and complementary new paradigm for the school.
7. Caldarone and Williams (2004).
8. Brook, P. (1988) *The Shifting Point: 40 Years of Theatrical Exploration; 1946–1987*. London: Methuen, p. 3.
9. John McCallum's text is an ideal entry to the Australian 'canon'. McCallum, J. (2009) *Belonging: Australian Playwriting in the 20th Century*. Sydney: Currency Press.
10. Mamet, D. (1999) *True and False: Heresy and Common Sense for the Actor*. New York: Vintage, p. 9.
11. Rodenburg, P. (2002) *Speaking Shakespeare*. New York: Palgrave Macmillan, pp. 191–222.
12. Ibid., p. 193.
13. Richard Nelson speaking at a Q and A session during the Perth International Arts Festival in 2017.

13

An Eye on the Exit: Actor Training in a Liberal Arts Environment

Ellen Margolis

The mission of this book, as I understand it, might be expressed as a question to a diverse group of acting teachers: What do you do for a living? That may not be the *best* way to describe this book, but if one is lucky enough to have not just a job but an identifiable career that spans decades, it's a question one should address voluntarily now and then, and with real curiosity.

What do I do for a living?

Today, I work in a liberal arts setting, in an American private residential college, where I serve as director of theatre. In a given week, I spend at least 50% of my time on email; course schedules; signing forms for students; curricular proposals; hiring, observing and mentoring adjuncts; serving on committees of mixed value; providing the upper administration with the urgently required outcome report du jour; noting calls for papers, talks, and workshops and watching their deadlines pass; and performing acts of diplomacy regarding guest artists.

Within this thicket of challenges, I maintain what space I can for my true calling, which is to teach and train aspiring artists and to learn from them relentlessly. The bulk of this work happens in a small, square, relatively clean studio with black walls and folding chairs. When teaching in this studio, I am at any given moment processing multiple—sometimes conflicting—values, though I may be aware of only one or two of them at a time.

What are the values or priorities I juggle as an acting teacher?

Reclamation

The first value is a sort of umbrella, which is to give my students the education I wish I'd had. I'm not sure I was ever trained as an actor. That is, I trained—I studied theatre and worked hard at my acting—but no one ever trained me in any systematic way in college. I spent most of my career thinking this was an unfortunate lack but now tend to view it with relief. Surely, there is good actor training that is systematic, but actor learning is a catch-as-catch-can matter of showing up, trying to discern a pattern, and then, as soon as one *does* see a pattern, killing one's teachers. So it may be for the best if those teachers are not too forceful in the first place. My undergraduate actor training, such as it was, took place within an immense public university in California and consisted of a couple of unconnected classes full of busywork that had little bearing on the guts of good performance. We typed up elaborate analyses for our scenes and guessed at how to rehearse them, let alone how to get past our limitations.

After graduation, I spent a few years working in cafés during the day and making experimental theatre with my friends at night, and then I went on to a graduate programme in acting at another huge public university. This felt more like *training* than my undergraduate work had—it was sweatier, at least—but it was still confusing. One of my two acting teachers was an intense Performance Group actor who had worked with Grotowski. His approach focused on impulse and accessibility; classes consisted of writhing toward and away from each other in minimal clothing. He treated us with a great deal of suspicion, certain that our aims were corrupt, which is to say he suspected that we hoped to make a living as actors.

The other teacher was a local favourite in the dinner theatre scene and drilled us in technical skills. This man communicated in every interaction that some of us had the magical *something* that would allow us to go on to careers and that some simply did not. Like his colleague, he also assumed that we all aspired to the profession, but his premise was that some of us would fail through no fault of his.

At both institutions, I absorbed a consistent message that power imbalances in the theatre were not my business as a mere actor, particularly a female one, whether those dynamics were expressed in canonical plays or the ways that casting and rehearsal were conducted.

For my part, I was driven by intense curiosity and ultimately patched together an understanding of how to work and how the profession operates. And in the meantime, I found myself powerfully called to teaching. The daily discovery-making and problem-solving with students, continual pressures and revelations, the challenges of articulating an elusive process all spark my creativity. But perhaps more than anything, I am drawn to revisit the scene of the crime, the crime being my teachers' failings no more than my own.

The Ideals of the Art

I imagine that each of us has an artistic idol or two residing in our minds and thus occupying a corner of our studios—the torchbearers for our most idealistic sense of what our art could or should be. After seeing the Saratoga International Theatre Institute's vibrant devised project *Cabin Pressure* at the Actor's Theatre of Louisville in 1998, I knew I needed to work with the company, and so I immediately applied for their summer intensive training programme. Training every day in Saratoga Springs that summer awakened my most precise and demanding aims for my acting and other creative work. Over the weeks of the workshop, artistic director Anne Bogart and a number of her hand-picked SITI actors who served as our teachers became true heroes of mine—not because they cultivated any sort of worshipful attitude in us, far from it, but because of their utter devotion to and discipline in pursuing their own best work. Our days were spent in practice of the gruelling Suzuki physical conditioning, learning Viewpoints and composition work under Bogart's demanding gaze and trying to hold ourselves to our teachers' utterly exacting and precise standards. On our last day of training, our teachers implored us to keep our aims high, even (or especially) when working with those who may not hold to the same ideals.

Others who call to me in a similar way include the great director Ariane Mnouchkine, whose 'we must have art the first day' I often invoke in class, not only on first days of class and rehearsal but perhaps even more often on ordinary Tuesday afternoons.

But though I returned to campus in the fall of 1998 more demanding, precise and cranky in my approach to training than my students had known me to be before, and though Mnouchkine's work remains a touchstone for me, I don't believe that failure to put a sort of idealist rigour above all else is truly a failure. There are moments when compassion, distraction, a joke, a misspeaking, even a messiness may best serve the training cause. It is, again, a matter of juggling priorities, including the following.

Liberal Education

At schools like mine, approximately one-third of a student's college credits are distributed among various general education requirements, one-third are dedicated to a major programme of study (such as theatre or biology), and one-third are elective credits—classes students take out of personal interest or, increasingly these days, for a second major, typically undertaken in the spirit of having 'something to fall back on'.

What is this education? What is a liberal arts education as currently administered in the United States? I believe that the average citizen, even one with a college degree, would be astonished to glimpse how little agreement there is among those of us in the academy about what we're trying to do. I have sat on one committee after another devoted to the definition of a core set of goals, participated cheerfully in countless meetings and town halls on this same topic, and researched or at least kept up with current thinking on best practices for a liberal education. After all of that, I can *almost* tell you what I think all students should be able to do by the time they've earned an undergraduate degree. I can *almost* tell you, and if you left it to me to determine general education requirements for my college, I could almost do it.

The complications, of course, arise when two or more gather to tackle these decisions. As well-educated, well-meaning, earnestly engaged and happy-to-research educators, we begin to map the desired outcomes and find that we can't even agree on the relative weights of the outcomes we can agree on. It's not unusual for an institution to appoint committees and spend years reviewing possible requirements before giving up on a redesign of core curriculum. But it's fair to say that most college-educated people in my country agree that our college graduates should be able to do the following:

- communicate well, specifically write clearly, exhibit decent social skills, present an idea or a project, and listen
- organize time, people, ideas and projects

- analyse arguments, including their own
- engage respectfully with people, places, and ideas, both domestic and foreign
- reverse climate change

The one-third of their college credits (roughly ten 15-week classes) reserved for general education could go a long way toward these objectives. But this doesn't relieve me, a theatre professor, of the obligation to tie training in movement, voice, text analysis and impulse to the greater set of skills required of a good citizen or the body of knowledge one might hope to find in an educated individual. In fact, one might expect that students will learn this other material in the best and most lasting way if practised in the area where their greatest passion lies. And so, the approach to a cluster of scenes from the Theatre of the Absurd is prefaced by an impromptu lecture on the movement as a whole, which then extends into a brief talk on existentialism, which can then take over a class session while *The Myth of Sisyphus* (and the myth of Sisyphus) are brought in, as, eventually, is Kierkegaard. And for the past several years, I have taken a few weeks out of scene study class, a nuts-and-bolts acting workshop, to have students do a research project, part of their graded work for the class, on issues like casting and representation in the contemporary theatre with reference to gender, ethnicity and disability. Such is the difference between the bachelor of arts degree at a liberal arts college and a conservatoire or bachelor of fine arts programme, both of which focus exclusively on praxis and aim to graduate hireable, working actors. And yet, neither can I neglect the hirability factor, which is therefore another priority for the acting teacher:

Professionalism

In *Being an Actor*, Simon Callow decries the actor he labels the 'Professional', whom he describes as a line-learning, trick-performing drone who may perform satisfactorily on command but never challenges a fellow artist or really digs into a role. And yet, even those putatively lacklustre professionals surely possess a set of skills without which one does not progress to a callback, a booking, a paycheque. Would it not be irresponsible of me to overlook the set of skills and behaviours that professional directors and producers will expect to see in a rehearsal room—and even to instil in my students some sense of expediency or at least efficiency?

As was probably the case in many fields at the time when I matriculated, my fellow students and I were offered no education in auditioning, resume-fashioning, or interviewing. It was taken for granted that we already knew how to do these things, that we wouldn't need to know, or that we would figure it out on our own. Consequently, most of us wallowed around for years trying to learn these things on the street, as it were. Can I in good faith refrain from telling students, at the potential cost of their self-expression, that they must wear shoes to an audition? Do I make time in my syllabus to teach slating, resume design and choosing audition pieces, even in cases where the students have not yet grasped the essentials of impulse, action and connection? We must, for the sake of our students, keep one eye on the world of the working actor, but to do so is not without cost of time that might (or so my artistic idols might say) be better spent on the fundamentals.

If I lock the studio door the instant class is scheduled to start, barring latecomers from entrance, am I doing so to teach a lesson about how things are (theoretically) done in New York, to uphold the values of my best teachers, or to avoid the annoyance of explaining an exercise more than once? And is it perhaps more important that the tardy student has the chance to show the work they have prepared or that a scene partner is not left stranded? Is the door locked in service of my students, my art, my convenience, or my ego? And who are these students, and does it matter? Of course it does.

The People in My Studio

Who they are and how they are growing as both actors and people matters enormously. Our greatest strength as teachers arrives when we move past dogma and begin to recognize our students as they are, and become willing to learn from them. We need to find space in ourselves to appreciate the spaces in the training, including those spaces that we do not, or could not, design. We must step back and respect the ways in which life experiences, including difficult ones, are critical to the maturing of a student actor, rather than being threatened by these factors or pretending they are insignificant.

I am reminded of a conversation with the actor Kelly Maurer of the SITI Company during the second or third week of my training. Then in my late thirties, I was hard-pressed to keep up with the younger students physically, but I did my earnest best while hoping I was bringing other worthwhile qualities to the table. One morning, Kelly plopped down next to me while I was warming up. "How's it going?" Kelly asked. "Not bad for an old lady?" I replied, instantly wishing I could take away that upward inflection. Kelly responded with some highly reassuring words about my work, then told me that Mr. Suzuki himself, surely the ultimate torchbearer for systematic training, often told young actors: "life will beat you up, and you will get more interesting, but until then, you must train very hard!"

Experiences like the loss of a grandparent, claiming gender and sexual identity, and living abroad—these maturing experiences are part of how a young human develops into someone who can hold space for complex given circumstances, such as those found in compelling dramatic literature. At any given moment in class, I may be aware of mixed priorities, yes, and also of the varied needs of young people who may be developmentally narcissistic, tough-minded, fragile, inept, or unsuited to the work and yet all of whom are drawn to it for profoundly individual reasons.

As mentioned earlier, I greatly admire the director Anne Bogart. Like many American directors and acting teachers, I rely heavily on techniques she has developed and frequently look to her for inspiration. Bogart's vision of directing has been a touchstone for me, and the summer when I studied with her I particularly absorbed her perspective on *decisiveness*. In her essay 'Violence', which appears in the collection *A Director Prepares*, Bogart writes,

> Something matters to an audience only if you make it matter. If something is not attended to decisively by the actor and the director, then it will not be attended to by the audience. ... The act of decision gives presence to the subject.[1]

Deliberation, intention and attention are prime values for me in all areas of theatre, starting with *casting*. I don't want to look at young actors plastered with fake age makeup and powdered hair, and I don't want our audiences to have to see that, either. I don't want to look at female students playing male characters and be pulled out of the action to the likely reality that not enough men auditioned for the show. I never want casting to signal 'compromise'. I'm not, of course, talking about various kinds of fluid, storytelling theatre—which is most of my favourite material. But in the kind of *representative* theatre where character identity is meant to be fixed and stable, I hold somewhat conservatively to the idea that there should be an artistic reason for an unconventional choice and a framing of it so that the audience can understand that reason, whatever it is. Or rather, I held to that idea until recently, when I came to understand how it affected one of my beloved students.

In 2013, a young woman named Larissa Wilde[2] started her freshman year at my university and enrolled in my beginning acting class. She was a bright, focused student; one couldn't be in Larissa's presence without being aware of a lively mind at work. To my delight, Larissa auditioned for our fall production of Seamus Heaney's *The Burial at Thebes* and was cast as Antigone. I was excited to see her in her first mainstage role. If she was not as effective in the role of a tragic princess as she had been in class, I chalked this up to the heavy line load, as compared to our relatively simple impulse- and movement-based work in the beginning acting class. The following spring, Larissa appeared in Sarah Ruhl's *Melancholy Play* on the mainstage, playing a lovelorn British nurse. Again, though she worked conscientiously, her performance was subdued. As the school year ended, I thought of her as a student with potential and discipline and looked forward to watching her develop.

I saw relatively little of Larissa the next year, however. Unlike in her freshman year, she didn't seem to be spending much time around the theatre building. I assumed she was leaning into her other major interest, creative writing and had less time for the theatre. When I did run into her, she seemed a little standoffish. At some point, I registered that she had cut her hair very short.

The following fall, I was happy to see that Larissa, now a junior, was enrolled in my playwriting class. When I took attendance the first day, she mentioned that she preferred to be called 'Larry'. Over the next few days, I heard other students refer to Larry as 'they'. By the second week of class, I wondered if I was doing something wrong. What followed was a conversation of barely five seconds but one I am unlikely to forget.

"I'm hearing that you prefer 'they.' Is that right?"

Larry's face lit up. Larry smiled, huge and nodded. "Yes! Thank you!" For a few days, I was awkward using 'they' and 'them' to refer to Larry, whether in their presence or when they were out of the room. A microscopic pause would enter unbidden after the word left my mouth. Still, remembering how Larry had responded when I asked, I pushed through, and within a week the new pronoun was an old friend.

The next spring, Larry Wilde auditioned for our mainstage production of *Rossum's Universal Robots*, or *RUR*, the modernist melodrama by Czech writer Carel Capek. Our student director chose (with the translator's permission) to re-set the show in 2045 and to investigate the idea of transhumanism in our present and near future. This director's vision for 2045, which he communicated in his casting notices, included an internationally diverse workplace and gender fluidity.

Larry, who is petite, with classically feminine features, gave a strong audition and was cast as the wise and sympathetic Alquist, the sole human character who works with their hands and who thus stands in for a dying sense of humanity. In callbacks, Larry's simple delivery and grounded physicality offered a centre of gravity in a frantic world. Alquist is the only human character left alive in the play's final scene, where he decries the current state of affairs and reviles man for playing god. It is a huge responsibility for a young actor at the end of a long show. Alquist attempts to create new life, argues and pleads with his god, and ultimately finds hope in the apparent love match of two robots. Larry's acting was bold, vulnerable and fully realized. Watching the show on opening night, as Alquist blessed the new world's 'Adam and Eve' and sent them on their way, I was moved to tears.

During the curtain call, I wondered ever so briefly how the audience around me—students, faculty, parents, community members—might be reading Larry-as-Alquist's gender. Did they imagine that we had run out of men, that this actor was playing across gender? In the same instant, I realized I couldn't possibly care less. All that mattered was the meeting of actor and character and the huge step that young actor had taken in realizing their talent. It was the flip side, I suppose, of Bogart's "Something matters to an audience only if you make it matter."

A few weeks after the show closed, I invited any willing students to chat with me about gendering as it had played out in their experiences of actor training. I am curious not only about how transitioning or non-binary individuals navigate the acting studio but also how we may inadvertently reinforce gender in exercises, scene assignments and even warm-ups. A number of students responded, and each spent 10 to 30 minutes speaking with me, but I'll focus on my conversation with Larry. That afternoon, I learned how important the *RUR* opportunity was to them and why they had been scarce in the department and not seen on stage the year before:

> Sophomore year was kind of a weird, in-between space, which is a huge reason I didn't do theatre. ... It wasn't because I didn't want to; it was because I felt uncomfortable, I guess. I [didn't know] where I could place myself in terms of ... roles. ... *I* didn't know what to do with me, so I didn't know what a *director* could do with me. ... I just didn't want to put either of us through that, I guess. So I just ended up ... I was miserable. I really, really missed doing theatre, but ... I didn't really know how to start those kinds of conversations. ... It was difficult, and it sucked, but it was kind of just what I ended up doing.

Larry reflected on *RUR* as a rare opportunity:

> I love to act, but I don't know how often I'm going to have the chance to do a character where it's like, oh, I can *really* do this. ... That's completely within my comfort zone of identity! Because even if I were cast as a cis male character, I don't look like a cis male, I don't sound like a cis male, and I know that that's a weird thing to deal with as an audience.

At the end of this long conversation, I asked Larry if they had any last words for the interview. Larry, who is 20 years old, responded:

> Even now I'm not totally sure what a trans person can do in theatre... and when I say 'trans people', I mean paying particular attention to ... people who haven't transitioned or don't plan to. ... It's really uncertain ground for those kinds of people in theatre. ... I don't know what I'm allowed to do; I don't know what I'm allowed to ask for; I don't know what expectations to have for myself or for directors.

Three months after this conversation, I was lucky enough to have Larry audition for my production of *The Good Woman of Setzuan*, in which they stole the show as the pompous, lovelorn barber, Mr. Shu Fu, displaying exquisite comic timing. The following spring in my scene study class, Larry broke our hearts as Dr. Rank, tickled us as Algernon, and chilled the room as Deeley in *Old Times*. (My fellow teachers will understand when I say that wonderful art that takes place in a musty studio in front of an audience of 15 students and an instructor is nonetheless … wonderful art.) At graduation, Larry received the department's highest award for a performer, by unanimous agreement among my colleagues. The space had been created for this gifted young person to flourish, which is all that was needed.

Meanwhile, I have completely let go of an agenda that was high-minded but that failed to respond to the actual needs of my actual students. Every curious, hard-working student must know there is a place for them on our stages. We may not, currently, be actively keeping anyone out, but we should be actively patrolling for the students who do not yet see a place for themselves. Today, I cast scenes and shows based on the actor's abilities, with gender contributing to my sense of type, but no more than that. Cross-casting of any sort that doesn't reflect a particular directorial choice is no longer second best in my mind; rather, it demands engagement of the audience's imagination, like all good theatre does in all kinds of ways.

My earlier agenda was perhaps a superficial one masquerading as artistic integrity. But what about my actual personal creative agenda at any given time? How does it play out in teaching?

My Personal Creative Agenda

I like to think that I have one. I like to think that, at the very least, I'm collaborating with students based on that which truly interests and challenges me currently. In fact, as I write this, it feels like it might be the most valid of the values, the 'desert island' value. Much of my artistic practice these days lies in the field of playwriting, but I am still a director and acting teacher—and, occasionally, an actor—for good reason. What excites me most in the studio is seeing what happens when a playwright's text takes over an actor's nervous system and trying to articulate *how* that happens—doing my best to help students recognize the set of conditions that may have allowed for it. Indeed, my personal creative agenda for the most part has to do with encouraging young people to be as bold and committed in their work as I wish I had been. I suppose this returns us to the value of 'reclamation', but not without one critical last stop.

Kill Your Teachers

There are moments when all the aforementioned values work together, and we feel like geniuses. Those are the moments we must be most wary of. The final value that I do my best to keep in mind when teaching is to remind my students that, regardless of how authoritative I may sound at times, I could be wrong. Once we have gotten past the panicked need to sound smart, knowledgeable and qualified for our jobs, we need to be conscientious about undercutting our own authority as often and genuinely as possible. The Japanese word 'sensei', I am told, literally translates to 'one who has gone before'. We ought to claim the authority of one who happens to have gone before, but not a jot more than that.

Summing Up

I sometimes wonder about applying for other jobs, not because I am discontent where I am or because I crave a change of that sort but because I wonder what my statement of teaching philosophy (a standard component of academic job applications in the United States) would look like now that I have so many years of actual teaching under my belt. If you have been on hiring committees at an American university, you'll know that these all tend to look alike. It's hard to distinguish yourself in a statement of philosophy. We all tend to say that we try to empower students, that we strive to combine appropriate levels of rigour with appropriate levels of flexibility, and that we draw advisedly from the same four or five proven and popular approaches (unless we are applying for the rare job that insists strictly on adhering to only one of them). We all mean these things, too. But our ability actually to implement these good aims and also to meet the students where they are varies widely, depending on our experience and our ability to learn from that experience.

Currently, my statement of philosophy for a job I'm not actually applying for would look like this:

1. I want them to be good at listening.
2. I want them to be curious.
3. I want them to love good sentences.

4. I want them to stay in touch, especially when it's hard to stay in touch.
5. I want them to sing every day.

(Number 5 may sound a little soppy, but I am a little soppy and also half Irish. People need to sing, in my opinion and in the opinion of every ancestor on my mother's side. And certainly, *actors* need to sing.)

But what about the students' ambitions? What are the ambitions of theatre students in a something-to-fall-back-on world? Where will they go from here? What do we have to offer a student who can neither express that their dream is to work in the theatre nor honestly say that they don't want that? What, in other words, can we do for a student who is always keeping an eye on the exit, downplaying their desire for a life in the arts?

Here I sigh, pushing aside my deep desire for them to at least try to leap forward before they fall back. What I want most is for them to lunge into theatre wholeheartedly, to risk failure and embarrassment, to fall in love with projects and sacrifice for them, and to spend some years making goofy experimental theatre and starting their own companies. Few of them will do any of these things. And though many of them do begin to book good acting jobs even before graduation, others won't make it to a single professional audition. So how can I claim to have served them?

At the same time that we work them hard in voice and speech, movement, text analysis and scene study, we are, whether or not we intend it, offering theatre as a guide to effective citizenship. In their time in our studios, they practice these critical skills:

- negotiating actual (not virtual) space, physical intelligence and paying attention (a dying skill)
- treating a theatre space as sacred and treating every place as potentially sacred to *someone*
- recognizing the contributions of team members from diverse backgrounds
- through devising work, encouraging themselves to love living with questions rather than valuing quick solutions
- embracing a rigorous process of pushing themselves hard and emphasizing balanced self-care.

The tired truism repeated by every theatre jade advises "if you can be happy doing anything besides theatre, do that instead." But I believe we are called to the arts for any number of reasons, and the arts need people who are capable of (and happy in) any number of pursuits. Nor is the world of work for adults these days so linear as it once was or defined along a narrow track. Millennials are more likely than not to change *careers* (not just jobs) multiple times in their working lives. An ability to see one's identity as malleable is critical.

Workshop Exercise

Group Composition Assignment

This group composition assignment partakes of the SITI Company's composition work, Laban training and the tools my students work on over the first months of class. The description that follows is as given to the students I work with.

This assignment requires students to work in groups of two to three to create an original piece of theatre, three to four minutes long, illuminating a piece of text.

TEXT: You will use material from the *Tao Te Ching* by Lao-tzu, in the Stephen Mitchell translation. Please select material that addresses the city-state or leadership, and choose a verse that *all* group members respond to well.

GUIDELINES: You should work with part or all of one verse (i.e. one numbered chapter); your text can be anywhere from 6 to 15 lines. You may break up the text as you see fit and return to certain lines or phrases, and so on. In fact, you probably *should* do these things.

STAGING: Your composition will incorporate three scenes of different lengths, separated by blackouts, which you will create through our eyes-open/eye-closed convention. Your illumination of the text should make deliberate use of the Laban efforts you have been working with. Be mindful of the direct/indirect, fast/slow, free/bound and heavy/light qualities of both movement and vocal delivery throughout the piece. Establish two to three gestures as the main vocabulary for the piece (remember that gestures can be transformed through tempo, size and effort quality while still remaining essentially the same gesture).

You should create a sense of location through your work with space and through a vocal soundscape. Please do not use recorded music, but using the voice musically is welcome. Include two to three entrances/exits and vary their speed. Include ten seconds of simultaneous slow-motion movement (synchronized or not) at least once. Include simultaneous fast speech (synchronized or not) at least once.

Include one explosion.

Add beauty through judicious use of costumes and decoration.

TIMELINE:

Week 1: select your verse, memorize it and work for at least 90 minutes as a group. (At that meeting, experiment openly until you arrive at a strong shape for your piece.)

After a warm-up, show your tutor a rough draft of your project, and then schedule and plan Week 2 rehearsals as follows:

In Week 2, rehearse three more times for approximately one hour each. Throughout your rehearsals, do your best to connect with each other in real time onstage and remain present at every moment. End each meeting by articulating goals for the next one. (Goals might include pushing tempos, experimenting with a different orientation in the room, or spending a determined amount of time on a moment that you're not yet satisfied with.)

At the end of Week 2, all finished projects are seen in class.

Have fun, be wonderful and don't be afraid to astonish your tutors.

Notes

1 Bogart, A. (2001) *A Director Prepares: Seven Essays on Art and Theatre*. London & New York: Routledge, p. 59.
2 As this a story of identity transition, I use first a female and then a male name for this student; I fabricated both names to protect the student's privacy.

Bibliography

Adler, S. (2005). *Stella Adler on Ibsen, Strindberg and Chekhov*. New York: Random House.
Alberge, D. (2013). 'Imogen Stubbs Hits out at Mumbling Actors'. https://www.theguardian.com/stage/2013/jun/22/mumbling-actors-theatre-chiefs
Artaud, A. (1958). *The Theatre and its Double* (translated by Mary Caroline Richards). Artsminds: Grove Press. http://www.artsminds.co.uk
Assist, E. (2018). *About Us*. https://www.entertainmentassist.org.au
Baldwin, J. (2003). *Michel Saint-Denis and the Shaping of the Modern Actor*. Westport: Praeger Publishers.
Baptiste, B. (2003). 'Journey into Power: Power Vinyasa Yoga, Level 1'. DVD Release. *Good Times Video*. Touchstone.
Baudrillard, J. (1983). *Simulations* (translated by Paul Foss, Paul Patton and Philip Beitchman). New York: Semiotext(e).
Benedetti, J., ed. (1991). *The Moscow Art Theatre Letters*. New York: Routledge.
Berry, C. (1973). *Voice and the Actor*. New York: Collier Books.
Berry, C. (1973). *Voice and the Actor*. London: Virgin, 1993.
Berry, C. (1975). *Your Voice and How to Use It Successfully*. London: Harrap.
Berry, C. (1987). *The Actor and His Text*. London: Harrap.
Berry, C. (2001). *Text in Action: A Definitive Guide to Exploring Text in Rehearsal for Actors and Directors*. London: Virgin.
Berry, C. (2008). *From Word to Play: A Handbook for Directors*. London: Oberon Books.
Berry, C. & Linklater, K. (1997). 'Shakespeare, Feminism and Voice: Responses to Sarah Werner', *New Theatre Quarterly* XIII(49), 48–52.
Billington, M. (2009). 'Method in the Madness'. *Guardian*, May 9, 2009. https://www.theguardian.com/stage/2009/may/09/stanislavski-method-acting-michael-billington
Bogart, A. (2007). *And Then, You Act: Making Art in an Unpredictable World*. London & New York: Routledge.
Bogart, A. (2007). *A Director Prepares: Seven Essays on Art and Theatre*. London & New York: Routledge.
Bogart, A. & Landau, T. (2005). *The Viewpoints Book*. New York: Theatre Communications Group.
Bogosian, E. (1994). *Pounding Nails in the Floor with My Forehead*. New York: Theatre Communications Group.
Brook, P. (1988). *The Shifting Point: 40 Years of Theatrical Exploration; 1946–1987*. London: Methuen.
Buchanan, J. (2016). '"Look Here, upon This Picture": Theatrofilm, The Wooster Group Hamlet and the Film Industry', in G. M. A. Z. Wilcox (ed.), *Shakespeare in Ten Acts*. London: British Library, pp. 204–299.
Burns, R. (2015). *The Complete Songs and Poems*. Glasgow: Geddes and Grosset.

Butler, J. (1988). 'Performative Acts and Gender Constitution: An Essay in Phenomenology and Feminist Theory'. *Theatre Journal*, 40, pp. 519–531.
Caldarone, M. & Lloyd-Williams, M. (2004). *The Actors' Thesaurus*. London: Nick Hern.
Callow, S. (1991). *Acting In Restoration Comedy*. London: Applause Theatre Books.
Callow, S. (2009). 'Can you spot the difference?'. *Guardian*, 11 May 2009. https://www.theguardian.com/stage/2009/may/11/simon-callow-theatre
Carnicke, S. M. (2010). 'The Knebel Technique: Active Analysis in Practice', in Hodge, A. *Actor Training* (2nd edn). London & New York: Routledge, pp. 99–117.
Carson, A. (2016). *Antigone*. London: Oberon Books.
Chambers, C. (2004). *Inside the Royal Shakespeare Company*. London & New York: Routledge.
Chekhov, A. (1998). *The Plays of Anton Chekhov*. New York: Harper Perennial.
Chekhov, M. (2000). *Lessons for Teachers of His Acting Technique*. Tuscon: Dovehouse Editions.
Chekhov, M. & Du Prey, D. (1985). *Lessons for the Professional Actor*. New York: Performing Arts Journal Publications.
Claxton, G. (2009). *Intelligence in the Flesh: How Scientific Understanding Can Help Practical Education Regain the Respect It Deserves*. Centre for Real World Learning University of Winchester.
Claxton, G. (2015). *Intelligence in the Flesh: Why Your Mind Needs Your Body Much More than It Thinks*. New Haven: Yale University Press.
Climenhaga, R. (2007). *Pina Bausch*. London & New York: Routledge.
Collins-Hughes, L. (2017). Need to Fake an Orgasm? There's an Intimacy Choreographer for That. *New York Times*, 15 June 2017. https://www.nytimes.com/2017/06/15/theater/need-to-fake-an-orgasm-theres-an-intimacy-choreographer-for-that.html
Colman, G. (2008). 'Reality TV Taking Over Acting Talents'. http://www.youtube.com/watch?v=scHZJmcFB8I
Congreve, W. (1999). *Love for Love*. London: Methuen Drama.
Cowie, A. (2016). *Blogging Shakespeare*. http://bloggingshakespeare.com/is-troilus-and-cressida-as-bad-as-everyone-says
Coyle, J. (2011). 'Fassbender Fleshes Out Characters With Physicality'. *Backstage*, 30 November 2011.
Crohn Schmitt, N. (1990). *Actors and Onlookers: Theatre and Twentieth-Century Scientific Views of Nature*. Evanston, IL: Northwestern University Press.
Cumberlege, G. (1948). *Report of the Oxford University Drama Commission*. Oxford: Oxford University Press.
Dalton, L. (2000). 'The "Other" Chekhov'. *Backstage West*. http://www.michaelchekhov.net/otherchekhov.html.
Daphna, B. C. (1981). *Distance in the Theatre: The Aesthetics of Audience Response*. Michigan: UMI Research Press.
Darnley, L. (1994). *A History of Voice Teaching in Britain*. University of Birmingham.
Darnley, L. (2013). *Artist Development and Training in the Royal Shakespeare Company: A Vision for Change in British Theatre Culture*. PhD thesis, University of London.

Davis, N. & Sample, I. (2017). 'Nobel prize for medicine awarded for insights into internal biological clock'. *Guardian*, 2 October 2017. https://www.theguardian.com/science/2017/oct/02/nobel-prize-for-medicine-awarded-for-insights-into-internal-biological-clock

Diamond, D. (2009). 'Balancing Acts: An Interview with Anne Bogart and Kristin Linklater', in *The American Theatre Reader: Essays and Conversations from American Theatre Magazine*. New York: Theatre Communications Group, pp. 480–489.

Dixon, S. (2007). *Digital Performance*. Cambridge, MA: MIT Press.

Donnellan, D. (2006). *The Actor and the Target*. London: Nick Hern Books.

Drain, R. (1995). *Twentieth-Century Theatre: A Sourcebook*. London & New York: Routledge.

Duckworth, A. (2017). *Grit. Why Passion and Resilience are the Secrets to Success*. London: Vermilion.

Elkin, S. (2011). *University or Theatre School*. http://blogs.thestage.co.uk/education/2011/03/university-or-theatre-school/

Emerson, R. W. (1893). *Essays and Lectures*. New York: Library of America.

Etherege, G. (2015). *The Man of Mode*. London: Methuen Drama.

Ferguson, F. (1949). *The Idea of a Theatre*. Princeton, NJ: USA University Press.

Fischer-Lichte, E. (2012). 'Appearing as Embodied Mind: Defining a Weak a Strong and a Radical Concept of Presence', in G. Giannachi, N. Kaye & M. Shanks (eds), *Archaeologies of Presence: Art, Performance and the Persistence of Being*. London & New York: Routledge, pp. 103–118.

Fischer-Lichte, E. & Saskya, I. J. (2008). *The Transformative Power of Performance*. London & New York: Routledge.

Foucault, M. T. & Hurley, R. (1985). *The Uses of Pleasure. A History of Sexuality* (vol. 2). London: Penguin.

Franck, F. (1981). *Art as a Way: A Return to the Spiritual Roots*. New York: Crossroad Publishing Company.

Frost, A. (1998). 'Timor Mortis Conturbuit Nos: Improvising Tragedy and Epic', in C. McCullough (ed.), *Theatre Praxis*. Basingstoke: Macmillan, pp. 151–173.

Frost, R. (1920). *The Road Not Taken*. www.poetryfoundation.org

Fuchs, E. (1996). *The Death of Character: Perspectives on Theatre after Modernism*. Indianapolis, IN: Indiana University Press.

Fuchs, E. (2004). '*EF's Visit to a Small Planet*: Some Questions to Ask a Play'. *Theater Magazine* 34(2), pp. 4–9.

Gardner, L. (2008). 'Not Puppets, but Thinking Actors'. *Guardian*, 15 July 2008.

Gillett, J. (2014). *Acting Stanislavski: A Practical Guide to Stanislavski's Approach and Legacy*. London & New York: Bloomsbury Methuen.

Ginters, L. (2008). 'Lindy Davies: A Path to A Process, Part 2'. *Australasian Drama Studies* 52(April), pp. 78–90.

Glinert, E. (ed.) (2006). *The Complete Gilbert and Sullivan*. London: Penguin.

Goebbels, H. (2015). *Aesthetics of Absence: Texts on Theatre*. London & New York: Routledge.

Goldman, W. (2001). *Which Lie Did I Tell?* New York: Bloomsbury.

Gomez-Pena, G. (2005). *Ethno Techno*. London: Routledge.

Gorchakov, N. M. (1954). *Stanislavsky Directs*. London: Minerva Press.

Gough, R. (2018). 'Future Proof (With Courage & Curiosity): Training for a Theatre that Does Not Yet Exist', *Polish Theatre Journal* 1(5), pp. 1–12.
Govedic, N. (2014). 'Questions about Secret Service' *Novi List*, Zagreb 3.7.
Gray, P. (1965). *Stanislavski and America*. New York: Hill and Wang.
Grotowski, J. (1966). *Plea for a Poor Theatre Flourish*. Stratford-upon-Avon: Royal Shakespeare Company.
Grotowski, J. (1968). *Towards a Poor Theatre*. New York: Simon and Schuster.
Gutekunst, C. & Gillett, J. (2014). *Voice into Acting: Integrating Voice and the Stanislavsky Approach*. London: Bloomsbury Methuen Drama.
Hartenberger, U. (2011). 'Why Buildings Matter'. https://www.parliament.uk/about/living-heritage/building/palace/architecture/palacestructure/churchill/
Hazlitt, W. (2004). *Selected Essays of William Hazlitt 1778–1830*. Whitefish, MT: Kessinger Publishing.
Heddon, D. & J. Milling (2015). *Devising Performance: A Critical History*. Basingstoke: Palgrave Macmillan.
Heidegger, M. (1960). *Origins of a Work of Art*. isites.harvard.edu
Henri, R. (1960). *The Art Spirit*. Philadelphia: J. B. Lippincott Company.
Hite, B. C. (2015). *Positive Psychological Capital, Need Satisfaction, Performance, and Well-Being in Actors and Stunt People*. Thesis, Minneapolis: Walden University.
Hobart, A. (2003). *Healing Performances of Bali: Between Darkness and Light*. Oxford: Berghahn.
Hodge, A. (2006). *Twentieth Century Actor Training*. London & New York: Routledge.
Houseman, B. (2002). *Finding Your Voice: A Step-By-Step Guide for Actors*. London: Nick Hern Books.
Houseman, B. (2008). *Tackling Text (and Subtext): A Step-By-Step Guide for Actors*. London: Nick Hern Books.
Huang, A. C. (1973). *Embrace Tiger, Return to Tiger Mountain: the Essence of Tai Chi*. Salt Lake City, UT: Real Peoples Press.
Huxley, M. & Witts, N. (1996). *The Twentieth-Century Performance Reader*. London & New York: Routledge.
Ingold, T. (2000). *The Perception of the Environment Essays on Livelihood, Dwelling and Skill*. London: Routledge.
James, D. J. (1952). *The Universities and the Theatre*. Sydney: Allen & Unwin.
Janisheski, J. (2014). 'Empire of Stillness: The Six Essential Aspects of Japanese Noh'. *Conversation*, 18 June 2014. http://theconversation.com/empire-of-stillness-the-six-essential-aspects-of-japanese-noh-27517
Jones, T. (2009). 'Toby Jones: "I delve into a character's physicality"'. *Guardian*, 9 May 2009. https://www.theguardian.com/stage/2009/may/09/toby-jones-character-physicality
Joseph, B. L. (1959). *The Tragic Actor*. London: Routledge and Kegan Paul.
Joseph, B. L. (1960). *Acting Shakespeare*. London: Routledge and Kegan Paul.
Joseph, B. L. (1964). *Elizabethan Acting*. Oxford: Oxford University Press.
Kazan, E. (2013). 'Notebook for A Streetcar Named Desire', in T. Cole and H. Krich Chinoy (eds), *Directors on Directing: A Source Book of the Modern Theatre*. Indianapolis, IN: Bobbs-Merrill.

Kemp, R. (2012). *Embodied Acting: What Neuroscience Tells Us about Performance*. London & New York: Routledge.
Knowles, R. P. (1996). 'Interrogating the Natural Voice', in J. C. Bulman (ed.), *Shakespeare, Theory and Performance*. London & New York: Routledge, pp. 92–113.
Kostelanetz, R. (2003). *Conversing with Cage*. London: Psychology Press.
Kunio, K. (1983). *The Noh Theatre: Principles and Perspectives*. New York, Tokyo: Weatherhill/Tankkosha.
Kunitz, S. (2002). *The Collected Poems*. New York: W. W. Norton & Company.
Laing, B. (2013). 'Who Needs Live Art. An Ongoing Rant', in Lois Keidan, L and A . Wright (eds) *The Live Art Almanac* (vol. 3). London: Oberon Books.
Lakoff, G. & Johnson, M. (1999). *Philosophy in the Flesh: The Embodied Mind and Its Challenge to Western Thought*. New York: Basic Books.
Larkin, P. (1988). *Collected Poems*. London: Faber and Faber.
Leabhart, T. (2004). 'Jacques Copeau, Etienne Decroux, and the "Flower of Noh"', *New Theatre Quarterly* 20(4), 315–330.
Lechte, J. (1994). *Fifty Key Contemporary Thinkers*. London: Routledge.
Linklater, K. (1992). *Freeing Shakespeare's Voice: The Actor's Guide to Talking the Text*. New York: Theatre Communications Group.
Lyotard, J. F. (2011). *Discourse, Figure*. Minneapolis, MI: University of Minnesota Press.
Machon, J. (2009). *(Syn)Aesthetics: Redefining Visceral Performance*. Basingstoke: Palgrave MacMillan.
Machon, J. (2013). *Immersive Theatres: Intimacy and Immediacy in Contemporary Performance*. Basingstoke: Palgrave MacMillan.
Mamet, D. (1997). *True and False: Heresy and Common Sense for the Actor*. New York: Pantheon Books.
Mandell, J. (2017). 'Cooling Down: How Actors Unwind After Taxing Performances', *American Theatre*, March 2017.
Maxwell, I., Seton, M. & Szabó, M. (2015). 'The Australian Actor's Wellbeing Study: A Preliminary Report', *About Performance* 13, pp. 69–113.
McCallum, J. (2009). *Belonging: Australian Playwriting in the 20th Century*. Sydney: Currency Press.
McGilchrist, I. (2009). *The Master and His Emissary: The Divided Brain and the Making of the Western World*. New Haven and London: Yale University Press.
McMahon, B. (2012). 'Unemployment is Lifestyle for Actors'. http:www.huffingtonpost.com/Brendan-mcmahon
Mehrabian, A. (1972). *Silent Messages: Implicit Communication of Emotions and Attitudes*. Belmont: Wadsworth Publishing Company.
Meisner, S. (1987). *Sanford Meisner on Acting*. New York: Vintage.
Merrifield, N. (2013). 'Three-year drama training not needed by 'majority of actors'. *Stage*, October 24 2013.
Ming, Y. J. (1996). *Tai Chi Theory and Martial Power*. Wolfeboro, NH: YMAA Publication Center Inc.
Moor, A. L. (2013). *Contemporary Actor Training in Australia*. QUT eprints. https://eprints.qut.edu.au/63083/

Moore, T. (2016). 'Why Theater Majors are Vital in the Digital Age', *Chronicle of Higher Education*, 3 April 2016. http://www.chronicle.com/article/Why-Theater-Majors-Are-Vital/235925
Morris, E. (2005). *Being and Doing: Workbook for Actors*. Los Angeles: Ermor Enterprises.
Moss, L. (2005). *The Intent to Live: Achieving Your True Potential as an Actor*. New York: Bantam Dell.
Motokiyo, Z. (1984). *On the Art of the No Drama: The Major Treatises of Zeami* (translated by J. Thomas Rimer and Yanazaki Masakazu). Princeton, NJ: Princeton University Press.
Mroz, D. (2011). *The Dancing Word: An Embodied Approach to the Preparation of Performers and the Composition of Performances*. Amsterdam and New York: Rodopi.
Nachmanovitch, S. (1991). *Free Play: Improvisation in Life and Art*. New York: G. P. Putnam.
Nagler, A. M. (1959). *A Sourcebook in Theatrical History*. New York: Dover Books.
Nitschke, C. (1988). *Ma: Place, Space and Void*. Kyoto Journal 38. http://www.kyotojournal.org/the-journal/culture-arts/ma-place-space-void/
Noe, A. (2008). 'Précis of Action In Perception: Philosophy and Phenomenological Research', International Phenomenological Society. LXXVI(3, May). University of California, Berkeley.
Noe, A. (2012). *Varieties of Presence*. Cambridge, MA: Harvard University Press.
Odets, C. (1998). *Waiting for Lefty*. New York: Dramatists Play Service.
Ohno, K. & Ohno, Y. (2004). *Kazuo Ohno's World: From Without & Within* (translated by J. Barrett & T. Mizohata). Middletown: Wesleyan.
Oida, Y. & Marshal, L. (1997). *The Invisible Actor*. London: Methuen.
Olsberg, D. (1944). *Freedom, Structure, Freedom: Anne Bogart's Directing Philosophy*. PhD Thesis, Texas Tech University.
Olson, S. A. (2002). *Qigong Teaching of Taoist Immortal 'The Eight Essential Exercises of Master Li Ching-Yu'*. Rochester, NY: Healing Arts Press.
Oteri, F. (2000). 'Pauline Oliveros Interview: Creating, Performing and Listening', *New Music Box*. https://nmbx.newmusicusa.org/pauline-oliveros-creating-performing-and-listening/10/
Palmer, P. (2007). *The Courage to Teach: Exploring the Inner Landscape of a Teacher's Life*. San Francisco: Jossey-Bass.
Papacharissi, Z. (2010). *A Private Sphere: Democracy in a Digital Age*. Malden: Polity.
Pascal, B. (2006). *Pensees*. New York: Open Road Integrated Media inc. Philosophical Library, https://ebookcentral.proquest.com/lib/unimelb/detail.action?docID=4353553#
Patanjali (2017). *The Yoga Sutras of Patanjali*. Buckingham: Digireads.com Publishing.
Paul, A. M. (2012). 'School of Hard Knocks: "How Children Succeed," by Paul Tough'. *New York Times*, 23 August 2012.
Pavis, P. (1987). *Dictionary of the Theatre: Terms, Concepts, and Analysis*. Toronto, ON: University of Toronto Press.
Pavis, P. (1992). *Theatre at the Crossroads of Culture*. London & New York: Routledge.
Pitches, J. (2012). 'Lexicon of Training Terms', *Theatre Dance and Performance Training* 3, 3.
Plunka, G. A. (1992). *The Rites of Passage of Jean Genet: The Art and Aesthetics of Risk Taking*. Madison: Fairleigh Dickinson Associated University Presses, Inc.

Prior, R., Maxwell, I., Szabó, M. & Seton, M. (2015). 'Responsible Care in Actor Training: Effective Support for Occupational Health Training in Drama Schools', *Theatre Dance and Performance Training*. Taylor and Francis online.
Rabkin, G. (1983). The Play of Misreading: Text/Theatre/Deconstruction. *Performing Arts Journal* 19, 7.
Ramzyk, S. M. (2002). *Delicious Dissembling*. London: Heinemann.
Reed-Danahay, D. (1997). *Auto/Ethnography: Rewriting the Self and the Social*. Oxford & New York: Berg.
Reeve, J. & Jang, H. (2006). 'What Teachers Say and Do to Support Students' Autonomy during a Learning Activity', *Journal of Educational Psychology* 98(1), 209–218.
Ren, H. (2016). 'Digital Performance: How representations of physical and virtual bodies inform identity construction/deconstruction'. MPhil Thesis, Brunel University.
Robb., A. E. & Due, C. (2017). 'Exploring Psychological Wellbeing in Acting Training: An Australian Interview Study', in J. Pitches and L. Worth (eds) *Theatre Dance and Performance Training*. Taylor and Francis online.
Robinson, D. (1999). *Nietzsche and Postmodernism*. Cambridge: Icon Books.
Rodenburg, P. (2002). *Speaking Shakespeare*. London: Methuen.
Rogers., C. (1961). *On Becoming a Person: A Therapist's View of Psychotherapy*. New York: Houghton, Mifflin, Harcourt.
Rosen, C. (2000). *Creating the 'Berkovian' Aesthetic*. PhD Thesis. https://www.iainfisher.com/berkoff/berkoff-study-a1.html
Safir, M. A. (2011). *Robert Wilson from Within*. Paris: The American University of Paris.
Salter, D. (1996). *Acting Shakespeare in Postcolonial Space Shakespeare, Theory, and Performance*. London & New York: Routledge.
Sardi, P. (2016). 'When acting techniques become dogma and acting teachers become gurus'. https://www.linkedin.com/pulse/when-acting-techniques-become-dogma-teachers-gurus-peter-sardi
Schechner, R. (1968). '6 Axioms for Environmental Theatre', *The Drama Review: TDR* 12(3, Spring), 41–64.
Schechner, R. (1970). *Dionysus in 69*. Performance Group. New York: Farrar, Straus and Giroux.
Schechner, R. (2006). *Performance Studies: An Introduction* (2nd edn). London & New York: Routledge.
Schechner, R. (2010). on rites and rituals in *Dionysus in 69*: Online Dramaturgy, 20 November 2010. Part 3: https://www.youtube.com/watch?v=bcZvjm6fHqs&t=2s
Schell, H. (2011). *Casting Revealed: A Guide for Film Directors*. Studio City: Michael Wiese Productions.
Schlovsky, V. (1917). *Theory of Prose*. G. L. Burns (trans.) Illinois: Dalkey Archive Press.
Schnizler, A. (2004). *Round Dance and Other Plays*. Oxford: World Classics.
Schonmann, S. 'Ethical Tensions in Drama Teachers' Behaviour'. https://view.office-apps.live.com/op/view.aspx?src=http%3A%2F%2Fwww.theatroedu.gr%2Fportals%2F38%2Fmain%2Fimages%2Fstories%2Ffiles%2FArthra%2FSCHONMANN_Ethical%2520Tensions%2520in%2520Drama%2520Teachers.doc

Seton, M. (2010). 'The Ethics of Embodiment: Actor Training and Habitual Vulnerability', *Performing Ethos* 1(1), 5–20.
Sextou, P. (2016). 'The Pedagogy of Drama Supervision in Higher Education', *Brookes eJournal of Learning and Teaching* 3, 1. http://bejlt.brookes.ac.uk/paper/the_pedagogy_of_drama_supervision_in_higher_education-2/
Shakespeare, W. (2006). *Hamlet: The Texts of 1603 and 1623*. London, New Delhi, New York, Sydney: Bloomsbury.
Snow, G. (2018). 'Drama schools commit to ethical guidelines to tackle sexual harassment'. *Stage*, 19 April 2018. https://www.thestage.co.uk/news/2018/drama-schools-commit-ethical-guidelines-tackle-sexual-harassment/
Sörensen, S. (2017). 'Constructed reality or deconstructed fiction – immersive strategies in the work of SIGNA'. Summer Scriptwriting Camp TAM, Velico Tarnovo. https://www.youtube.com/watch?v=5DwUBeT9v8c
Stanislavski, K. (1987). *The Stanislavski Technique Russia: A Workbook for Actors*. New York: Applause.
Stanislavski, K. (1989). *An Actor Prepares*. London & New York: Routledge.
Stanislavski, K. (2008). *An Actor's Work: A Student's Diary* (translated by Jean Benedetti). London & New York: Routledge.
Stanislavski, K. *Stanislavski Quotes*. www.azquotes.com
Steadman, M. J. (1998). *The Presentation of Shakespeare's Plays on BBC Radio*. Birmingham: University of Birmingham.
Strasberg, L. (1988). *A Dream of Passion: the Development of the Method*. New York: Plume.
Suzuki, T. (2015). *Culture is the Body: The Theatre Writings of Tadashi Suzuki*. New York: Theatre Communications Group.
Swanson, L. (2011). 'Exploring Taksu & Meditation – Mysterious Power and the Tools to Realize It'. Independent Study Project (ISP) Collection. Paper 1242. http://digitalcollections.sit.edu/isp_collection/1242
Taylor, G. & Wilson, P. (2015). *Dramatic Adventures in Rhetoric*. London: Oberon Books.
Taylor, S. L. (2016). *Actor Training and Emotions – Finding a Balance*. Thesis, Western Australian Academy of Performing Arts (WAAPA).
Teatret, O. (1989–2012). *JUDITH*. Holstebro, Denmark: Odin Teatret Film.
Trevis, D. (2011). 'Are Drama Schools Training Actors for Real Life?'. *Guardian*, 5 October 2011. https://www.theguardian.com/stage/theatreblog/2011/oct/05/poor-actors-training-job-opportunities
Trussler, S. (1994). *The Cambridge Illustrated History of British Theatre*. Cambridge: Cambridge University Press.
Tuppen-Corps, A. (2017). https://www.alicetuppencorps.com/about
Tysome, T. (2004). 'Focus Theatre'. *Times Higher Education*, 16 April 2004 (23–24).
Vanbrugh, J. (1971). *The Relapse*. London: Methuen Drama.
Vaughan, R. (2018). 'The i: Mental health crisis among students "must be a top priority"', Office for Students, UK, 13 August 2018.
Viala, J. & Masson-Sekine, N. (1988). *Butoh: Shades of Darkness*. Tokyo: Shufunotomo Co.
Walker, M. B. (1979–1980). *East 15 Acting School Prospectus*.

Wangh, S. (2013). *The Heart of Teaching: Empowering Students in the Performing Arts*. London: Routledge.

Wegner, H. W. (1976). 'The Creative Circle: Stanislavski and Yoga', *Educational Theatre Journal* 28(1, March), 85–89. https://www.meetup.com/Wellbeing-for-the-Arts/

Werner, S. 'Performing Shakespeare: Voice Training and the Feminist Actor', *New Theatre Quarterly* XII(47), 249–258.

Werry, M. & Róisín, O. (2012). 'The Anatomy of Failure: An Inventory', *Performance Research* 17(1), 105–110.

Willis, B. (2008). *Text, Subtext and Vocal Resonance: Speaking Shakespeare on the Twentieth Century English Stage*. Birmingham: University of Birmingham.

Worthen, W. B. (1997). *Shakespeare and the Authority of Performance*. Cambridge: Cambridge University Press.

Worthen, W. B. (2008). 'Hamlet at Ground Zero: The Wooster Group and the Archive of Performance'. Oxford University Press: *Shakespeare Quarterly* 3(59, Fall), pp. 303–322.

Zarrilli, P. ed. (2002). *Acting (Re) Considered: A Theoretical and Practical Guide*. London & New York: Routledge.

Zarrilli, P. (2009). *Psychophysical Acting: An Intercultural Approach after Stanislavski*. London & New York: Routledge.

Zarrilli, P. (2015). 'The Actor's Work on Attention, Awareness, and Active Imagination: Between Phenomenology, Cognitive Science, and Practices of Acting', in M. Bleeker, J. F. Sherman & E. Nedelkopoulou (eds), *Performance and Phenomenology: Traditions and Transformations*. London & New York: Routledge, pp. 75–97.

Index

Note: Page numbers with n refer to notes.

A

Abdelazar, 76
Aboriginal Australians, 148
Aboriginal Tent Embassy, 148
accompanying circumstances, 204
acting
    as action, 199–214; *See also* active analysis
    in immersive and interactive performance, 158–176; *See also* interactivity and immersion
    introduction to craft of, 86–94; *See also* scene or monologue, beginning work on
    styles, 202; *See also* acting-training methodologies
Acting in Restoration Comedy (Callow), 66
Acting Shakespeare (Joseph), 120
Acting Shakespeare in a Postcolonial Space (Salter), 130
Acting Stanislavski: A practical guide to Stanislavski's approach and legacy (Gillett), 19n5
acting-training methodologies
    establishing understanding of, 35–37
    physical actions as official government-sanctioned approach, 198
    possible harmful effects of, 37
Acting Up, 23n53
actions
    acting as, 199–214
    blueprint of, 201–204
    change of, in process of evaluation, 205, 207
    counteraction and, 212
    definition of, 90–91
    doing, 201
    driving/controlling, 147, 152
    exercise, 231–232
    feelings rising from, 211
    invisible action, 200–208
    living believably, 201, 208
    physical, 139, 198
    play, 196, 201, 209–211
    in script analysis, 147, 148
    visible action, 200–201, 208–213
    See also active analysis; terminology, action-based acting
active analysis, 196–201, 208, 212, 214
    acting as action, 199
    cognitive analysis in, 198, 199, 200, 201–208, 212–213
    ownership and, 213–214
    physical actions in, 139, 198
    physical analysis in, 198, 199, 201, 208–213
    Stanislavski's development of, 198–199
activities, 205
Actors Center, 197
Actors Center Alliance of Teachers, 20n7
Actor's Equity, 14
actor–spectator relationship, 10
Actors Studio, 17, 19n4
Actors Wellbeing Academy, 28
actor training
    across borders, 177–193
    attaining individual virtuosity in, 116n51

257

258 Index

biases, 15, 16
conservatoire model schools, 40–41
contexts, 15–16
devised work and, 5, 34, 136
diversity in, 3, 5, 15, 23n53, 228
foundation training, 100–102, 105, 106–108, 112
histories, 13–16
impulse training, 32, 108
inclusion in, 5, 16
interactivity and immersion, 158–160
in liberal arts environment, 233–247
Method-based teaching, 36
new dramaturgical and interdisciplinary paradigms in, 5
practitioner/teacher in, 37–40
safe practices in, 5
skill-based, 123
teachers in, 37–42
teacher–student ethics in, 5
value and, 17–19
welfare in, 5, 31
wellness in, 5, 27; *See also* mental health; well-being
widening participation in, concerns over, 5, 15–16
workload, 41
See also acting-training methodologies; holistic actor training
Actor Training and Emotions – Finding a Balance (Taylor), 28
acupuncture points, Tai'ji, 115n33
Adler, Stella, 218
aesthetics of interactivity and immersion, 160–162
agency, developing, 30, 34
aletheia, 58
All My Sons (Miller), 221
American Society for Theatre Research, 20n7
American Theatre, 27, 146, 197
Amphitryon, 76
ankoku butoh, 157n42

Annual International Conference on Visual and Performing Arts, 7th, 125
Antigone (Carson), 148, 149–153
Antigones, contemporary, 148
antithesis, 82
Antoine, André, 136
arc
  in composition work, 152
  in script analysis, 147
architecture, 145, 156n32
Artaud, Antonin, 153, 161
Artist Development and Training in the Royal Shakespeare Company (Darnley), 121
Artsminds, UK, 27
Art Spirit, The (Henri), 151
asanas (body poses), 184–185
Ashtanga, 178
Assange, Julian, 148
assessment tasks, 41
As You Like It (Shakespeare), 54
athletes, parallels between actors and, 184
Attenborough, Richard, 13
attention
  energy flows and, 210
  target of, 205, 206–207, 210
  in yoga, 187–188
Australasian Drama Studies Conference, 20n7
Australia, 2, 14
  aboriginal practices of yoga in a circle, 180
  diversity of texts in, 222
  improving curriculum in, 40
  Stanislavski and, 218–219
  well-being initiatives in, 26–27, 28
  See also National Institute of Dramatic Art (NIDA); Queensland University of Technology (QUT)
Australian Actors Wellbeing Study, The (Maxwell), 27, 28, 29
Australian Society for Performing Arts Healthcare (ASPAH), 28
Autonomous Actor, 32–33
autonomy, establishing, 29, 32–34

B

bachelor of arts in theatre (BA theatre), 4, 14, 16, 20n10, 31, 46, 85–86, 158, 174, 196
bachelor of fine arts (BFA), 23n48, 26, 27–28, 85, 154n3, 196
back stage behaviour, 10
BA(Hons) acting, 158
Bausch, Pina, 138, 163
BBC advisory committee on spoken English, 119
Beale, Simon Russell, 120
beat, 91–92
beats, in script analysis, 147
Becher's Brook, 65, 83n4
Beckett, Samuel, 205
behavioural characteristics class, 51–52
'being in the moment,' 38
Benedetti, Robert, 21n19
Beque, Henry, 47
Berry, Cicely, 126
biases, 15, 16
    training approaches impacted by, 15
Bikram, 178, 180
Billings, Alexandra, 197
Birmingham City University, 16
Black Lives Matter, 148
Blatchley, John, 45
blocking, 98, 147, 153, 187, 226–228
Blonska, Agnieszka, 158
Boal, Augusto, 154
Body Speaks, The (Marshall), 113n10
body training, 7
Bogart, Anne, 6, 21n17, 140, 143, 144–146, 147, 151–152, 153, 155n19, 156n29, 184, 235, 239, 241
Bomber, Alison, 126
Booth, Edwin, 120
Branagh, Kenneth, 124
breathe, understanding when and when not to, 220–221
Brecht, Bertolt, 126, 161, 173–174
Brechtian displacement, 126
Bretton Hall College, 20n9
briefing sheet, 48, 55, 56, 60
Bristol Old Vic Theatre School, 23n53
Bristol University, 13–14
British acting schools
    received pronunciation (RP) in, 118–119, 123–124, 126
    teachers in the establishment of, 118
Brook, Peter, 154, 221
Brown Ash, Margi, 31–32
Bruford, Rose, 118
Bryars, Gavin, 20n9
Buchanan, Judith, 127
Burns, Robert, 48
Burton, Richard, 124
Bury Walker, Margaret, 45, 47, 51
butoh, 136, 137–138, 148–149

C

Caban, Andrea, 197
Cage, John, 20n9, 149, 161
Calderone, Marina, 19n5
California Repertory Company, 197
California State University, 21n18
California State University Long Beach (CSULB), 6, 196–197, 214
Callow, Simon, 66, 81
Cambridge University, 7
Cameron Mackintosh Visiting Professor of Contemporary Theatre, 13
Canberra, 148
Cannon, Dee, 17
Cannon, Doreen, 52
Cannon, Walter, 103
cant, 82
Cariston, Mark, 5
Carnegie Institute of Technology, 13
Carnicke, Sharon Marie, 197
Carreri, Roberta, 127
Carson, Anne, 148
Cart Macabre (Living Structures), 176n11
Central Saint Martins, 16

Central School of Speech and Drama, 118
centred, 107
Chambers, Colin, 124
character
   archetypes, 66
   driving force of, created by playwrights, 219
   études in character work, 150–151
   exercises ('who' in you), 229–230
   Mamet's idea of 'no such thing as character,' 222–223, 225
   objective of, 88–89
   obstacle of, 89–90
   out of, 11, 163
   playwrights on actors becoming, 222–223
   psychological life of, 141
   reasons for being in scenes, 212
   spine or super-objective of, 142, 155n23
   time provided for interaction, 203
   work, 150–151
   writing in character exercises, 229
'Chasing Sheep Is Best Left To Shepherds,' 77
Chekhov, Michael, 20n9, 45, 51, 112n1, 138, 153, 197, 198, 199, 208, 210, 221
Chinoy, Helen Krich, 155n23
choral work, 148–150
choreography, 28, 153, 179, 184
Churchill, Winston, 144
City University of London, 16
Claxton, G., 112n1, 114n22
Clay, Jack, 197
Clouzot, Catherine, 51
cognitive analysis, 198, 199, 200, 201–208, 212–213
Cole, Toby, 155n23
Colman, Geoffrey, 21n22
Columbia University, 140
composition work, 151–153
Condron, Aiden, 158
Confederation of Australian State Theatre Companies (CAST), 28

confident command of and holding the space exercises, 75–81
   I'm worth your attention, 77–78
   king/queen and the peasants, 76–77
   relish the words, 78–81
   unassailable opinion – the epigram, 78
conflict, 89–90, 92–93
Congreve, W., 82
conservatoire training
   academy supporting, 40–41
   at East 15, 46, 58
   at QUT, 40–41
   at RBC, 16, 118–121, 125, 130
   at RSC, 129
   Stanislavski based, 218
   T/A/S in, 228
   at WAAPA, 218, 228
conventions, 6
Copeau, Jacques, 45, 112n1
corpus callosum, 103
cost of auditioning for drama school, 23n53
counteraction, action and, 212
Cowan, Edith, 23n54
creative process, neurological application to, 103–104
cultural necromancy, 127, 128

D

Dadaism, 161
Dajerling, Ula, 176n11
dan tian, 107
Dan Tian, 115n40
Darnley, Lyn, 118, 121
Dartington College of Arts, 20n9, 158
Davies, Lindy, 32–33, 108, 112, 116n51
deep listening philosophy, 149
delicious movement, 149
d'Emilia, Dani, 176n11
devised work, 5, 34, 136
Dey, Misri, 158
Dicks, Rob, 128
Dionysus in 69 (Schechner), 161–162

Directors on Directing: A Source Book of the Modern Theatre (Cole and Chinoy), 155n23
discovery, 93
'Disposition of the Linen, The,' 77
Distinguished Lecture Series, University of Southampton, 18
diversity, 3, 5, 15, 23n53, 228
Dixon, Steve, 11
doing, in interactivity and immersion, 158–160
doing as energy, 210–212
Dolgachev, Viacheslav, 197
Donnellan, Declan, 64, 65, 200, 210, 218
double entendres, 82
Draffin, Robert, 8
Drama Centre London, 16, 45, 47
drama school
    access to training in, equitable, 15
    cost of auditioning for, 23n53
    defined, 20n8
    financial support through government grants, 20n11
    purpose of, 16
    selection processes in, 15
    United Kingdom's Conference of Drama Schools, 16
    university theatre programmes compared to, 15
    validation of, 16
    values, 24n54
dramatic conflict, 142, 147
dramaturgy, 10
Draughtsman's Contract, The (Nyman), 77
dreamthinkspeak, 160
driving/controlling the action
    in composition work, 152
    in script analysis, 147
Duckworth, Angela, 35
Due, Clemence, 27, 28, 37
duration, 145, 156n31
dynamics
    competing forces for, 212
    in composition work, 152
    group, 34, 55, 139, 143
    of shapes, 145

East 15 Acting School, 3, 16, 24n54, 45–47
    approach to acting training in psychological and behavioural realism, 45–48
    non-judgemental space to explore, 47
    overall objective of, 45–48
    specialized courses, 45–48
    three strands of initial acting training, 45–46
Edith Cowan University, 23n54, 24n54
EF's Visit to a Small Planet (Fuchs), 147
Eiko and Koma, 149
Eisenberg, Alan, 14
Elizabethan Acting (Joseph), 120
embarrassment, 229–230
emotion, actor's experience of, 39, 140–141
employment opportunities, 7, 15, 159, 217
empty space, Brook's, 154
energy
    Chinese concept of, 102, 106–108, 115n40; *See also gōng fēng shuǐ*
    doing as, 210–212
    flows, attention and, 210
    human, 198
    work, 198
entering the gap, 104–105
Entertainment Assist, 28
environmental theatre, 161
epigrams, 81
Essex University, 46
Etherege, George, 67–68
ethics
    of consent, 5, 12, 162, 230
    integrity and, 12, 85, 183–184, 192
    of interactivity and immersion, 162–165
    physical contact and, 10, 12, 162, 165

études
  in active analysis, 199
  in character work, 150–151
  in choral work, 150
  nonverbal or 'silent, 138, 142, 155n12
  in observation exercises, 138–139
  patterns and, 142
  in physical analysis, 208
  pressures and, 143
  two- to three-minute, 150
  in work in rehearsal studio, 212–213
event, 93–94
  in composition work, 152
  defined, 204–205
  as a noun, 204
  in script analysis, 147
experimentation, 159, 164, 165, 198
Exploring psychological wellbeing in acting training: an Australian interview study (Robb and Due), 28
eyes, interacting, 166–168

F

Facebook, 64, 78
Faculty of Fine Arts and Music (FOFAAM), 113n2
failure, 218
fairy tale project, 56–57
Falmouth University, 6, 158–176
  aesthetics of interactivity and immersion, 160–162
  courses, 160
  ethics of interactivity and immersion, 162–165
  Living Structures, 166, 176n11
  process-based methods of training, 160
  professional practice, 165–166
  training, thinking, doing, 158–160
  workshop, 166–175
fang xin, 105–106, 114n26
Farrelly, Dan, 173
Fassbender, Michael, 139

Federation of Drama Schools, 12
feeling of ease, 210
feelings rising from actions, 211
Fender, Terrie, 158
fēng energy, Chinese concept of, 102, 107
  See also gōng fēng shuı̌
Ferguson, Dugald, 176n11
Fergusson, Francis, 59
Fettes, Christopher, 45
Financial Times, 121
first read-through, 96, 223–224
Fischer-Lichte, Erika, 9
five openings, 106
flock of birds, 185–186
floor pattern, 145
Flourish Magazine, 129
focus – attention/intention, in yoga, 187–188
Fogerty, Elsie, 118
Foucault, M., 50
foundation exercises, 108–111
foundation training, 100–102, 105, 112
  gōng fēng shuı̌ and, 106–108
frontal cortex, 103
front stage behaviour, 10
Frost, Robert, 48
Fuchs, Elinor, 146–147
Futurism, 161

G

Gallese, V., 103
gap
  entering, 104–105
  minding, 105–106, 112
  See also space or gap, in-between *(ma)*
General Certificate of Secondary Education (GCSE), 22n42
Gesamtkunstwerk, 161
gesture, 145, 156n32
Gielgud, John, 119, 124
Gilbert and Sullivan, 80–81
Gillett, John, 19n5

Ginters, L., 33
Gister, Earle, 197, 199, 211
given circumstances, 87–88, 96–98
goals, 35, 153–154
Goffman, Erving, 10
Goh Lay Kuan, 114n18
golden age of verse speaking, 121–122
gōng energy, Chinese concept of, 102, 107
   See also gōng fēng shuĭ
gōng fēng shuĭ
   foundation exercises, 108–111
   foundation training, 106–108
   rise and the fall (up is down, down is up, in is out, out is in), 109–110
   wind between object, body and hard surfaces, 110–111
   working the extremities (hands and feet), 109
   you are the horizon (experiencing spatial, textual and temporal energies), 111
Gough, Richard, 12, 158
Graham, Martha, 139, 155n15
grants, 20n11
Greer, Germaine, 119
Grotowski, Jerzy, 112n1, 128, 129, 153, 161, 234
grounded, 107
group composition assignment, 246–247
group dynamics, 34, 55, 139, 143
Guardian, 119–120
Guildford, 16
Guildhall, 16, 23n53
Guthrie, Tyrone, 13–14
Gu Yian, 105–106, 113n4, 114n24, 114n27

Hackey Sack Tag, 231–232
Hagen, Uta, 45
Hall, John, 20n9
Hamlet (Shakespeare), 64, 119, 124–129, 199, 221
   Branagh's movie, 124
   gender expectations, 127
   1603 quarto version of, 125–130
   Wooster Group version of, 124–125, 127
Handel, 76
hands and feet (working the extremities), 109
Hatha, 178
Hazlitt, William, 64, 65
Heddon, Deirdre, 15
Heidegger, Martin, 1, 58
heightened language plays, 136
hemispheres of the brain, 103, 105, 113n12, 114n23
Henri, Robert, 151
Herzberg, Amy, 197
higher education (HE), 46
Higher Education Funding Council, 14
History of Voice Teaching in Britain, A (Darnley), 118
Hite, Brian C., 28
holistic actor training, 26–43
   academy supporting the conservatoire, 40–41
   agency, developing, 34
   autonomy, establishing, 32–34
   awareness of actor's health and well-being, 28–29
   identity, establishing and supporting, 30–32
   knowledge of acting methodologies, 35–37
   principles of teaching actors, 41–42
   recommendations into practice, 29–30
   recommendations to drama schools, 26–28
   skills for well-being (mindfulness practices), 34–35
   teacher in, 37–39
   teaching practices, new model of, 39–40
   workload, 41
horizontal/intention practice, 187–188

hours of study, 23n52
Houseman, Barbara, 126
human behaviour, 62, 141, 199, 201–202
human relationships, 61, 65–66
Hytner, Nicholas, 13

'I am' (poetic text assignment), 48
Idea of a Theatre, The (Fergusson), 59
identity, establishing and supporting, 29, 30–32
imaginings, neurological creative process involving, 103–104
immersive theatre, 9–10, 160–162, 166
improvisations, 21n17, 54, 55, 150–151, 153, 162, 171, 213
improvisatory exercises, 230–231
   Mike Leigh Hands, 230
   She Went to Sea in a Sieve, 230–231
   Status Game, 231
impulse training, 32, 108
incidents from the high street (exercise), 51–52
inclusion, 5, 16
Indonesia, somatic training in, 8
Infamous, 140
Ingold, T., 104
Inside the Royal Shakespeare Company (Chambers), 124
integrity of the circle, 183–184
intention, in yoga, 187–188
interactivity and immersion, 158–176
   aesthetics of, 160–162
   ethics of, 162–165
   instructions to students, 169–171
   interacting eyes, 166–168
   intimacy, exploring boundaries of, 171–175
   professional practice, 165–166, 174
   range, 168–169
   teachers asking questions of their/our own practice concerning, 164–165
   training, thinking, doing, 158–160
   workshop, 166–175
International Platform for Performer Training, 20n7
interpersonal interaction, 10
interpretation, 62
intimacy, exploring boundaries of, 171–175
Intimacy Directors International, 163
invisible action, 200–208
   blueprint of, 201–204
   definition of, 200
   event as a noun, 204
   event defined, 204–205
   process of evaluation, 205–208
   reading, 201–208
Invisible Actor (Marshall and Oida), 113n10
Ionesco, Eugène, 161

Jackson, Kevin, 220–221
James, Adrian, 8
Janisheski, Jeff, 1, 6, 9, 21n18
Jenkins, Mark, 197
jian (downward energy), 115n40
Jīng Lu, 115n34
Jo-ha-kyu, 149
Jones, Toby, 140
Jordan, Richard, 17
Joseph, Bertram, 120
JUDITH, 127

kai xin, 105
kamae, 149
kāng (upward energy), 115n40
Kazan, Elia, 17, 155n23
Kean, Edmund, 64
Kemble, John Philip, 64
Kemp, Edward, 119–120
Kemp, Richard, 103, 115n43
kinesthetic response, 145

Kings College London, 16
Knebel, Maria Osipovna, 197, 198, 199
knowledge
  in establishing understanding of acting methodologies, 30, 35–37
  mental health/well-being and, 30, 35–37
  somatic, 101, 105, 106, 107, 112, 112n1
koans, 138, 154n6
Koestler, Arthur, 162–163
Komparu, Kunio, 102
Krantz, James, 42
Kruse, Klaus, 5, 9, 12, 158, 176n11
Kuan Yin, 104
Kulit, Wayang, 101
Kundalini, 178, 187
Kunitz, Stanley, 141
Kuo Pao Kun, 104, 114n18

Laban, Rudolph, 20n9
Lakoff, G., 103
language
  heightened language plays, 136
  as persuasion, 65
  power of, 65, 81
  taste of, 66
  teaching text in era of language loss, 84–99
  See also text
large circle of circumstances, 203
leading circumstances, 203–204
Lebank, Ezra, 197
left hemisphere of the brain, 103, 105, 113n12, 114n23
Lehmann, Hans-Thies, 12
liberal arts environment, actor training in, 233–247
  ideals of the art, 235–236
  liberal education, 236–237
  people in studio, 238–243

personal creative agenda, 243
professionalism, 237–238
reclamation, 234–235
summing up, 244–246
teachers being wrong, 244
workshop exercise, 246–247
Linklater, Kristin, 126
Littlewood, Joan, 45, 46
living believably, 201, 208
Living Structures, 166, 176n11
London's Central School, 21n22
Love for Love (Congreve), 82

ma, Japanese concept of, 102–103
  See also space or gap, in-between *(ma)*
Macauley, Alistair, 121
Mahler, Gustav, 153
Malmgren, Yat, 45, 51
Mamet, David, 17, 222–223, 225
Manning, Chelsea, 148
Man of Mode, The (Etherege), 67–75, 81, 82
mantra, 188–189
Margolis, Ellen, 5
Marshall, Lorna, 102–103, 113n10
master in fine arts (MFA), 19n4, 46, 125, 126, 154n3, 155n19, 196
master of arts (MA), 53
mastery, requirements to arriving at, 196
Maxwell, I., 27, 28, 29
McCall, Michael, 6, 8–9
McCarron, Cathleen, 81
McGilchrist, Iain, 103, 113n12
Mechs, Rude, 162
Medea, 155n19
Media Entertainment and Arts Alliance (MEAA), 28
meditation and mindfulness, 190–192
Mehrabian, Albert, 146
Meisner, Sanford, 201, 208, 210
Melbourne University, 24n54

mental health, 4–5
  acting methodologies, establishing understanding of, 35–37
  agency, developing, 30, 34
  autonomy, establishing, 29, 32–34
  identity, establishing and supporting, 29, 30–32
  initiatives in Australia, 26–27, 28
  knowledge, 30, 35–37
  mindfulness practices, 34–35
  recent developments in awareness of actor's, 28–29
  recommendations into practice, 29–30
  skills for, 30, 34–35
Merlin, Joanna, 197
metaphors, 10, 82
method acting, 24n58
#MeToo movement, 29, 165
Meunier, Danielle, 158
Meyerhold, Vsevolod, 146, 161, 199
middle circle of circumstances, 203
Mike Leigh Hands, 230
Miller, Arthur, 221
Miller, J. Michael, 197
Milling, Jane, 15
mimeticism, 18, 44, 47, 55
mind, definition and experience of, 105
  See also xin
mind–body connection, 141
mindfulness practices, 34–35
mind the gap, 105–106, 112
Ming, Yang Jwing, 114n23
Miss Julie (Strindberg), 147
Mitchell, Stephen, 221
Mnouchkine, Ariane, 235–236
moment before, 88
monkey mind, 191
Montessori Education System, 31
Moor, Andrea L., 5, 23n48
Moore, Tracey, 11
Morris, E., 218
Moscow Art Theatre (MAT), 181–182, 197, 198–199

Moss, L., 218
Mousetrap, The, 126–127
movement, 7
  assessment tasks, 41
  in character work, 151
  in choral work, 149
  gestures, 145
  in *gōng fēng shui*, 106–111
  patterns of, 142
  relaxation and breathing techniques, 34
  rise and the fall, 106, 109–110
  space and, 144
  T/A/S, 226–231
  tempo and, 145
  training, 34, 192
  in yoga, 178, 186, 190
Music for the Royal Fireworks (Handel), 76

N

National Alliance of Acting Teachers, 197
National Institute of Dramatic Art (NIDA), 1, 6, 15, 136–157, 220–221
  application to a play *(Antigone)*, 148
  character work, 150–151
  choral work, 148–150
  composition work, 151–153
  course satisfaction, 32
  courses offered, 154n3
  founding of, 154n3
  Fundamentals of Acting class at, 140
  goals, 153–154
  observation exercises, 138–139, 144
  patterns, 141–142
  people, 137–138
  physical life, 139–140
  pressures, 143
  psychological life, 140–141
  quotes guiding the NIDA actor, 137–138
  script analysis, 147–148
  space and time, 143–146
  strengths of, 137

text, 137, 146
Viewpoints, 6, 21n17, 136–137, 144–146
world of play, 146–147
National Student Satisfaction Survey, 122
National Theatre, 22n32
National Youth Theatre, 17
naturalism, 47, 57, 120, 123, 127–129, 136, 146, 225
Nelson, Richard, 227
neurological application to creative process, 103–104
New Drama Theatre of Moscow, 197
New National Theatre, 113n10
Nitschke, C., 102
Noe, Alva, 103–104, 108
noh, 148–149
non-naturalistic approach, 122, 126, 129
Norton, Edward, 21n19
'Notebook for *A Streetcar Named Desire*' (Kazan), 155n23
Nyman, Michael, 77
Nyong'o, Lupita, 153

object exercises, 52–57
objective
 character's, 88–89
 exercise, 231–232
 in script analysis, 147, 148
observation, 60–62
 exercises, 138–139, 144
 phenomenological, 53–54, 61
obstacles
 of character, 89–90
 Stanislavski's idea of, 219
Occupy Movement, 148
Odet, Clifford, 141
Odin Theatre, 127
'Of Her Chamber Poems' (Waller), 68
O'Gorman, Hugh, 8–9, 21n18
O'Gorman, Róisín, 218

Ohno, Kazuo, 138
Oida, Yoshi, 51, 113n10
Oldham, James Christopher, 126–127
Oliveros, Pauline, 149
Olson, Stuart Alve, 114n30
om, 183, 188–189
'On Actors and Acting' (Hazlitt), 64
online environments, 10–11
online identity construction, 10–11
Ostermeier, Thomas, 64–65
Other, the, 102, 103, 104, 105, 106
out of character, 11, 163
Overlie, Mary, 144, 156n29
Oxford University, 7, 13

Pace University New York, 19n4
Papacharissi, Zizi, 10
Parks, Suzan-Lori, 136
participatory performance, 163, 166
patterns, 141–142
Pavis, Patrice, 9
Pearson, Mike, 14–15
people, connecting to and/or collaborating with, 137–138
perception, neurological creative process involving, 103–104
Performance Group, 161, 234
Performing Arts Learning and Teaching Innovation Network, 20n7
Performing Arts Scoping Study, 20n7
performance, defined, 213
permission, 12, 33, 45, 47, 77–78, 213
personal communication, Mehrabian's ratio of, 146
phenomenological observation, 53–54, 61
physical actions, 139, 198
physical analysis, 198, 199, 201, 208–213
physical contact, 10, 12, 162, 165
physical life, 139–140
physical tactics, 148
Piscator, Erwin, 161

play
　application to, 148
　world of, 146–147
playing action, 196, 201, 208–211
playwrights
　actions of, 200–201
　on actors becoming characters, 222–223
　actors connecting to, 137
　approach to text, 221
　arbitrary approach by, 225
　biography of, analysing, 224
　creative agenda of, 243
　driving force of character created by, 219
　to give reasons for characters being in scenes, 212
　intentions of, 88, 91, 201
　leading circumstances and, 204
　movement and, 227
　playing (visible) action and, 209
　river of action designed by, 210
　in second read of the play, 224
　text punctuated by, 220–221
　time provided by, for characters to interact, 203
　traps written by, 94–95
Plough and the Stars, The, 22n32
poetry, 48–49
Positive Psychological Capital, Need Satisfaction, Performance, and Well-Being in Actors and Stunt People (Hite), 28
post-dramatic theatre, 9, 11–12, 119, 125
postmodern theatre, 9, 12, 119, 123, 125
potential, defined, 213
power imbalances, 12, 234
Powers, Mala, 197
practical aesthetics, 33, 38
Practice as Research in Performance, 20n7
practitioner *See* teacher
pranayama, 187
Presentation of Self in Everyday Life, The (Goffman), 10

pressures, 143
Prior, R., 27, 36
process of evaluation, 205–208
　accumulation of information, signs, signals, or attributes, 205, 206, 207
　assignment of highest value, 205, 207
　case of the fireman, 206–208
　case of the late student, 206
　change in target of attention, 205, 206–207
　change of action, 205, 207
professional practice, 165–166, 174
proprioception, 115n43
psychological life, 140–141
psychological tactics, 148
psychophysical approaches, 198–199
psychophysical events, 205
psychophysical exercises, 179
psychophysical level of training, 162
psychophysical life, 141, 146, 152
psychophysical manner of memory, 213
psychophysical practice, 192
psychophysical relationship, 131
psychophysical techniques, 159
Punchdrunk, 160
Purcell, Henry, 76
Pussy Riot, 148

Q

qigong, 106, 114n28
qualifications, 1
Queensland University of Technology (QUT), 26–43
　agency, developing, 34
　autonomy, establishing, 32–34
　course satisfaction, 32
　identity, establishing and supporting, 30–32
　knowledge of acting methodologies, 35–37
　principles of teaching actors, 41–42

skills for well-being (mindfulness practices), 34–35
success of, 23n48
supporting the conservatoire, 40–41
teacher, personal experience of, 37–39
teaching practices, new model of, 39–40
workload, 41
quest project, 57–58
Quick and Dirty Guide to Acting Terminology, 86

Rahardjo, Slamet, 101–102, 105, 116n48
raillery, 81
range, 168–169
rants, 82
Ravens, The (Beque), 47
reading invisible action, 201–208
'Reality TV Taking Over Acting Talents,' 21n22
Rebeck, Theresa, 95
received pronunciation (RP), 118–119, 123–124, 126
rehearsal process, 39, 56, 94, 112, 126, 159, 162, 163, 181
rehearsal space, 75, 229
rehearsal studio, work in, 212–213
rehearsal time, 217
Reinhardt, Max, 161
Relapse, The (Vanbrugh), 81, 82
relational impulse cultural collaborative (RICC) training, 31–32
relaxation and breathing techniques, 34–35
ren, 107, 115n37
Ren, Helenna, 11
repartee, 81
repetition, 4, 6, 31, 145, 150–151, 156n31, 184, 197
resistance, acknowledging, 42
Restoration comedy, 65, 66–67, 79
Restoration drama, 65–66
Restoration theatre, 7, 75

re-traumatization, 229–230
Rich, Paul, 144
Richards, Lloyd, 197
Rigg, Diana, 13
right hemisphere of the brain, 103, 104, 113n12
rise and the fall, 106, 109–110
River Fal Estuary, 173
roadmaps, student, 49–51
'Road Not Taken, The' (Frost), 48
Robb, Alison E., 27, 28, 37
Robson, Susan, 20n14
Rodenburg, Patsy, 225
Rondo, 76
Roseby, Paul, 17
Royal Academy of Dramatic Art (RADA), 3, 16, 17, 23n53, 65, 113n10, 119–120
Royal Birmingham Conservatoire, 16, 118, 119, 122, 125, 130
Royal Central School of Speech and Drama, 23n53
Royal National Theatre, 113n10
Royal Shakespeare Company (RSC), 81, 113n10, 119–120, 121, 124, 129
RSC Studio, 124
rtricolon, 82
Ruckert, Felix, 163–164
Russia, 138, 148, 197, 198

Sadak, Diane M., 5
safe practices, 5
Saint-Denis, Michel, 45
Salter, Denis, 130
salutations, yoga, 179
San Francisco State University (SFSU), 84–86
Saratoga International Theater Institute (SITI) Company, 6, 21n17, 184, 235, 239, 246
Sardi, Peter, 21n19

scene analysis, 38
   detailed biographical questions, 97–98
   given circumstances, 96–97
   scoring, 98
scene objective, 219–220
scene or monologue, beginning work on
   beat, 91–92
   character's objective, 88–89
   character's obstacle, 89–90
   conflict, 92–93
   discovery, 93
   event, 93–94
   given circumstances, 87–88
   group exercise, 94–96
   moment before, 88
   stakes, 92
   tactics, 90–91
   trap of the scene, 94–95
   See also terminology, action-based acting
Schechner, Richard, 12, 161–162, 164
Schlovsky, Viktor, 46
Schonmann, Shifra, 5
School of Dramatic Arts, University of Southern California, 197
school of fish, 185–186
School of Humanities at Essex University, 46
School of Theatre and Dance at San Francisco State University (SFSU), 84–86
scoring a script, 221
Screen Producers Australia (SPA), 28
script analysis, 147–148
second read-through, 224
Secret Cinema, 160
Secret Service (Ruckert), 163–164
self-actualization, 58–60
self-identification, 48, 180
self-model, study of, 48–49
Seton, Mark Cariston, 5, 28, 36
Sextou, Persephone, 5
Shakespeare, William
   British tradition in acting, 118–135
   dilemma of action *versus* inaction, 221
   first recording of Shakespeare, 120
   golden age of Shakespearean acting, 122
   naturalism in, 120, 127
   non-naturalistic approach, 122, 126, 129
   Sonnet 129 (Shakespeare), 130–134
   Willis's research on, 120–121
   word statues in acting Shakespeare (workshop exercise), 130–134
Shakespeare and the Authority of Performance (Worthen), 124–125
Shanghai International Performing Arts Research Centre (SIPARC), 113n4, 114n24, 114n27
Shanghai Theatre Academy, 113n4, 114n24
shape, 145
Shared Experience, 113n10
Shaw, Fiona, 140, 155n19
'She/He is' (poetic text assignment), 48
She Went to Sea in a Sieve, 230–231
Shifting Point, The (Brook), 221
shuī energy, Chinese concept of, 102, 107–108
   See also gōng fēng shuī
Shunt, 160
SIGNA, 162–163
Silent Messages (Mehrabian), 146
similitudes (similes), 81
Simms, Stephen, 9, 12
Sina, Tonia, 163
Singapore, somatic training in, 8
singing, 45, 118, 119, 123
'6 Axioms for Environmental Theatre' (Schechner), 161
1603 quarto *Hamlet* (Shakespeare), 125–130
skill-based training, 123
skills for well-being, 30, 34–35
small circle of circumstances, 203–204
   accompanying circumstances, 204
   leading circumstances, 203–204
Snowden, Edward, 148

somatic knowledge and practices, 8, 101, 105, 106, 107, 112, 112n1
Sonnet 129 (Shakespeare), 130–134
Sontag, Susan, 164
Sopel, Jon, 18
Sörensen, Signa, 162–163, 164
space
  Brook's empty space, 154
  connect to and/or collaborate with, 137
  time and, 143–144
  Viewpoints of, 145–146
space or gap, in-between *(ma)*
  between the actor and the tree, 101–102
  defined, 101
  entering the gap, 104–105
  gōng fēng shuǐ foundation exercises, 108–111
  gōng fēng shuǐ foundation training, 106–108
  mind the gap, 105–106, 112
  neurological application to creative process, 103–104
  origins and meaning, 102–103
Spacey, Kevin, 13
spatial elements, 156n32
spatial energies, experiencing, 111
spatial relationship, 145
Speaking Shakespeare (Rodenburg), 225
speech, 7, 45, 118, 121, 124, 127, 146, 225, 227
Speed of Light (Tan Swie Hian), 114n20
spine, character's, 142, 155n23
stages of life project, 53–56
staging, 150, 153, 172, 246–247
stakes, 92
standard English, 118
Standen, Verity, 176n11
Standing Conference of Drama Departments, 20n7
Stanislavski, Konstantin, 9, 12, 17–18, 19n4, 24n61, 45, 66–67, 121
  active analysis and, 196–201, 208, 212, 214
  activities, 205
  advice given to NIDA actors, 137–138
  as artistic director of MAT, 198
  character's psychological life, 141
  in contemporary practice, 196–215
  études, 208, 212–213
  experimentations, Soviet doctrine and, 198
  idea of obstacles, 219
  influences, 126
  interpretation of 'character,' 123
  model of, 86
  observation exercise, 138–139
  philosophy of, 138
  playing action, 208–210
  principles of, 6
  process of evaluation, 205–208
  scene objective, 219–220
  Stanislavski-based questions, 67
  Strasberg's interpretation of, 124
  super-objective, 142, 209–210, 219–220
  system of, 85, 136
  techniques of, at WAAPA, 218–220
  three circles of circumstances, 202–204
  yoga practice, writings on, 179
Star Wars: The Force Awakens, 153
Status Game, 231
St Denis, Michel, 124
Stewart, Patrick, 13
story, in script analysis, 147
St Petersburg State Theatre Arts Academy in Russia, 138
Strasberg, Lee, 124, 218
Streep, Meryl, 138
Strindberg, August, 147
structural bias, 15
Stubbs, Imogen, 119
student loans system, 20n11
student productions, 166, 174
studio rules, 59–60
studio world, 58, 59
study of another in the group (exercise), 51

Sulerzhytski, Leopold, 198
super-objective, 142, 209–210, 219–220
Suri-ashi, 149
Sutarja, Ida Bagus, 107
Suzuki, Tadashi, 6, 21n17, 112n1, 115n40, 235, 239

table work, 148, 212, 223–224, 227
tactics
    criteria for, 91
    defined, 90
    framing, 91
    in script analysis, 148
    See also actions
Tai'ji, 105, 106, 107, 114n28, 115n33
Taksu, 107, 115n39
Tan Swie Hian, 104–105, 114n18–20, 116n49
Tao Te Ching (Lao-tzu), 221
T/A/S (towards/away/stay), 226–231
Taylor, Susan Leith, 28
Tcherkasski, Sergei, 138, 139–140
teacher, 37–42
    asking questions of their/our own practice concerning interaction, 164–165
    autonomy-supportive, 40
    conservatories and academics, 40–41
    new model of, 39–40
    personal account of, 37–39
    principles of, 41–42
    research, embracing, 40–41
    student workload and, 41
teacher-as-expert model, 39
teacher-as-facilitator model, 39–40
Teacher Development Program (TDP), 197
teacher director, 39, 216–219, 226, 229
teacher–student ethics, 5
techne, 58
temenos, 181, 192
tempo, 145, 152, 156n31

temporal energies, experiencing, 111
Terence, 44
terminology, action-based acting, 85–98
    acting, introduction to craft of, 86–94
    applying, 94
    group exercise, 94–96
    individual paperwork, 96–98
    introducing, 85–94
    See also scene or monologue, beginning work on
text, 7, 146
    approach to, 221–222
    beat in, 91–92
    character's objective, 88–89
    character's obstacle, 89–90
    concepts, applying, 94
    conflict in, 92–93
    connect to and/or collaborate with, 137
    discovery in, 93
    event in, 93–94
    given circumstances, 87–88
    group exercise, 94–96
    individual paperwork, 96
    moment before, 88
    punctuating, 220–221
    scene analysis, 96–98
    in script analysis, approach to, 146
    serving, 225
    stakes in, 92
    tactics in, 90–91
    teaching, in era of language loss, 84–99
    terminology, 85–86, 94
    textual energies, experiencing, 111
Text, Subtext, and Vocal Resonance: Speaking Shakespeare on the 20th Century English Stage (Willis), 120–121
Theaterwissenschaft (science of theatre), 14
Theatre and Performance Research Association, 20n7
theatreness of theatre, 154
Theatre School at Melbourne University's Faculty of VCA-MCM, 100, 112, 113n2

Theatre Training Research Program (TTRP), 104, 114n18
Theatre Workshop, 46
theatricality, 9, 65–66, 136, 154
theories of performance, 121, 159, 160, 161
thinking, in interactivity and immersion, 158–160
three circles of circumstances, 202–204
  large circle of circumstances, 203
  middle circle of circumstances, 203
  overview of, 202–203
  small circle of circumstances, 203–204
time
  for character interaction, 203
  connect to and/or collaborate with, 137
  rehearsal, 217
  space and, 143–146
  Viewpoints of, 145
Tolokonnikova, Nadezhda, 148
tongue twisters, 80–81
Tragical History of Doctor Faustus, The (Grotowski), 128
Train to Brooklyn (Rebeck), 95–96
transitions, 153
trap of the scene, 94–95
True and False (Mamet), 222
truth, 1, 153
'truth, the post truth, and nothing but no truth, so help me God, The' (Sopel), 18
Tuppen-Corps, Alice, 9
turning point
  in composition work, 152
  in script analysis, 147
12 cavities, 106, 114n30
12 Years a Slave, 153
'Two Sosias, The,' 76

Uncle Vanya (Chekhov), 139–140, 179
unconscious bias, 15, 16
understanding, phases of, 31
unemployment rate for actors, 14–15
unison forms, in yoga, 185–186
United Kingdom
  academic study of performance in, beginning of, 13–14
  Conference of Drama Schools, 16
  degree courses in, 14
  Higher Education Funding Council in, 14
  Office for Students, 4–5
  unemployment rate for actors in, 14–15
United States
  first drama department in, 13
  unemployment rate for actors in, 14–15
unity, yoga for building, 181–182
Universities and the Theatre, The, 13–14
University of Arkansas Fayetteville, 197
University of Essex, 16, 24n54
University of Huddersfield, 6–7
University of Leeds, 20n9
University of Melbourne, 113n2
University of Notre Dame, 6–7, 217
University of Southampton, 18
University of Southern California's School of Dramatic Arts, 197
University of Surrey, 16
University of the Arts London, 16
University Performance Centre, 158
university theatre programmes, drama schools compared to, 15
unjaii breathing, 187
up is down, down is up, in is out, out is in (rise and the fall), 109–110
Urfaust (Goethe), 173–175, 176n11

Vakhtangov, Evgeny, 136, 146, 199
van Hove, Ivo, 64–65
Van Lieu, Ron, 197
Varyon (Living Structures), 176n11
vertical/attention practice, 187–188
Victims of Duty (Ionesco), 161

Victorian College of the Arts (VCA), 23–24n54, 32–33, 113n2
    course satisfaction, 32–33
Victorian College of the Arts and Melbourne Conservatorium of Music (VCA-MCM), 100, 112, 113n2
Viewpoints, 6, 21n17, 136–137, 144–146, 156n29
    of space, 145–146
    of time, 145
    vocabulary of, 145
Vincent, Sam, 76
Vinyasa, 178, 180, 187
Vinyasa Power Flow, 178, 180
virtual reality (VR), 22n32
visible action, 200–201, 208–213
    counteraction and, 212
    definition of, 200–201
    energy flows, attention and, 210
    making the action of the story happen, 210–212
    playing, 208–210
    in rehearsal studio, 212–213
visiting teacher director, 217
vocational training, 5, 15, 20n10, 40, 158
voice, 3, 7
    assessment tasks, 41
    imaginative exploration of text in relation to, 225
    in mantra, 189, 190
    in observation exercises, 138
    in RBC curriculum, 118–119, 120, 121, 123, 124, 126
    relaxation and breathing techniques, 34
    tone of, 146
    voice-overs, 26, 160
von Goethe, Johann Wolfgang, 173, 176n11

W

Wagner, Richard, 161
Waiting for Lefty (Odet), 141–144
waiving of fees, 23n53
Waller, Edmund, 68
Wangh, S., 42
Warner, Deborah, 155n19
WAWPT (Whole Actor, Whole Person Training), 26, 43
Wayth, Laura, 8–9
welfare, 5, 31
well-being, 5–6
    acting methodologies, establishing understanding of, 35–37
    agency, developing, 30, 34
    autonomy, establishing, 29, 32–34
    identity, establishing and supporting, 29, 30–32
    initiatives in Australia, 26–27, 28
    knowledge, 30, 35–37
    mindfulness practices, 34–35
    recent developments in awareness of actor's, 28–29
    recommendations into practice, 29–30
    skills for, 30, 34–35
Wellbeing for the Arts, UK, 27
Werry, Margaret, 218
Western Australian Academy of Performing Arts (WAAPA), 6, 23n54, 216–232
    approach to text, 221–222
    blocking, 226–228
    character exercises ('who' in you), 229–230
    contact hours per day expected of students, 217
    contemporary performance stream, 232n6
    course satisfaction, 32
    failure, 218
    first approaches, 223–224
    first impressions, 217–218
    improvisatory exercises, 230–231
    Mamet's idea of 'no such thing as character,' 222–223, 225
    objective/action exercise, 231–232
    punctuating the text, 220–221
    serving the text, 225

Stanislavskian techniques, 218–220
T/A/S, 226–231
teacher directors, 216–219, 226, 229
workshop, 229–232
'Western,' defined, 21n20
Westminster Forum Projects, 17
Whelan, Gregg, 158
white noise, 225
'who' in you (character exercises), 229–230
Willis, Brian, 120–121
Wilson, Robert, 2
wind between object, body and hard surfaces, 110–111
wit, 67, 79
  delineating types of, 81–82
Wooster Group, 124–125, 127
word is a weapon, 66
word statues in acting Shakespeare, 130–134
working the extremities (hands and feet), 109
workshop exercises
  confident command of and holding the space, 75–81
  group composition assignment, 246–247
  incidents from the high street, 51–52, 60, 61
  in interactivity and immersion, 166–175
  WAAPA, 229–232
  word statues in acting Shakespeare, 130–134
Worthen, W. B., 124
writing
  about practice, 13
  about somatic knowledge and practices, 101
  arbitrary approach to, 225
  capturing descriptions by, 2
  in character exercises, 229
  generic guides as parameters to shape, 221

personality of individuals emerging through, 48
principle of, 225
style of, 202
wu, 107, 115n38

xin, 105–106, 115n34, 115n36
xin yi, 105, 113n6

yáng energy, 106
Yau, Andy, 126
yi, 105
yīn energy, 106
yoga, 34–35, 177–193
  ancient practice of, 178
  asanas (body poses), 184–185
  Ashtanga, 178
  Bikram, 178, 180
  building unity, 181–182
  in a chair, 180
  in a circle, 177–193
  focus – attention/intention, 187–188
  in four components of acting, 190
  Hatha, 178
  incremental development, 182–183
  integrity of yoga circle, 183–184
  Kundalini, 178, 187
  making the foreign habitual and the habitual beautiful, 183
  mantra, 188–189
  meditation and mindfulness, 190–192
  om, 183, 188–189
  popularity of, 177–178
  practice of unison forms, 185–186
  pranayama, 187
  salutations, 179
  Stanislavski's writings on, 179
  successful, 181
  traditional practice, 180

Vinyasa, 178, 180, 187
Vinyasa Power Flow, 178, 180
you are the horizon (experiencing spatial, textual and temporal energies), 111
You Me Bum Train, 160
Young Gallant's Academy, The (Vincent), 76

Z

Zarrilli, P., 103–104, 112n1
Zen, 138, 149, 154n6, 191
Zinder, David, 197
Zon, Boris, 198

www.ingramcontent.com/pod-product-compliance
Lightning Source LLC
Chambersburg PA
CBHW072126290426
44111CB00012B/1795